Oil painting by Lorna Mason, "Grandma's Tea Leaf."
Gift to the Author, 1974.

Grandma's Tea Leaf Ironstone

A History and Study of English and American Potteries

Annise Doring Heaivilin

Published by

Wallace-Homestead Book Company
580 Water's Edge Road
Lombard, Illinois 60148

This Book is Dedicated To the
ONE
Who Made It All Possible

"The potter who gives us our table service, and imbues the things of daily use with artistic expression is perhaps more entitled to our thanks than the manufacturers who furnish, sometimes, very useless ornaments exclusively for the wealthy."

*From **A Pottery Primer**, W. P. Jervis, 1911*

Contents

Foreword

The history of people, their lives, their ways, and of the progress which they achieved and passed on to us is a vital, thrilling saga. The very nature of the way of life we now enjoy was made possible by the hardships endured by our ancestors. Much of this narrative has been provided by our association with our neighbors as well as our families. Their influence was by daily customs established with tolerance and generosity.

Yesterday, today, and tomorrow are all chapters in one book; to know only the chapter of today is not enough to satisfy our human spirit — it only spurs us to study and record the accomplishments of our forefathers so that tomorrow's children may be more enlightened and appreciative of earlier struggles.

In compiling this book, much effort was expended to set forth the history and development of the sturdy earthenware utilized by those who chose to forge our frontiers of yesterday. Much evidence has already shown that fine porcelains were produced and imported for some of the early American consumers, but the major portion of the consumption was relegated to the sturdy ironstone china produced in numerous English and American potteries. Little, very little, has ever been published about the Tea Leaf Ironstone china so widely used in all parts of the United States, Canada, and other areas of the world.

In preparing this book, the author has enjoyed the opportunities of examining and photographing hundreds of pieces of Tea Leaf Ironstone china with a thoroughness made possible only by the unbounded generosity of the collectors and owners of many major collections throughout the United States.

This is a chronicle of the origin of the Tea Leaf design, the development of a struggling industry, and the fabrication and distribution of this popular ware. It is an in-depth study, presented in a very human manner, to provide the novice as well as the advanced collector with invaluable reference material and classic information not found in any other single volume.

Nevertheless, the author regards this publication as only an introduction to the subject. Much remains to be discovered or confirmed. Her hope is that this book may stimulate others to pursue, along with her, the continued identification and recording of related material and thus to bring proper appreciation to the tableware of our grandmothers — "Grandma's Tea Leaf."

— Jack Lawton Webb

Acknowledgements

This book was born of frustration at not being able to find a complete history of my beloved Tea Leaf Ironstone. As time skittered by, it became very evident that other collectors had the same problem . . . with one difference; I set about compiling such a volume, never dreaming how far this quest would lead, or how many wonderful people would cross my path on this journey into the past.

Up to this time I had written nothing more serious than school term papers, Sunday School lessons, or P. T. A. devotions and programs. I have always been as hungry to read as to eat, so possibly this is one reason for the compulsion to put my findings on paper. I speak a common, everyday language to you who care deeply for the simple, homey atmosphere created by our kind of people who lived in the latter part of the last century.

This volume is not in any way to be considered a complete history of all English and American potteries. Rather, it is a resumé of those potters who produced our lovely Tea Leaf pattern, limited to those examples I have actually seen and photographed. It is not a scientific treatise but rather a calculated effort to record the myriad of items potted by these old-time craftsmen. My aim has been to be as comprehensive and accurate as possible; my contacts have been from all sections of our country as well as Canada, and naturally the Staffordshire District of England. My one disappointment in this project was being unable to make a planned visit to England in 1973, because of illness in my family. I am always eager and grateful to hear from others concerning history of the potteries and their own treasures of the past.

Next best to a personal visit to Stoke-On-Trent was the countless correspondence with:

Mr. Arnold Mountford, M. A., F. S. A., F. M. A., Director of the City Museum and Art Gallery, Hanley, Stoke-On-Trent, England

Mr. Geoffrey Godden, F. R. S. A., Worthing, Sussex

Mason's Ironstone China Ltd., Staffordshire

E. H. Edge, The Wedgwood Group, Barlaston

F. Kotek, Chairman, A. J. Pointon, General Sales Manager, and F. Spooner, from the Enoch Wedgwood (Tunstall) Limited Group

Peter J. Holmes, Barker Bros., Ltd., Longton

Tony Houldsworth, Sales Manager at Myott-Meakin (Tunstall) Ltd. (the Alfred Meakin Group)

The Washington Pottery (Staff.) Ltd.

The City of Stoke-On-Trent for their fine Handbooks sent to me by Mr. Mountford

On this side of the Atlantic my task was made easier by assistance from E. H. Brown at the British Consulate Office in St. Louis and the New York office of Wedgwood through Claudia Coleman, Sales Manager.

Mr. David Buten, Director of the Buten Museum of Wedgwood, Merion, Pennsylvania, and Mr. Albert Banton Jr., Director for the National Park Service, in charge of the Abraham Lincoln Home in Springfield, Illinois, were most knowledgable and helpful. More information came from J. Jefferson Miller II, Director of Ceramics and Glass of the Smithsonian Institution. Virginia Voedisch, and Ms. Joana Dobson, Librarians at the American Ceramic Society offices in Columbus, Ohio, were invaluable in finding answers for me.

Betty C. Monkman, Registrar, Office of the Curator at the White House, was gracious to answer my inquiry about Mrs. Lincoln's dishes.

James L. Murphy, Curator of the Ohio Historical Society, Columbus, and James Hickey, Illinois historian, were both very helpful on several occasions, and a special thank-you goes to the Claysville Illinois Historical Restoration Society where I took pictures all one Sunday afternoon.

Ruth Salisbury, Archivist at the Historical Society of Western Pennsylvania, was very patient with my inquiries there.

James Van Trump, Vice President of the Pittsburgh History and Landmarks Foundation, and Philip Curtis of the Newark Museum, Newark, New Jersey were also very kind, as was Robert G. Carron of the Milwaukee County Historical Society.

Norman Allen, head of the Science and Industry Division of the Youngstown and Mahoning Public Library; Rachael Gulickson, Curator, West Salem Wisconsin Historical Society; Janis Obst, Curator, Minnesota Historical Society, Fulsom House, Taylor Falls, Minnesota; Glenna Mosgrove, Curator, Illinois Pioneer Heritage Center, Monticello, Illinois each gave thoughtful answers and shared pictures/information which enhance this book.

Special "thank you" to the staffs of various other libraries is in order: The Linda Hall Library of Science and Technology at the University of Missouri at Kansas City; The Public Libraries of Kansas City, Missouri and Kansas City, Kansas; and the Riverside, Antioch, Gladstone, and Platte Woods, Missouri branches of the Mid-Continent Library system, along with the Carnegie Library at Park College in nearby Parkville, Missouri. John Crearer Library in Chicago, The Kittanning Free Public Library, Kittanning, Pennsylvania, and the Free Public Library in Trenton, New Jersey, along with the Ohioana Library Association, Columbus, Ohio, were all most thoughtful and cooperative.

My task would have been much harder without the Carnegie Public Library in East Liverpool, Ohio and the guidance and patience of Mrs. Margaret Guyton and Mrs. Janice Brookman. Mrs. Guyton, head librarian and granddaughter of the editor of the *Potters' Gazette* shared much background material, old newspapers for my perusal, made ever so many copies of reference material, and gave me a unique city map which brought early ELO history to life. Mrs. Brookman, her assistant, is a granddaughter of Gus Trenle, one of the owners of the East End Pottery. Without her, my story would have been much less complete. At the East Liverpool Historical Society headquarters, after the passing of Harold Barth, help came from William H. Vodrey Jr., Mr. Jack Lanan, Mr. and Mrs. Samuel Gates, and Eva Wasbutsky; along with Mr. and Mrs. Clarence Moore, Marion (Mrs. J. D.) Thompson, and the Burford sisters, Jean and Grace, and Mr. and Mrs. Willis Gaston. Olive Allison,

Edith Harker Goodwin, and Louise Newall Cook were living encyclopedias on East Liverpool history, while W. L. Smith added information about the old K.T.K. Co. and the current Taylor, Smith & Taylor Company.

All my East Liverpool sources of history were thoughtful and kind, but the Prince of the Potters was Mr. Arthur Wells, of the Homer Laughlin works in Newall, West Virginia just across the river, who took me through their pottery "morgue" for a memorable visit to yesteryear. His sixty-plus years with that company were evidenced in the history he recalled for me. Later Mr. Ed Carson graciously answered numerous inquiries.

Of no less importance was the day I spent at Hall China Co. when Skip Dawson missed his lunch in order to be my guide, while *John T.* and *Everson Hall* tied all the information together with such simplicity and clarity that I felt as if I could walk in and go to work . . . at some very menial job.

The crowning glory in East Liverpool history came the day Mr. Fred Clifford called me from Chicago and for almost an hour answered questions, and shared information, about the Red Cliff ware made for him by the Hall China Company. He promptly sent beautiful 8″ x 10″ glossy prints to show all the Tea Leaf items in their line. No one could have been more gracious.

There would have been a lackluster story of the Mayer China Company without all the help from Lois McKean who has a special gift of knowing all the interesting tidbits which should go into a history such as company history brochures and copies of awards earned at International Expositions.

The Buffalo Pottery story would have been dull reading without much assistance from Violet and Seymour Altman who had previously published their *Book of Buffalo Pottery*, and other faithful company employees who answered extensive correspondence.

Other working potters who allowed me to observe and ask questions as work went on were Mr. Pomeroy at the Sterling Pottery along with George Vardy at the Cardinal Stonecraft Works, both in Wellsville.

Joe Trupia of Syracuse China Corporation, Maury Dickson, of Canonsburg Pottery, and W. C. Weinhold, Sales Manager for the Walker China Company, each took time to answer my letters and phone calls, as did Gordon T. Entwistle from Jeanette Glass Co. who now owns Walker China Company, and L. E. Tway for Interpace Corporation in reply to my query about Shenango China.

Our story would not be complete without help from old catalogs and newspapers including Sears, Roebuck, and Co.; Montgomery Ward and Co.; Butler Brothers; excerpts from *Drovers Journal*; *The Peoria Journal Star*, along with the *Evening Review of E.L.O.* and numerous clippings from the *Kansas City Star and Times*.

Recognition is due the Hillcrest Shop for reprints of old catalogs and brochures along with the History Book Committee of Beaver Falls for their Centennial booklet.

My heartfelt thanks to other writers who taught me much and were so encouraging; Johana Anderton, my friend and mentor who guided me as we worked together and made it possible for this book to be written. Lois Lehner, more than all the rest, was an endless source of information and inspiration. She shared with me her expertise in writing techniques, plus tremendous valuable knowledge of pottery history. Others include Elizabeth Collard, Esther Dawson, Grace Allison, Gladys Caruso, and R. E. Wheat. Also important to me are Betty Grissom, Mamie Hackley, Vera Kneeland, Ann Lamp, Mildred Russell and my good friend Jack Lawton Webb.

A skeleton story was possible but full coverage was complete with gleanings from ever so many magazines. Help was found in the *American* (Feb. 1, 1890) on through the calendar and alphabet: *Antique Digest*; *Antique Journal* and the *Antique Trader* with Connie Morningstar's columns which I have used numerous times; *The Antique Monthly* and the *Antique Reporter*, along with *Antiquing*, and the simply named *Antiques Magazine* were wonderful. *The Crockery, Brass, and Glass Journal*, though out of print, still lives for me. (Wish I could find a huge collection of them!) *Ceramic Age*, *Good Housekeeping*, *National Antique Journal*, *National Antiques Review*, *Hobbies* and *Harpers* provided occasional help, but the American Ceramic Society's *Bulletins* and their *Journals* supplied much important information for our story. Naturally the *Collectors' News*, with words from Esther Croker, along with the old *Collectors' Weekly* which carried Jabe Tarter's column were always thought provoking. I miss the *Western Collector* and the *Mid-America Reporter*, but Jo Cunningham's new *Glaze*, Nora Koch's *Daze*, and the *Tri-State Trader* leave little time for any other reading/clipping. (But I do manage, though often leaving other duties for later!) I pestered *Spinning Wheel* magazine ever so often, but A. C. Revi, Paul Evans, the late Marcia Ray, or one of several staff members always took time to provide beneficial answers.

My dear friend Lucille Wren has been a wonderful sounding board; provided a free clipping service; worked on my mailing list; kept track of my correspondence, and put at my disposal a listening ear at all times.

Not one line of this book would have been written without the approval and encouragement of my husband Jim along with our five children. Even though the children are all gone from home, each in his/her own way has been a "very present help." My "family" also includes a faithful employee for over ten years, Eileen Vassmer Hein. Without her, my research trips, photographic appointments, time to think, read, and write would have been an absolute impossibility.

Not to be overlooked are various typists: Jewel Heaivilin, Crystal Overman, Nancy Sand, Joyce Sanders, Debra (Prins) Heaivilin, Cherry Kuhn, Helen (Heaivilin) Long, and Jeanne Hulick.

Everyone else is listed in alphabetical order because, by measure of importance to me, most all of them should be listed first . . . an impossible situation.

Among these are many who provided photographs not used in this book: Norman W. Alford, Abegail Alley, Adele Armbruster, Eleanor Ball, Mr. and Mrs. T. A. Baker, Mr. and Mrs. Bernard Barton, Rosemary Beardsley, John Bennington, Blankenship's Antiques, Frank and Katie Bourke, Jim and Barbara Bowling, Mrs. Charles E. Burgess, Lynn Burnett, Lynn Collins Cassady, Mr. and Mrs. Glen Church, The Colonel's Cupboard, The Corner Cupboard, Mary Jane Dewender, Ken Doll Antiques, Evelyn Fangetti, Esther Flowerday, Mrs. Max France, Linda Garrison, Gene and Gwen's Antiques, Gunnel's Antiques, Lee Hardin, Skip and Mary Jane Hastings, Zaneta Meakin Hatten, Virginia Heinman, Margaret Herberger, Dick Herm, Richard R. Houser, Thelma W. Hudson, Carolyn Hurdle, Ruth Hutchinson, Clive Iman, Henry and Myrtle Jorgenson, Frances Johnson, Delores Julian, Mrs. E. K. Koos, Anna Long, Lola's Antiques, Margaret Manning, Billie Martin, Mrs. Robert T. Mayer, Oletha McAdams, J. V. McCann, Margaret McIntosh, Shirley McKibbin, Helen L. Mershon, Mr. and Mrs. Sid Moore, Dr. Paul Mosele, Dorothy Oard, Mrs. W. H. Oberholtzer, W. Wm. Ogborn, D.V.M., Omega Belle O'Connor, Marie Polkington, Mrs. Clara Price, Mr. and Mrs. Olin Pryor, Mr. and Mrs. William Pryor, Gertrude Renfro, Margaret Revers, V. N. Rhea, C. A. Riley, Margaret Roe, Doris Rule, Mr.

and Mrs. Robert Sandfort, Elsie Sexton, Mr. and Mrs. E. M. Shore, Mrs. John R. Shores, Ruth Slick, Ruth Smiley, Dorothy Smith, Mrs. J. Sneddon, Mrs. Reva Sobolka, Del Vonne E. Soule, Tish Soucy, Bill and Carol Starr, Mr. and Mrs. Rick Stein, Frances Taylor Antiques, Juanita Unruh, Shirley Van Clott, Ruth Van Kuren, Ann Vanlandingham, Anna Mae Van Patten, Marcella Vincent, Mr. and Mrs. Harry Wagoner, Lorraine Walters, Grace Weatherby, Beryl Webb, Inez Wheeler, James Seeley White, Annise White, Mrs. Nobel Whitney, and Lydia Wise.

Owners of photographed collections are listed alphabetically and numbered. Credit is shown at the end of each picture caption by the corresponding number in parenthesis (xx). Author's own photographs are unmarked.

1. Collection of Laura Ady
2. Drawings by Johana Gast Anderton
3. Collection of Ron and Marcia (Heaivilin) Balloun
4. John Banks' Collection
5. H. B. Barth — East Liverpool Historical Society
6. Ruth Bloomcamp
7. Collection of Irene Borre — Photos Courtesy John Finney
8. Courtesy of Mrs. Jack Bridges
9. Mrs. Floyd Brown
10. Mrs. E. N. Collins
11. Courtesy of Agnes Cott
12. Collection of Katie Dukes
13. Janet Larsen Dunbar Collection
14. Permission by Mrs. Carl Durban
15. Courtesy of Bertha Fanning
16. Collection of Robert V. Fisher
17. Folsom House, Minnesota Historical Society; Curator, Janis Obst
18. Courtesy of Tom Fountain
19. Courtesy of Avia & Beverly Lind Garbee of the Sunrise Antique Shop
20. Photographs by Harold J. Gerwien at the Request of Frances Spinner — Permission "Star of India" Director
21. Glick's Antiques — Eldon Glick
22. Golden Unicorn — Anna Lisa Klenk
23. Edith Harker Goodwin
24. Mrs. John J. Gray
25. Betty Grissom Antiques
26. Leona Haley's Tea Leaf Collection
27. The Collection of Doris and Burdell Hall
28. Mr. and Mrs. David Hansen
29. Roger and Helen Harper of Harper's Korner
30. Mrs. Leo Harrison's Collection
31. Mrs. Lloyd Hayworth of Brass Bucket Antiques
32. Dean and Debra (Prins) Heaivilin
33. The G. E. Heaivilin Collection
34. The Private Collection of Jeff and Dorothy Heaivilin
35. Hearth Stone Antiques — Ruth Mast
36. David and Eileen (Vassmer) Hein
37. Dorothy (Samuelson) Heavilin
38. Ann Hick's Collection
39. Hospice Antiques — William Durham and William Galloway
40. Collection of Mr. and Mrs. Michael Humphrey
41. Courtesy — The Marie T. Jansen Collection
42. Mr. and Mrs. E. W. Karger

43. Betty Kirkpatrick — Old Brick House Antiques
44. Adeline Kruse
45. The Rob Lee Collection
46. Mrs. Nellie Lewis — Mark Twain Trading Post
47. Lincoln Home, Springfield, Illinois — Albert Banton, Jr. Director for National Park Service
48. The Lock Collection
49. Carl M. and Helen K. (Heaivilin) Long
50. Kelly Karl Long
51. Mrs. David Mann
52. Courtesy of Lloyd and Lorna Mason
53. The Kathy Mast Collection
54. Courtesy of Mrs. Clem F. Maurer
55. Mayer China — Interpace Corporation
56. Mrs. J. B. McClure
57. Courtesy of John McCrann
58. Collection: Lester McLenon and Charles Ohrazda
59. The Rev. and Mrs. Harry Menzies
60. Courtesy of Larry and Carol Miller
61. Permission: Arnold R. Mountford, Director: City Museum and Art Gallery, Hanley, Stoke-on-Trent, England (trademark information)
62. Glenna James Mosgrove, Curator, Illinois Pioneer Heritage Center
63. Courtesy of Murray's Antiques
64. The Povenmire Collection
65. Theran Rand
66. The late Mrs. Louis P. Rausch
67. Courtesy Mr. and Mrs. Dick Reed
68. Margaret Revers
69. Teet Reynold's Collection
70. The Roughton Collection
71. Courtesy — Mrs. Roger Schneman
72. Mrs. C.O. Schulten
73. Collection of Mrs. James Scott
74. Shake's Antiques — Mr. and Mrs. W. K. Shake
75. The late Nathan Shannon
76. Courtesy of Clara Sharp
77. Collection of Mrs. John Sommers
78. Summer's Museum
79. Courtesy of Bertha Cottrell Stumpff
80. Courtesy of Margaret Taylor
81. Frances Trowbridge
82. Courtesy: Collection of Mark Ward — Photographs by Loren Leiseberg
83. Paul and Marie (Murdock) Whittenhall
84. Collection of Mrs. Opal Wilcoxon
85. Hazel L. Windle
86. Courtesy of Mrs. Tom Wornall, Jr.
87. Collection of Fritz and the late Mrs. Wort
88. Lucille Wren
89. Sally Wright Collection
90. Ruth and Leon Young — Country Cousin Antiques
91. Collection of the late Sylvia Daily
92. Courtesy of Mrs. Ethel Teagarden
93. Frances Spinner
94. Jabe Tarter, Akron Beacon Journal, Akron, Ohio

Trademark Key

English Companies

AD	Adam, Wm. & Sons (Potters) Ltd.
AL	Alcock Potters
BC	Baker & Chetwynd Co.
B.S.	Bishop & Stonier
BW	Bridgwood (& Son)
BU	Burgess, Henry
CH	Challinor, E. & C.
CL	Clementson, Jos. (& Sons)
C.E.M.	Cork, Edge, Malkin & Co.
CO	Corn, W. & E.
DA	Davenport, John
E.M	Edge, Malkin & Co.
ED	Edwards, John
E.F	Elsmore & Forster
EL	Elsmore, Thos. (& Sons)
FU	Furnival, Thos. (& Sons)
GR	Grindley, W. H. & Co.
HU	Hughes, Thos.
JO	Johnson Bros.
MAD	Maddock, John
MEA	Meakin, Alfred
MEA J.G.	Meakin, J. & G.
M.T.	Mellor, Taylor & Co.
P.B.	Powell & Bishop
P.BS	Powell, Bishop & Stonier
A.S	Shaw, Anthony
W.E	Walley, Edward
W.W	Wedgwood, Enoch (Tunstall) Ltd.
W.M	Wileman, James F.
WI	Wilkinson, Arthur J.

American Companies

BR	Brunt, Wm. Jr. & Sons Co.
BUF	Buffalo Pottery
CA	Cartwright Bros
CU	Cumbow China Decorating Co.
EEP	East End Pottery
G.B	Goodwin Bros. Pottery Co.
RC	Hall China Co. (Red Cliff)
H.P	Harker Pottery Co.
HLC	Laughlin, Homer — China Co.
K.T.K.	Knowles, Taylor & Knowles Co.
JEM	Mayer, J. & E.
R.C.	Red Cliff — see Hall China
SB	Sebring Pottery Co.
C.C.T.	Thompson, C.C. — Pottery Co.
V.P	Vodrey Pottery
WAC.	Walker China Co.
WH	Wheeling Pottery Co.
WC	Wick China Co.
CTS	Children's Tea Sets
OE	Odds and Ends
UM	Unmarked
REP	Reproductions

Table of Registration Marks 1842–1883

A beneficial system of marking wares with an elaborate key, which makes it possible to identify the exact date, month, year, and class (type of ware, for example ceramics is shown as IV), was termed a Registry Mark on English manufactured goods, and was implemented by the British Patent Office from 1842 to 1883. Following is the Year Letter Index from 1842–1867 and 1868–1883:

1842 X	1857 K	1871 A
1843 H	1858 B	1872 I
1844 C	1859 M	1873 F
1845 A	1860 Z	1874 U
1846 I	1861 R	1875 S
1847 F	1862 O	1876 V
1848 U	1863 G	1877 P
1849 S	1864 N	1878 D and
1850 V	1865 W	(1878 W – 1-6 March)
1851 P	1866 Q	1879 Y
1852 D	1867 T	1880 J
1853 Y		1881 E
1854 J	1868 X	1882 L
1855 E	1869 H	1883 K
1856 L	1870 C	

Below are pictured the two Design Registration Marks used from 1842–1867 and 1868–1883.

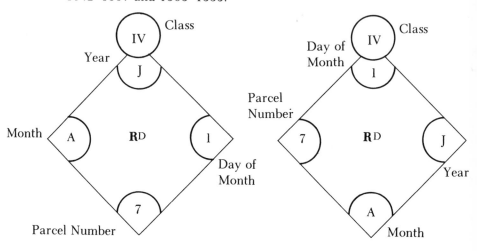

In addition to the Year Letter Index shown above, the Month Letter Index is indicated below; these are the same for both periods of the Year Letter Index.

January	C (or O)	August	R
February	G	(Plus September	
March	W	1–19, 1857)	
April	H	September	D
May	E	October	B
June	M	November	K
July	I	December	A

Table of Design Registration Numbers Found on Wares From 1884

Rd. No.	Registered in Year	Registered in Month of
1	1884	January
19754	1885	January
40480	1886	January
64520	1887	January
90483	1888	January
116648	1889	January
141273	1890	January
163767	1891	January
185713	1892	January
205240	1893	January
224720	1894	January
246975	1895	January
268392	1896	January
291241	1897	January
311658	1898	January
331707	1899	January
351202	1900	January
368154	1901	January
385500*	1902	January
402500*	1903	January
420000*	1904	January
447000*	1905	January
471000*	1906	January
494000*	1907	January
519500*	1908	January
550000*	1909	January

* *Approximate numbers only.*

Americana

Much has been written about the covered wagons, stage coaches, and riverboats; muskets, coon-skin caps, and Indian scouts; as well as gold miners, homestead ranchers, and railroaders in the early days of this country, but virtually nothing has been recorded about the dishes our hardy ancestors used three times a day.

We can be sure that few dined at fine mahogany tables, draped with spotless white linens, set with glistening silver and fine English or European porcelain. Rather, they used heavier, more practical ware that would stand long moves by river boats, heavy wagons, or the new-fangled steam-engine trains. Dishes had to withstand countless washings, often by careless, childish hands using homemade lye soap.

Most American housewives followed the fashions set by their English and European sisters, and, in fact, many of them were truly blood sisters because of immigration. They were exactly like we are today — always yearning to "keep up with the Joneses." The popularity of pewter plates, mugs, and tankards had passed. Then came yellowware and Rockingham, followed by cream-colored Queensware, Gaudy Dutch, and Welsh, multicolored Staffordshire, and finally plain white ironstone.

And then! Tea Leaf caught the ladies' fancy because it was simple, yet elegant. The bluish white body looked clean, the simple spray and band in copper lustre satisfied their hunger for a bright spot of color; and elegance was evident in the shapes used in the hollowware. And it was cheap!

By 1900 at least twenty-five English potters had started producing their own variations of Tea Leaf, and perhaps a dozen American contemporaries were trying to get their share of the market.

English Tea Leaf was sent to the United States by the shipload. It was packed in barrels and these were distributed throughout this country by the cheapest method possible. One young matron collector told me that in her reading as a journalist she had found Tea Leaf was used as ballast in ships landing along the Atlantic Coast. After discharging the Tea Leaf they loaded with cotton, wood, tobacco, and clay (to make more English pottery). If rocks and stones had been used as ballast, they could only be dumped in the bay and there is evidence this was done at times. The Tea Leaf ballast made the trip more profitable because there was a ready market for white dishes.

At this time England and America were in the midst of an Industrial Revolution which ultimately resulted in better wages and working conditions as well as improved living conditions — an overall higher standard of living. The use of electricity, machinery, and natural gas helped speed up the manufacturing processes with assembly line methods, thereby resulting in greater production at lower cost. This in turn increased employment, giving more people regular cash incomes with which to purchase some luxuries as well as necessities. These hardy people dug the clay, coal, and ore for the factories and mills; built and operated the ships, railroads, and other common carriers; others raised the livestock, harvested the grain, picked the cotton, or made them into products ready for use. Others preached the gospel, taught the schools, and printed the newspapers. These are the people who ate from Tea Leaf dishes and made them one of the most popular patterns ever made.

Early Memories

My Tea Leaf story begins in the early 1920s at Shell Knob, Missouri. This sleepy little community in Barry County, deep in the Ozark Hills, was the home of my maternal grandparents, George G. and Louisa Tennessee Winn Cottrell. She was born in the state for which she was named but the date of her birth and how she came to southwest Missouri are unknown to me. Grandpa was born October 22, 1859 at Marshfield, Missouri, and migrated, while still a youth, to the Shell Knob area with his widowed mother and at least two brothers, Joel and Tom. As Tom still had the wanderlust, he eventually left for the great northwest and Joel followed, but he returned later, married, and set up housekeeping near Shell Knob.

It was common practice for a widowed parent to live with one of his or her children, so Grandpa naturally invited his mother to live with him and his new bride when Joel first left. A set of Tea Leaf dishes, purchased by Joel before he left home, was taken along and became part of the George Cottrell household. To my knowledge, that is the only set of dishes my Grandma Cottrell ever had.

I was with my grandparents a good part of the time because my mother, Vesta Cottrell Doring, lived only four years after I was born. After she passed away in 1921, I spent the better part of the next two years in this wonderful, yet simple, home. Even after my father, William F. Doring, married Emma Mason from Chanute, Kansas, I spent many, many summers at Shell Knob with my grandparents.

Louisa and George G. Cottrell, grandparents.

Among my earliest memories was Grandma's brown gravy, made after she had cooked homemade sausage. It was served in her square open Tea Leaf bowl. There were fluffy white biscuits and lots of freshly laid eggs served on her Tea Leaf plates and the platter. I cannot remember other pieces of the Tea Leaf service.

We had no pitcher and bowl sets in the bedrooms, but rather a galvanized water bucket with a tin dipper and a granite wash basin on a "wash stand" in the corner of the kitchen. In the summertime these were moved to the back porch along with the plain white, oval open soap dish — not a fancy Tea Leaf one with a lid. I cannot remember the chamber pot but I assume it was plain white ironstone, also. It seemed everyone had one of those.

Grandpa Cottrell was a large man; although of average height, he was stocky and broad shouldered. With his thatch of jet-black hair, his heavy mustache, his bushy eyebrows, and his dark brown eyes, he presented a foreboding appearance. His hands were huge from his long use of well drilling and blacksmithing tools, and his booming voice matched the sound of his hammer as he struck the anvil while shaping a piece of iron for a horseshoe. He spoke with a voice of authority, because for over forty years, he was also a Church of Christ preacher; yet to me as a small child, he was love personified. His religious beliefs were to be lived, in fact were lived for over fifty years.

Notice I did not say he was a minister. To me, that denotes formal education. Grandpa could neither read nor write until after he was married, when Grandma taught him. She must have been a good teacher for he went on to serve many years on the local school board and was elected to one term, 1924–1926, in the Missouri House of Representatives from his home Eleventh District. Jefferson City was "too big and too wicked" and he would have no part of a second term. In his estimation, his success was measured not by the money earned but by the 517 baptisms by which souls were added to the Church of Christ.

Grandma was a perfect complement to him. She was a tall, slender woman of Scottish descent. Her blond hair was straight, combed back severely from her face, and fastened in a tight knot on the crown of her head. Her voice was so soft I had to listen intently to catch what she had to say, but she was joyous to listen to, because she invariably had a pleasant story, a Bible verse, or a song to share. Her blue eyes and sweet, sincere smile always said to me, "You are loved." Because of her capable hands and infinite patience through the years I learned to sew, to churn butter, and to wash the Tea Leaf dishes. If I promised to be careful I could also handle the blue carnival Grape and Cable glasses she had received as premiums with Arbuckle brand coffee. Every Saturday morning she gave me a "dose" of epsom salts, "whether I needed it or not." (It was good for me.) On these occasions I was permitted to drink from one of those beautiful blue glasses. "Happiness" was breakfast at sun-up, dinner with company more often than not, and supper by lamplight, using the Tea Leaf plates and bowls. What was missing in worldly goods was more than compensated for by the security and stability, simplicity and honesty, hospitality and love we knew in this home. This is what Tea Leaf means to me today!

In 1935 Grandpa's heart failed and a few months later Grandma went to join him. Shortly before her death Grandma appropriately gave the one remaining plate to her niece, Joel's daughter, Bertha Cottrell Stumpff. That is the 8″ plate shown here.

Tea Leaf plate, sole surviving item of the Cottrell dishes.
(79)

For the next thirty years, I was busy growing up, finding a husband, building a home, rearing five children, and helping establish a business. I had neither time nor money for frills, and Tea Leaf was relegated to the back of my mind.

One Sunday in 1965, my husband Jim and I attended an antique show. There, in the back of an obscure booth, hung a lone Tea Leaf plate that opened a floodgate of memories for me. As soon as I learned the pattern name, I began my relentless search for history about this symbol of happiness, as well as for the dishes themselves.

Little did I dream I would be sharing through the pages of a book what has come to me so far. I am very sure I have only begun to learn the history of the many companies, both English and American, that have produced Tea Leaf through the years. Even though this book has many illustrations, there must be countless items I have not seen. I will welcome additional Tea Leaf stories and information about companies and items not mentioned, as well as those covered herein.

My present collection serves twenty to twenty-five, which is more than enough for our five children and their families. At my latest count there are pieces in my cabinets representative of twenty-five potters.

As my collection and my own knowledge of the subject grew, frustration at being unable to find even one book that contained a complete Tea Leaf story was just too much! I spoke to Johana Gast Anderton, my good friend and mentor, about this lack of information, with the suggestion that *she* write a book about this Tea Leaf. Since she had written several collectors' books, I felt she would be an ideal author. Johana recalled an oft-quoted cliche', " 'If you want something done — do it yourself!' I think it is a wonderful idea, go to work!" She has provided invaluable instruction and advice in every area of production, for which I am most grateful.

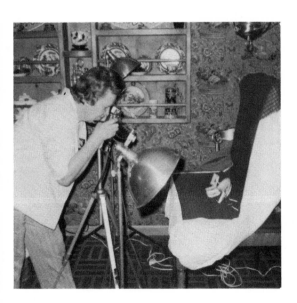

Research has been sheer joy! Thousands of miles of travel were easy because I enjoy driving alone. Sleepless nights were caused by my excitement at finding so many items in a single collection to photograph and catalog — not from worry or unhappiness. Long, long hours of work were fun because I enjoyed bending over the camera, setting the lights just right to eliminate reflections, setting up displays of several related items, and taking the pictures. What fun it was to hand a Polaroid print to my hostess and see the surprise and satisfaction on her face when she viewed her very own Tea Leaf in a new light. The cataloging was a pleasure because I could do it alone, talking to myself and making mental notes as I went along.

Haunting libraries has taught me patience and tolerance. Many people knew nothing about Tea Leaf and I developed my own methods of spotting usable printed information. Modern copying machines are miracle workers, but they will never replace, completely, the 3″ x 5″ note card and a ballpoint pen.

My son Jeff was with me on an early research trip, and after photographing three collections in one day, we were both dead tired but brim full of ideas — one was to use a different background for each collection. It has proved to be a lifesaver because it has been positive identification of individual collections. This is the reason for the varied backgrounds.

Collectors have opened their collections for photographing; shared nostalgic stories to be retold; extended hospitality to a tired, hungry stranger; and written countless enthusiastic letters. By such gifts of sharing many have become a part of this book.

To my familiar question, "Why do you collect Tea Leaf?" the answer nearly always has been "My Grandmother had . . ."

Our youngest child was married in March, 1973 and at the family dinner (served on our Tea Leaf, of course) discussion turned to the title of this book. Nothing was settled, but a few days later the following letter arrived from my 11-year-old grandson, Kelly Karl Long, of Pekin, Illinois.

Dear Grandma,   March 20, 73

We got your letter today. The book you are going to write about Tea Leaf is a good idea I think. When you go to England to get information I hope you have good luck.

The main reason I wrote this letter is to tell you a name I thought of. It is GRANDMAS TEA LEAF I sure hope you like it. I think you will.

If I come down this summer, I'll be down around the first of July, you probably know why (to get fireworks). Well, I'm gonna sign off now.

Good luck for the time being. I love you!

Your Grandson,
Kelly Long

"Grandma's Tea Leaf" is truly the only name that could apply to a collection of so many wonderful stories by good friends from all over these United States.

Lydia Wise wrote from Connecticut to say that when her mother, who was past eighty-five years old, was about seven years old, Lydia's grandmother moved from Iowa to West Virginia and took her Tea Leaf dishes with her, a kind of reverse migration.

A friend in Michigan wrote saying Tea Leaf had graced her grandmother's table as long as she could remember and it is still in use every day.

"Grandma's Tea Leaf" also brought back memories of a southern plantation childhood home of an elderly acquaintance. At her grandmother's home, Tea Leaf dishes were used by their faithful Negro workers, some of whom had been former slaves, while the family ate from imported porcelain.

Another lady in south central Illinois recalls by word and picture the story of her grandmother's Tea Leaf.

These pieces of Tea Leaf copper lustre remain from the complete dinnerware service for twelve and the bedroom set used by my grandmother, Martha Jane Rinehart, at Martha, Illinois (15 miles north of Monticello). The table setting was used at my mother's wedding in 1896, when there were five courses of meat served to the wedding guests. The table was re-set for twelve five times! Grandmother often said that she was so proud of her lustre Tea Leaf because Mary Todd Lincoln used the same pattern in the White House.

May 21, 1973   Glenna James Mosgrove

I shall long remember the Pryor family in which there were Tea Leaf owners on both sides of the family. Mrs. Pryors' grandparents were married in England, but left there the day after their wedding, bringing a set of Tea Leaf with them, which they used for many years on their farm near Spickard, Missouri. This is the only reference to Tea Leaf having been seen in English homes. It was all made for export. Mr. Pryor's interest in Tea Leaf was sparked by his grandmother, Minnie Schaffer, who used this lovely ware for many years in her home near Jamesport, Missouri. In turn, her daughter became a long time collector-user. Now, Mr. and Mrs. Pryor are avid collectors and enjoy using their dishes for special occasions. Their son Bill is a fourth generation collector who, with his wife, have become the new owners of his great-grandmother's pride and joy. He is one of many young men I have met who thoroughly enjoy and appreciate this simple memory of the past.

Another of these young men is Rob Lee, whom I first met when he was a 17 year-old junior in high school. While we were "trading" Tea Leaf, I asked my usual question, "Why do you collect Tea Leaf?" He exclaimed, "I just love it! The browner the better! My Grandmother Collins gave me her Tea Leaf and I just want to complete a set." Rob now owns some rare pieces and has brought me several unusual items. I am not sure when a set could be considered "complete" as there are so many different items to be found. This is evidenced by the photographs shown in this book.

"Grandma's Tea Leaf" fits this account from Clinton, Illinois. From the late 1880s until 1900 a general store was operated by Mr. C. N. Hammond and Mr. Ely. In 1900–01 Mr. Elmer Hammond bought Mr. Ely's interest and business was carried on until the early 1940s as C. N. Hammond and Sons. They sold groceries and Queensware, as dishes were called in those days. The English ware was Blue Willow by Allerton and Son and Tea Leaf Lustre by Alfred Meakin. They were delivered by freight train in one-hundred pound barrels that held a service for twelve. Part of the barrels were unpacked, and the straw in which the dishes had set was soon scattered everywhere. Of course, the dishes had to be washed before they were displayed on the shelves on either side of the long narrow building. These shelves extended to the ceiling and were reached by a ladder that was moved on a track mounted from the ceiling. All the dishes in the store were washed each November so they would be "clean and shiny for the Christmas trade." This was one of the early memories of Frances Trowbridge as she helped her mother and sister repeat this operation many, many times.

C.N. Hammond & Sons General Store, Clinton, Ill.
(81)

Some of the dishes were delivered from riverboats that operated on large rivers such as the Ohio, Illinois, Missouri, and Mississippi.

Freight was less expensive but sometimes the sinking of a boat was a catastrophe for many. Probably there are Tea Leaf dishes still in barrels in some of the old buried hulks.

Wreck of 19th century vessel discovered in Delaware Bay

The unmarked wreck of a 19th-century ship, possibly a British cargo vessel, has been discovered in Delaware Bay between Lewes, Del., and Cape May, N.J.

The wreck was found by two ships of the Commerce Department's National Oceanic and Atmospheric Administration, the RUDE and HECK, while dragging the bay for submerged navigational hazards.

Lt. Cdr. Merritt N. Walter, of Martin, Mich., commanding officer of the two wire drag vessels, said the wreck lay in 39 feet of water about 15 miles from Lewes, 7½ miles south of Cape May and 12 miles east north east of Cape Henlopen, Del.

Scuba divers aboard the wire drag ships found nothing remaining of the wreck's superstructure. Portions of the hull protruded from the bottom, and more was apparently imbedded in the mud. Walter said he found the wreck laid open on the bottom with part of its cargo, consisting of thousands of pieces of neatly packed Britishmade chinaware, exposed. The remainder of the cargo was imbedded in the bottom and covered with coral and silt.

On the basis of an examination of the chinaware by Jefferson Miller, curator of ceramic history at the Smithsonian Institution's National Museum of History and Technology, it was concluded that the wreck postdated 1876.

Miller said the all-white, undecorated pottery found in the wreck was manufactured in the 19th century from 1850 on. He identified the pottery as products of Powell and Bishop, of Hanley, Staffordshire, which operated between 1876 and 1878; J. W. Pankhurst & Co., of Hanley, Staffordshire, 1850–1882; and W. & E. Corn, Longport, Staffordshire, about 1864–94. Miller said practically all the chinaware was English "ironstone," a heavy, durable earthenware made for every-

day use and popular throughout the 19th century and to the present. One exception, a hand-enameled cup with simple polychrome flowers, a type of decoration favored at the time, was also English earthenware, manufactured between 1850 and 1900, and, like the ironstone pieces, an example of everyday useful china favored during the 19th century.

Walter said the cargo, which also included 19th-century washbowls and pitchers, and the debris were all in one pile about eight to ten feet tall and 25 to 30 feet across. The wreckage rises about 8 to 10 feet above the bottom.

The wreck's anchor was also hoisted to the surface. Of woodstock type, it weighed around 3500 pounds and measured approximately six feet across the flukes and eight feet along the shank. Walter said the size and weight of the anchor made it clear that the wreck was that of a seagoing vessel.

The Coast Guard was notified of the wreck's location, which will appear later on a nautical chart to warn ships of the underwater hazard.

The RUDE and the HECK are the only vessels of their kind in operation in the United States. The two craft, working together, locate underwater obstructions by towing a wire between them suspended from surface buoys. When the wire catches on an obstruction, it becomes taut, forming a V. If necessary, scuba divers examine the submerged object to determine the depth of the water above its highest point. The 90-foot, 176-ton sister ships each carry a complement of 10. They work in the offshore waters of the Atlantic and the Gulf of Mexico, seeking any objects which may be hazardous to shipping, including wrecks, protruding rocks and rock formations, abandoned oil derricks and pilings.

From the *Antique Trader*, date unknown.

December 2, 1977

Dear Ms. Heaivilin:

Thank you for your letter of November 7, 1977.

The article you enclosed is, as near as I can recall, correct. The people who worked that particular wreck came to the office several years ago. I gave them information on a number of pieces (as set forth in the article). Since that time, I have not had contact with these people, so I can give you no additional information. I do not recall any "tea leaf" design pieces, but it is possible there was some. I might add that over the years I have seen many sherds of English ironstone decorated with this design. They have come from digs in just about all parts of the United States.

Quite naturally, many ships carried ceramic cargos from England to the United States. Whether ceramics sometimes served as ballast I do not know. I'm sorry I cannot provide you with more specific information.

Good luck on your new book. When it comes out, should you wish to give us a copy for our library, we will be pleased to accept it.

Again, thank you for writing.

Sincerely yours,

J. Jefferson Miller II
Div. of Ceramics & Glass

One of the families who bought a barrel of dishes was vividly described to me by Mrs. Sally Wright. Her grandfather, Aaron Schrader, was a Methodist minister who lived in Illinois around the turn of the century. Because the Bishop was coming for a very rare visit, Grandmother just had to have a new set of dishes. Grandpa went to town in the wagon and brought home a barrel of dishes — the beautiful Alfred Meakin Tea Leaf service for twelve! What a lovely sight to set before the Bishop!

When Sally was four or five years old her grandmother gave her the butter pats from this set to use as doll-dishes. One day while having a "tea party" on the well-curb, their big old pet St. Bernard dog swept all the dishes off on the ground with one swish of his tail. Sally's broken heart seemed to match her broken dishes for quite some time. She told me she "can see that tail swishing yet!"

One of my prize possessions is a set of ten cups bought at an estate sale. Later, I became acquainted with Lucille Wren, a dear friend of the deceased, and she passed on this story:

"I don't know how Rita knew the dishes were for sale, but on a very hot Missouri summer day (long before air conditioning) Rita and daughter started from their home in south Kansas City, Missouri on a journey to Leavenworth, Kansas — a distance of thirty to forty miles. Because of poor roads this was a lengthy trip for two elegantly dressed women in a Packard of 1930s vintage.

At the proper address the trip ended with a climb up a lengthy set of rickety steps to a house on a very high terrace where they found the owner, a small white-haired woman in her mid-eighties, living alone. Her thoughts ran like this, it seemed: "City women — out of their minds — comin' so fur on sech a turrable hot day jes to buy these yhere ole things my kids growed up with. But enny way, I'll jes see how much I can git fur this yhere trash." Her prize possession seemed to be a dime store set of Blue Willow Ware!

The discussion lasted for hours, each haggling over the price. Their only respite was a glass of cold water from the ancient well in the yard.

The sale finally ended and a barrel full of Tea Leaf and Moss Rose dishes had to be taken down those lengthy, rickety stairs by two sweating women in their elegant apparel, and loaded into that Packard for the long, hot, but triumphant trip back to the city."

Another charming account comes from Laura in California. Her Tea Leaf Lustre went to church! She shared with me the account of the day their pastor asked permission to use her Tea Leaf pitcher and bowl set on Sunday morning to illustrate Jesus washing the feet of the disciples. A short time later Tea Leaf was used at her daughter's wedding. Humility and joy often walk hand in hand down life's highway.

One of the myriad of my correspondents is Esther Dawson who, in one letter, related how she found a set of ten Tea Leaf cups and saucers: A neighbor had seen them in the home of an elderly lady and hurried to tell Esther. Without waiting to finish supper for her family she scurried to see if she could buy those cups and saucers. The dear old lady was embarassed to finally ask if fifty cents was too much for a cup and saucer! They had gold lustre instead of the common copper and Esther has since told me some of the early day Tea Leaf was done in gold. (Recently some Tea Leaf decorated in gold came to me.)

She went on to say she grew up in a country house high on a hill. They had Tea Leaf for daily use, and when a piece was chipped or cracked her mother would stand on the back porch and sail these broken pieces down the hill into a ditch they were filling! So many times I have thought what a marvelous "dig" that would be. Maybe there are better pieces there than some we see today, and that is also one reason Tea Leaf is so scarce.

This is as good place as any to mention that archaeologists depend on pottery shards to tell the history of past civilizations. It is much more accurate than metals which are affected by moisture and earth chemicals, or wood and paper which soon decay. Pottery is the same when dug up after several thousand years underground as it was at the time it was buried. Also, pottery making methods have remained essentially the same from the very beginning. This puts us pottery lovers right on the ground floor with the archaeologists.

Mrs. Ellis Sharp has been a Tea Leaf collector much longer than many of us and proof of this is an article she wrote which was printed in the *Drover's Journal* in Chicago in 1948. I found Mrs. Sharp quite by accident and spent a wonderfully happy day in her home.

TEA-LEAF DISHES MAKE FINE HOBBY

Dear Household Friends: For serveral years I have been gathering information about Ironstone china, especially the old English dishes with the tea-leaf design. I have also been gathering the dishes, too. I inherited a few from my mother's set, later a few more from my step-mother's set. Then friends started giving me pieces and my family started buying them for me.

How does anyone know Ironstone china when they see an old dish? Look on the bottom, for most of it is plainly marked. There are many potters' stamps. The most common one shows a lion and a unicorn holding between them the Royal Arms of Britain and the motto of the Empire "Honi Soit Que Mal Y Pense," which means "Evil to him who evil thinks." Beneath this you will find the name of the potter, and above either Ironstone China or Royal Ironstone. The Mason Ironstone China stamp remained unchanged from 1813, to 1910 in England.

The tea-leaf pattern was first called Lustre Band or Sprig. Later it was called Tea-leaf. The design consists of three leaves with scalloped edges, usually five scallops. There is one bud on a long stem, curved sharply to the left, between the leaves. There is only one long stem but two smaller ones flanking it at the base of the design. This design is always brown. The potters printed

this brown design on the dish, then fired on a glaze over it, and then they put the lustre over the glaze exactly over the design, by hand. And on examining the dishes you will see many places where the lustre did not cover the pattern exactly. Besides the tea-leaf design there is usually a wide band of lustre around the rim of the dish and a narrower band around the base. On plates, sauce dishes and saucers there is only one wide band around the rim.

This pattern was used by many potters starting about 1800. From 1875 to 1890 it was the most popular design, but by 1910 it was no longer used. This design was made in many sizes, since each potter made his own pattern.

We see the name Alfred Meakin on most of our tea-leaf today. His pottery was at Tunstall, England, and many of his dishes were sent to United States from 1875 to 1900. Among the tea-leaf ironstone china that I have, besides Alfred Meakin are Wedgewood & Co., England, Mellor, Taylor & Co., England, Arthur J. Wilkinson, later R. Alcock Burslem, England, Thomas, Furnival & Son, England.

I have gathered this information from magazine articles and the book Old China by Minnie Watson Kamm I now have over 200 tea-leaf dishes. None are for sale or trade. But I am always hunting more of them.

On my buffet for all who come to see and enjoy are: a sugar bowl that was my mother's, a cream pitcher of my step-mother's, a spoon holder my husband bought at a farm sale, a coffeecup and large saucer that came from another household sale, a teacup and saucer that was my step-mother's, a teapot that was my mother's, a tureen with lid that my daughter bought for me at Marshall Field gift shop in Chicago, and three small side dishes another daughter found in a gift shop in Tennessee. I have soup dishes a son-in-law bought from a keeper of a motel in Wisconsin, some square dishes our hatchery man found in a chicken yard being used to water the chickens. So you see these old dishes came from many places.

I would like to find a ladle to go with my gravy dish, and some butter pats. I would also like to know if any of you know how to make the dishes that have turned dark white again.

Perhaps many of you know more about these tea-leaf dishes than I. I am always looking for more information about them.

May you all enjoy your hobbies as much as I enjoy my tea-leaf dishes.
—Mrs. Ellis S. Sharp, Route 1, Eureka, Ill.

Another friend is a dealer here in the Kansas City area who sold to me her copy of William Chaffer's *Marks and Monograms on Pottery and Porcelain*. The day I picked up the book she related the tale of a man who came to her shop to sell something he had no further use for. On her table was a Tea Leaf dish of some sort and he, in disdain, remarked, "Do you buy old junk like that?" To her affirmative answer, he responded, "Well! I have got something like that I feed the chickens and ducks out of in the chicken yard . . . even has a lid. Do you want that?" "What do you want for it?" asked Mrs. G. "Oh, I guess four bits will do," he replied. The bargain was completed — he brought it in straight from the chicken yard, without benefit of water or brush! Yes, it was a beautiful tureen and lid! This is a very good reason I always sterilize my Tea Leaf with a chlorine bath and soak — then wash it in hot soapy water and rinse well. At least I know they are clean and sometimes the dishes look much whiter. As a general rule cleaning and mending should be left to the professionals. Most cities of any size have at least one such business. Since there is so little Tea Leaf in mint condition, a piece mended by a professional should be welcome. Of course any reputable dealer will indicate any such departure from original perfection.

History and the Tea Leaf Legend

It is the general consensus the Tea Leaf "sprig" was patterned after the leaf of a real plant, but which one? Since the Oriental tea leaf is very unlike our modern motif we can enjoy as a pleasant superstition the story of the whole tea leaves left in the bottom of the cup bringing good luck. However, the Tea Leaf name is very appropriate because the China tea trade was the beginning of a new era in British history and subsequently of our own United States.

Chinese legend places introduction of tea as a beverage at about 700 B.C. but the earliest mention recorded in a Chinese dictionary is 350 B.C. Sometimes truth and fancy travel together but the story preferred by some Chinese is that tea was discovered in their country when Sheu Nung was Emperor in the first millenium. It seems water was unsafe for drinking until it was boiled. One day some tea leaves fell into the water he was to drink, unknown to him. But he noticed the aroma and was so pleased with the taste he ordered all his water to be prepared for him in this manner.

This could well have happened in the deep interior of China and the propogation and cultivation of these fascinating trees moved slowly down the Yangtze river to the coast. From there the growing of tea trees spread to Japan and the other Far East countries.

The Japanese have an interesting legend that credits the origin of tea to a Buddhist saint who meditated for nine years seated before a stone wall. During one of his meditations he fell asleep and upon awakening he was so humiliated that he cut off his eyelids to be sure the same sin did not recur. The severed lids, cast to the ground, took root and grew as a tea tree whose leaves, when steeped in hot water, made a drink capable of preventing sleep.

It is a well-recorded truth that long before the birth of Christ, countless Chinese people were hard at work making "china" of various sorts. They had discovered the art of firing pottery, thus making a very superior ware much in demand by peoples in their own part of the world.

By about 260 B.C., Shih Haung Ti, the "First Sovereign Emperor," had completed the Great Wall and standardized the country's script, laws, and system of weights and measures. In addition, by conquest, he completed unification of the northwest part of this vast land and named it in his own honor. It was natural their pottery was also identified by the same name — China.

The provinces of Honan and Kansu in this unified empire were famous for their ceramic wonders and Ching-tê-chêu was the "Stoke-on-Trent" of China. Their progress through the centuries is undisputed and by the early 1700s a Jesuit priest became instrumental in spreading to the European and Engish potters the ancient, well-guarded secret of porcelain-making in China.* He even pirated specimens of kaolin and pentuntsé and described in detail the industry in Ching-tê-chêu. Special mention was made of the expense and scarcity of raw materials such as wood for the furnaces, which had to be transported "a hundred leagues" (240–460 miles, depending on which league measurement is used). He commented also that anyone could find work and make a living. Another historian remarked that in this area "Formerly there were only three hundred furnaces, now there are nearly three thousand."†

In 1792–1794 Lord Macartney, English ambassador to China, reported there were "three thousand furnaces in Ching-tê-chêu for the baking of porcelain, all lighted at the same time, which at night presented the appearance of a town on fire!"‡

Various historians have recorded that immense forests were destroyed to supply these fiery monsters. In turn, soil erosion and lack of good conservation practices resulted in starvation, poverty, and misery for untold millions of Chinese people.

This was the supreme price paid for some of the most beautiful china and porcelain the world has ever known!

History was repeated in England in the sixteenth century in the Staffordshire area. Deforestation caused potters there to turn to coal for fueling their furnaces. Smog from the smoke-pall hung heavy over the Potteries, causing countless deaths and untold suffering among men, women, and children employees in the Five Cities.

Today in America, after only three hundred years, we are in the slow process of correcting some of our conservation practices with our programs of environmental control. It seems we will never learn.

Tea did not become a popular beverage in Japan until the thirteenth century; it was introduced into Java in 1684 by a German naturalist and doctor of medicine. In 1827 a young Dutch tea-taster, J.I.L.L. Jacobson, risked his life to go back into the forebidden interior Chinese gardens to bring seeds and workers out to the Dutch East Indies in order to propagate tea in that region.

Tea (and salt) have been considered legal tender and used in lieu of metallic coins in numerous countries at·various times; it may still be a common medium of exchange in the interior of Central Asia.

Impetus for this foreign trade all began with the Portuguese sailing ships in the 1400s when they first brought back from the Far East tea and spices, along with the beautiful ceramic wares of China. During the next century very little porcelain reached England but it was highly prized and the evident superiority of the ware whetted the desire for more.

Long before, 1559 to be exact, tea was mentioned in European history but it was the East India Company, the greatest tea monoply in the world, that made it popular and accessible in England. Tea was so scarce in England in 1660 that the prepared brew was taxed by the gallon just like chocolate. In 1659 a most valuable gift from the East

---

* William Chaffers, *The New Chaffers' Marks and Monograms on Pottery and Porcelain*, 14th Edition (London: William Reeves, Bookseller, 1954), pp. 317–321.
† Ibid., p. 320.
‡ Ibid., p. 320.

India Company to the King was two pounds and two ounces of tea from China.

The first exclusive shipment of tea was said to have been unloaded in Holland in 1610 and from there the tea customs spread to New Amsterdam (New York City) around 1650. The Dutch went all out for this new fad and with the actual tea-drinking came all the tea equippage: tea-boards, tea pots, silver teaspoons, tea strainers — but that is another story.

The Boston Tea Party is the one event in our own history, well known by every school child, and was a contributing factor to the American Revolution. Perhaps it was this quarrel with our mother country that created a bad taste in our mouths for tea. The end result: We never fully followed England in their national custom of tea-drinking. After the Revolution, trade increased at an accelerated pace between the United States, England, Portugal, and the Orient, and our young nation began trading directly with the Far East, instead of through Britain as we had been obliged to do previously.

By the time of Lord Macartney's report (1795–1800), Josiah Wedgwood I was passing from the scene and his sons were in charge of his beautiful Etruria. In the young American nation there were at least twenty-five well established potters and trade with England in raw materials for finished products was brisk on all fronts.

Indeed!! The lowly tea plant of China changed the course of history!

Competition has been the spark that ignited the fires of progress. The fierce competition of the clipper ships bringing tea from China to Britain was the basis of the great sagas of the English East India Company. We never tire of hearing about those eleven sailing ships which started the Great Tea Race of 1866 in Fouchow and arrived ninety-nine days later in London after a trip of 16,000 miles. First place went to the "Taipan" which docked in the London port; the "Ariel" beat the third competitor by only ten minutes when they both arrived at the Downs. These races were annual affairs until the picturesque clipper ships passed from the maritime scene.

Just a small part of the Tea Leaf dishes in the galley of the Star of India which is moored in the San Diego, California harbor. It is open to the public. (20)

Another of those sturdy sailing ships was the "Star of India" christened "Euterpe" in 1863 at a port in the Isle of Man. It sailed regularly from England to many ports of the world. Shortly after the turn of the century the "Euterpe" was sold to American interests and flew the Stars and Stripes until 1923 under the grand name "Star of India." Her final resting place is the port of San Diego, California where visitors may tour the ship and see the galley table set with Tea Leaf! The ship has been a tourist attraction since 1971 and one of my English-born friends, Frances Spinner, was instrumental in obtaining the pictures from the "Star of India" which accompany this story. I wonder how many of the other eighteen Star of India ships had also been outfitted with Tea Leaf.

Place setting plus serving pieces displayed on the table on board the Star of India. Eight of the potters works are represented. (20)

Regular shipments of tea to England had been firmly established by 1650. When first introduced there by the Portuguese, the tea was steeped, the liquid thrown out, and the leaves seasoned and eaten as a vegetable! However, this soon changed.

England held first place among the coffee-drinking countries of the world when tea was sold publicly for the first time at Garway's Coffee House in London in 1657. It was advertised as carrying the approval of physicians as well as having been presented to princes and other royal personages. It was coveted for its "scarcity and dearness."

To be totally acceptable a custom must be adopted by the ruler of a country and Queen Mary (1677–1694) was most enthusiastic after her initial tasting of this exotic beverage. It was customary for the porcelain imports from China to be accompanied by small packages of tea. (I wonder if this was the beginning of premiums — give-aways at the market place?) Queen Mary's seventeen-year reign with her beloved William means more to us when we recall it was she who first ordered tea services to match the oriental tea-bowls (cups). Soon she ordered complete dinner services to match those cups. This was such a beautiful display, she then asked for, and received, ornate wooden cabinets in which to display this dazzling porcelain. Thus, a new industry was born — the crafting of china cabinets.

Tea-drinking in the seventeenth century was a social occasion similar to our television parties in the 1950s, when only the privileged few had this modern miracle and were eager to share (or to showoff) with their friends and neighbors.

In England the custom of serving tea and cakes in the afternoon at five was originated in 1840 by Anna, wife of the Duke of Bedford. At that time it was the custom to eat a huge breakfast with no other meal until eight o'clock at night, so the respite of cakes and tea was most welcome. From this innovation many needs and necessities evolved. Serving the tea was taken very seriously. Much thought was given to the selection of sandwiches and pastries to be served on appropriate plates which were part of most tea services. A very simple service included only a tea pot with a sugar bowl and pitcher for milk or cream, but the usual set included two serving plates and a dozen cups and saucers. If the set was also used for high tea or Sunday night supper then a dozen tea plates and a dozen fruit sauce dishes along with a small waste bowl were added. A tea service also could include serving trays, one or two compotes, and a hot water jug. Tea pots were usually the last survivors of the sets.

In 1904 in New York City a tea merchant distributed samples of his tea tied up in small silk bags. The idea proved so successful that this type of packaging now surpasses all other forms. The iced tea fad began at the World's Fair in St. Louis, Missouri, also in 1904. A tea merchant there was having trouble getting rid of his product on a very hot day. By a brilliant idea born of desperation, he put ice in the beverage and added sugar. Eureka! Iced tea!

There is an old saying that others think we are crazy: We heat water to make tea hot and put ice in it to make it cold; put sugar in it to make it sweet and lemon in it to make it sour. I wonder what they think about the Russians, who serve tea in glasses and add lemon or jam. Tea is the most popular beverage in the U.S.S.R. today.

In Australia and New Zealand it is served at least seven times a day — from before breakfast to the last thing before retiring. It can be purchased in tea rooms, caravans, railway cars, offices, and factories. Even the farmers have tea brought to them in the fields. The dock workers won the right for a tea break when they struck, over this one issue. Perhaps this is one place where our union-approved coffee-breaks have garnered additional strength.

Sometimes I wonder what we would be drinking if that Japanese Buddhist saint had not cut off his eyelids! Or if the leaves of the tea tree had not accidentally fallen in the water, boiling for the safety of the Emperor's health!

I can think of no better way to honor this lowly evergreen plant than by the use and enjoyment of our simply elegant Tea Leaf dishes at every opportunity.

The Tea Leaf Design

The preceding historical background sketched how tea has changed the history of the world; thus, we can appreciate more fully why the "Tea Leaf" should be commemorated in a very special way. This is the time to "let our imaginations soar" and try to guess what might have happened in the evolution of our design.

Tea Leaf is the only name used in this book because it is the one name we all know to identify this popular old pattern. If you read "Lustre Band and Sprig," "Band and Spray," "Lustre Band and Spray," "Edge Line and Sprig," "Lustre Leaf," or "Lustre Spray," remember these are all early names used in both England and America.

At the outset of decoration with the Tea Leaf design, there was much plain white ironstone on the market, some very ornately embossed. The plain ware was a favorite in the world market, so it was reasonable for the manufacturers to do all possible to keep their customers interested in buying ironstone. Since firms used different basic shapes and the molds were readily available, it was a simple matter to apply the lustred design on the plain white ware.

Legends are legion as to just how the Tea Leaf design evolved since to date there is no known record of its beginning. The following ideas are listed alphabetically, not in any order of importance. In searching for possible models, I found the following illustrations of plants, all native to Staffordshire. You may have other suggestions you would like to share.

There is every possibility that more than one leaf was used as a model.

1. **Anemone** — a member of the buttercup family and some variety of it is in bloom most of the year. The wood anemone, a very beautiful flower, was a common sight around Staffordshire.

2. **Blackberry** — leaf designs were embossed on the body of some of the plain white ironstone and Alfred Meakin identified one of his ironstone patterns as "blackberry" in the trademark. It is possible this three-lobed leaf was looked upon as a pleasant pattern for this sprig design.

3. **Cinquefoil** — member of the rose family, many varieties are common in Great Britain. Most usual is the five-lobed variety but there is also a three-lobed plant; both designs are often seen in church windows. The accompanying picture of an old ironstone jug has a cinquefoil design on it. The common five-lobed variety was used on this old pitcher. It is entirely possible someone adapted the less common three-petal plant in the design of the Tea Leaf decoration.

Botanical drawings, Johana Gast Anderton

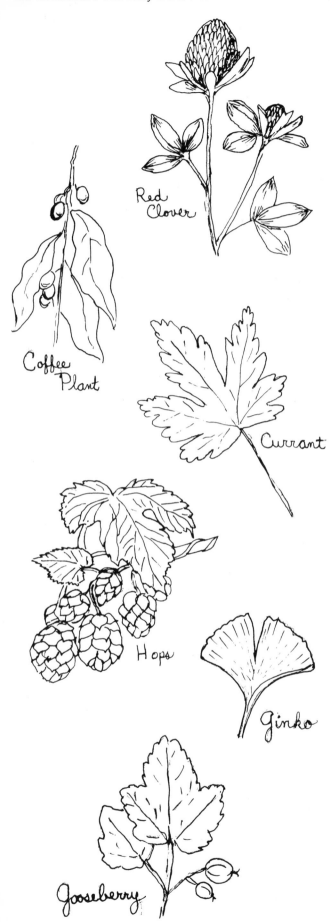

Red Clover

Coffee Plant

Currant

Hops

Ginko

Gooseberry

4. **Clover** — a good possibility for some of the potters' designers. Edge, Malkin Company Tea Leaf is a fine example. The flower looks somewhat like a clover flower and the clover leaf has three parts. Even though the common varieties we see here do not have serrated leaves, I think there is a possibility the clover was the model for this particular variant.

   In addition Powell and Bishop produced a variant in green underglaze design with copper lustre that resembles a clover flower and has been indentified by some collectors as such.

   The old Bridgwood Company clover leaf, as well as William Adams Company's variant, are considered forerunners of Tea Leaf. A clover design certainly could have been an expression of the artistic freedom of a designer.

5. **Coffee** — plant leaves do not resemble Tea Leaf but the sprigs of the berries may have been models for the variation by Clementson Brothers. I like to think there were potters in England who preferred coffee and wanted to show some recognition in their dinnerware, yet, not wanting to miss out on the Tea Leaf popularity in the market place, they settled on the combinations of dangling berries and a Tea Leaf, which now we know as the "coffee-berry" design.

6. **Currant** — leaves were a surprise to me in their likeness to our motif until I learned they are a member of the gooseberry family and native to Great Britain, which grows more black currants than any other country in the world. The fruit is used for flavoring as well as jams and jellies. They are grown under fruit trees because they like shade and gardeners can make better use of their ground. Since many potters were also farmers, currant bushes were quite a common sight.

7. **Hops** — also a native of England, grows profusely; hence it is a common sight and could very easily have been one of the inspirations for our design. Hops are used for brewing ale and beer, favorite beverages in the Potteries district. They are also used for medicinal purposes.

8. **Ginkgo Tree** — a model suggested by Frances Spinner, a native of Folkstone, on the southern coast of England. The history of this tree goes back to prehistoric times. It is a native of China, related to the palm family; the leaves fall after turning bright gold. It is known today as the Good Luck Tree (touching the tree is supposed to bring good luck). What better pattern could Powell & Bishop use for their variation to meet the Tea Leaf competition than this beautiful gold ginkgo leaf and the gold band which is the symbol of eternity? Our lone example of Tea Leaf by Cartwright Bros. of East Liverpool, Ohio is very akin to this gold serrated design of Powell & Bishop (later Bishop & Stonier).

9. **Gooseberry** — leaves have been mentioned numerous times as likely models for the Tea Leaf design, and they do bear a great resemblance. This is an excellent thought, as the gooseberry has been cultivated in England since the 1600s and today is very important in their agricultural production. Many of the potters were also part-time farmers or perhaps many of the farmers were part-time potters. The flower is also very similar.

10. **Pepper** — probably the least likely prospect for the pattern but when we look at a pepper plant leaf and then study the "Pepper Leaf" variation by Elsmore and Forster, the similarity is too noticeable to ignore.

11. **Ranunculus** — family of plants which includes thirty general types of approximately seven hundred species, among which are buttercups, larkspur, anemone, columbine, clematis, marsh marigold, peony and baneberry, crowfoot, spearwart, and celandine. Many of these varieties have gold flowers and three-lobed leaves; all are common in England. Some are herbs used for teas which usually have an acrid flavor. Many people have probably thought that tea was "good for them just because it. tasted so bad!" (when brewed from these herbs).

    Numerous plants were originally considered ornamental supplements to herb gardens or were used for medicinal purposes. In the 1800s many families grew their own medicinal plants and doctored themselves. This was long before the day of "take two aspirin with a glass of water" or "come to the office for a shot of antibiotic," so this particular family of plants was especially important to them. Any one of a number of them could have been the inspiration to a designer searching for a new idea.

12. **Rose** — was one of the most popular subjects for china decoration. We refer to a "rose sprig" or a "rose spray" and some others think the cabbage rose is very much like the green Tea Leaf pattern used by Powell & Bishop. Since the moss rose, the primrose, and the wild rose, as well as the cabbage rose, had already been used many times as models, stylization of the rose for yet one more design could have been a logical step. There is even a tea rose (not the hybrid tea roses we know) which has the fragrance of fresh green tea leaves. Rose leaves are found with three or five sections and some are more deeply serrated than others.

    It is interesting to note that the red rose of Lancashire and the white rose of Yorkshire were combined to form the symbolic Tudor Rose, the royal badge of England at the marriage of Henry VII of Lancashire to Elizabeth of York in 1486. Since then the Tudor Rose has been considered the national flower of England. The phrase, "there will always be an England" could have been in the mind of the designer as he transferred to a copper engraving plate, his hope that there would "always be a rose" to identify himself as Englishman. We might say it was his trademark on sturdy ironstone.

    With further study I note that in most cases the American potters omitted the flower from their Tea Leaf designs. I cannot help but wonder if this was a silent protest of the English domination, even long after we were a separate country.

13. **Strawberry** — has been called to our attention and is, in fact, mentioned in *Staffordshire Pottery** by Josiah C. Wedgwood M.P., and Thomas Ormsbee. There is a photograph of a creamer and sugar bowl in the Tea Leaf pattern with this notation: "Victorian lustre-ware creamer and sugar, part of the Staffordshire dinner service, circa 1850, decorated with strawberry leaves and flower in copper lustre." This is an

---

* Josiah C. Wedgwood M.P. and Thomas Ormsbee, *Stafforshire Pottery* (Robert M. McBride & Co., 1947), p. 152.

Strawberry

Teaberry

Avens

Tea Plant

example of Victorian china made by Anthony Shaw. The text does *not* state it was made by Wedgwood. (See chapter on the Enoch Wedgwood (Tunstall) Ltd. Company.) The co-author, Josiah C. Wedgwood, was a descendant of the master potter Josiah of Etruria, and not related in any way to Enoch Wedgwood.

14. **Tea Berry** — refers to the checkerberry or wintergreen berries. This plant is quite hardy in England; the leaves are sharply astringent with the taste and smell peculiar to wintergreen. The tea made from the leaves is known as mountain tea and is taken to relieve muscular aches and pains.

The red spicy berries, when roasted and ground, were used by some as tea or coffee substitutes; this custom carried over to the United States because the plant was also found here. Use of this substitute by the colonists in New England led to great dissension among the women concerning the unreasonably high tax on tea, as well as other imports from England. Tea berry, (or checkerberry, or wintergreen berry) tea was a very poor second choice to the Oriental tea they had come to enjoy. It was not long before the women's dissatisfaction spurred the men into action and the Boston Tea Party was the end result of this bitter resentment. History was once again affected by the tea leaf.

15. **Tea Plants** — small white fragrant flowers, similar to the bud on the dish design, but as noted before, the tea leaves are totally different.

16. **Water Avens** — another member of the rose family with the tri-part, coarsely serrated leaf, very common in Britain.

May I suggest that every individual Tea Leaf design is the expression of some long ago artist who created by "artistic license" what he saw around him. By adding a line or two, or by omitting a detail, he gave us something special which we all love. The sizes of the motif vary so much even within the line produced by one company, I can just hear some pot-bank owner or foreman saying, "Now don't you make that flower too big . . . you know this copper-lustre we have to buy is too expensive to waste." Another may have taken the opposite view: "Say, make that leaf sprig bigger! The women are all crazy for the new-fangled copper lustre stuff and since we don't have to put any other colors on, we can afford to give 'em more of this! Besides, it's prettier, isn't it?"

My one last suggestion as to why a three-part leaf was chosen: Perhaps some designer chose this method to express his belief in the Trinity. John Wesley, the founder of the Methodist church, was a frequent visitor to the Potteries and many potters were family friends of the Wesleys. In fact, one potter made, as a special gift for Susanna Wesley (John's mother), a huge pitcher that held enough milk to serve her entire family of fifteen children! Evidently John Wesley's work was successful because Josiah C. Wedgwood II, one hundred years later, reported the average potter was a Methodist.

Tea Leaf is a catchy name and its "popularity has spread like pollen in the wind" as expressed by the late Gladys Caruso. She continued, "It was the Elisa Doolittle of the Pottery trade: and I feel it has come into its own again. Its present popularity has resulted in a resurgence of collecting, of unprecedented proportions."

It appears there were a number of reasons for this broad appeal in the very beginning:

1. The designers must have liked it because it had to be well executed to look its best.

2. The decorators must have liked it because it was quick and easy to apply.

3. The jiggermen must have liked to have it applied to their wares because there was no overall design to cover the quality of their workmanship. Previously designs had often been used to cover flaws and imperfections in the body of the ware. Even without proper equipment and controls consistently good quality ironstone was produced as evidenced by the work of potters such as Davenport and Anthony Shaw.

4. Tea Leaf ironstone appealed to the average American housewife because it was white, durable, and simply elegant. There were none of the gaudy colors and overpowering designs to distract from a tasty meal. Elegance was in the body shape and variety was in the individual Tea Leaf designs on each item of the set. Each motif was made with an outline from an engraving plate, filled in by hand, then glazed and fired. Afterward, the design was covered exactly, with a thin coat of copper lustre and the band applied by a continuous turning of the item beneath a hand held brush. The piece was fired the second time at a much lower temperature in order to not burn off the copper lustre or distort the color.

The quiet dignity of such ware was familiar to countless children who sat through "grace" by a long-winded preacher. They waited, half-starved, while Sunday dinner of fried chicken, corn-on-the-cob, and apple pie grew colder and colder. All they could do was stare at the plate, turned upside down on the table, with the words Anthony Shaw, Alfred Meakin, or Wedgwood and Co., and wonder about those names and the funny looking marks with horses, unicorns, crowns, shields, ribbons, anchors, or the like.

More often than not the plates were placed upside down to keep the ever-present flies off them. (Screen wire was not invented until the 1850s and was not in general use until the 1890s.) Girls or women stood around the table, fanning the flies away from the waiting food, all the while hoping for a quick "Amen." Those were the "good ole days."

Because of this universal appeal, Tea Leaf caught on quickly and sold so well, and the potteries had to turn to assembly line production. No longer was each plate, cup, or bowl thrown by hand; they were pressed by machines. Someone writing in a 1948 *Farm Journal*† has called Alfred Meakin and Johnson Bros. the Henry Fords of the pottery industry.

Even more production was needed with the opening of the West here in the United States, when many new homes were established and ironstone was the preferred dinner ware and Tea Leaf was probably the most popular pattern in ironstone ever sold.

Today, most of the unpleasant jobs in the pottery industry are performed automatically by a machine or have been simplified by use of modern means of production. Even so, there is more hand labor in this industry than in any other I know of.

Let us now delve into the history of the pottery and the potters.

---

† Grace Ellis, *Farm Journal* (1948).

Some Early Staffordshire Pottery History

We cannot fully appreciate our heritage of the dishes on our tables until we know something of their early beginnings and the men who made them. Josiah Clement Wedgwood M.P., a great grandson of the famous Josiah Wedgwood, in his *Staffordshire Pottery and its History* published in 1913 brings this area to life. This chapter is a composite of his story, along with gleanings from other well known English historians including: Dr. Plot, writing before 1700; Simeon Shaw, writing in 1828; Llewellynn Jewitt, in 1878; William Burton, in 1902; W. P. Jervis and J. F. Blacker, each writing in 1911; William Chaffers' 14th edition history, published in 1954; and Bevis Hillier, who wrote in 1968. Each writer makes a unique contribution to this saga of ceramics. The time considered is approximately 1600–1970. The history of this district **is** the history of potting and the social history of the inhabitants has changed the course of events for over four hundred years. No other district in the world is so completely identified with one trade as the Potteries (Paw'-trees), but *not* because there was only one trade followed there. Before 1650 potting was incidental to agriculture, and as potting grew, so did the mining of coal and iron ore. The real reason for the name "The Potteries" was simply one of convenience. It was so much easier to say than "Tunstall-Burslem-Hanley-Stoke-Longton"; or to add "Shelton-Cobridge-Fenton-Dale Hall-or Longport." Few people outside of these towns wanted to refer to them individually, nor could they distinguish one from the other. The same is true today. This term came into common usage in the latter part of the 1700s.

This small lizard-shaped area is in the northern part of the County of Staffordshire, about one hundred fifty miles northwest of London and encompasses an area only about nine miles long and three miles wide.

Before the 1300s men often took as their last name that of their trade or form of employment. However in a Tunstall Manor List of common people dated 1299, which included Burslem, there were no names listed as indicating any association with the pottery trade; but in another similar list for nearby Audley, several were listed such as: Robert le Pottere, Thomas Pottinger, and Richard le Throware. Nor were similar names found on the Tunstall tax rolls for 1326, 1327, or 1333 but several years later, in the Court Rolls of that town there were several listings:

1348 — William the Pottere was given a license to make pots
1353 — Thomas the Througher was fined for non-payment of debt
1363 — John Pottere was fined for fighting in Burslem
1369 — Robert Le Potter was given a license to get clay to make pots
1372 — Thomas le Thrower bought land
1405 — Robert Potter died
1448 — Richard and William Adams were taken into court for digging clay on a common road

Digging clay on public property or along the roadside was a serious problem and heavy fines were levied against the culprits. This was the crime of the Adams brothers, William and Richard, as recorded above as well as in the chapter on the Adams Pottery. Filling up the pot-holes was invariably part of any rent or lease agreement. Even then many gaping holes marred the countryside but some few were used for various other purposes. Since these early-day potters were handymen of many trades, not hampered by ecologists, they sometimes placed their "pot-banks" right at the back of their houses by the cow sheds and dug the clay from their own land.

Other very early "pot-banks" were placed wherever clay was found. The clay was mixed with water, often from a nearby stream, and baked on the spot with wood which was also abundant and near at hand. All good things come to an end though; the wood was burned faster than it grew and it soon became rare and costly. As a result, coal was the fuel replacement and families began to specialize because of their own needs or the demands of their neighbors. Their kilns to bake the pots were often right in the banks of clay — thus the term "pot-banks."

There was, before 1600, no need for specialization in one district, as the art of potting is as old as the art of cooking, and it was considered a branch of housekeeping to supply the family with whatever pots needed for the household. Many of these crude utensils are on display in various Staffordshire area pottery museums.

In a brief geographical survey we can learn where our Tea Leaf was made.

Stafforshire Potteries District
Tunstall
Brownhills
Burslem
Longport
Cobridge
Hanley
Shelton
Etruria
Stoke-on-Trent
Fenton
Lane Delph
Lane End
Longton
River Trent

Maps by Helen K. (Heaivilin) Long

Tunstall — Beginning in the north end we find Tunstall which came from the Anglo-Saxon word "tun," a town, and "stall," an elevated seat. It was held as a feudal estate under the manor of New Castle by Henry de Audley and had belonged to John Frost in the reign of Henry VIII. The ironstone with which Tunstall abounds was worked as early as 1316, but it took three hundred years for the town to become of any importance. It is on a main road about four miles northeast of Newcastle and on a cross road from Lawton to Burslem. In the beginning of the nineteenth century there were only about sixty houses and three churches. One of the most famous potters of all time was from Tunstall — William Adams. But we must not forget Enoch Wood who introduced fluid glazes into the potting industry, or Richard Champion who in 1781 sold his patent to make the first true English porcelain to a group of Staffordshire potters that worked for a time in Tunstall at the Anthony Keeling works. This was the patent Champion had purchased from William Cookworthy. However more Tea Leaf lovers will recognize Tunstall as the home of Alfred Meakin potteries, which provided more of this design than any other company. Others included Edward Challinor; Elsmore and Forster; W.H. Grindley; Johnson Bros.; Enoch Wedgwood, Ltd.; and Anthony Shaw.

Burslem, called the "Mother of the Potteries," was two miles south and slightly east of Tunstall. The name had several possible meanings: "A bower in the wood" (there was a great amount of wood around Burslem area before 1600); another more likely one: "Bulwordslen" which referred to bull-baiting or a bull-keeper. Another authority gave "boars lane" from wild boars which ran rampant in the area.

Mr. Wedgwood in 1913 projected the possibility that

> . . . the impetus for local manufacture may have come from the dissolution in 1536, of the monasteries. There is reason to believe, judging from the remains at the Cistercian Abbey of Hulton that the monks made there such encaustic tile as they are to this day called *Cistercian*. Hulton Abbey and the Abbey's grange of Rushton both lie in the Burslem parish. Some rudimentary practice in the art and mystery of potting may well have come from the seven scattering brethren of this dissolved monastery and may account in part for the development which was to come. From now on we begin to find potters thick on the ground in Burslem . . .*

The Cistercians, who originated in France as a branch of the Benedictine order, were established at Hulton Abbey in 1222. It was destroyed about 300 years later along with numerous other monasteries and religious institutions during the reign of Henry VIII.

One of the unusual characteristics of this self-sustaining group was that each monastery had to have a plentiful supply of clean, fresh running water *inside* the buildings for drinking and sanitation purposes. Later excavations brought to light various types of tile which had been used to carry the fresh water in from nearby springs and others to carry the waste water away.

With this background I feel it is logical to conclude that potting was one of the trades that flourished inside the monastery through necessity, to provide for their daily needs, and later in the outside world of the Potteries district. As a result I like to think that many of those monk-brethren-potters were destined to benefit mankind in this very practical trade, another proof that all good things come to us from God who loves and cares for us.

Dr. Plot, the noted ceramist-historian, paid a visit to Burslem in 1677 and made copious comments on the diversity of the good clays available within a half-mile radius with plenty of coal also nearby.

---

* Wedgwood, Josiah C., *Staffordshire Pottery and its History.*

One of the greatest demands was for cheese and butter-pots for the dairy produce market at Uttoxeter. Because many early butter-pots were so porous and retained some of the water from the butter that incorrect weight or measure was given, a law was passed in 1757 regulating the size to hold fourteen pounds of butter and be glazed inside the container. One of the early potters mentioned in Burslem was one Cartwright who was referred to as a "poor butter-pot maker." He evidently was not so poor because it is recorded he gave twenty pounds annually to the poor — quite a tidy sum in that day and time. (See the Cartwright Bros. chapter.)

But Burslem had something else — the land was split up between many small copy holders (owners) and after 1600 these copyholders were enfranchised. There was no more baronial or manorial land! The people were free! They were independent of both the big farmers and the great landlords. They had security of ownership and greater opportunity for progress. They naturally turned to potting as they had the basic requirements mentioned before: clay, fuel, and skilled workmen; now there was incentive, and by 1790 another dimension was added — transportation — by way of the Trent-Mersey Canal of which Josiah Wedgwood was the mastermind.

As late as 1740, according to Simeon Shaw† "any manufacturer who was a freeholder" (a property owner that had inherited part of an estate) usually "exercised his right of taking clay or coal (or both) from any unenclosed or unenfranchised land in the area at any time and in any quantity he wanted." All the clay and coal used in the Burlsem ovens which were filled and fired once each week, were obtained "from holes in the streets and sides of the lanes and were not all filled up with refuse" when Shaw wrote his history in 1828 — almost 90 years later!

Our introduction to the most famous Burslem pottery family in their Court Rolls was when, in 1656, one John Calclough (alias Rowley) in his will gave: "To Thomas Wedgwood of the Churchyard of Burslem all my potting boards and all other necessary implements and materials belonging to the trade of potting (lead and lead ore only are excepted)." The same Thomas Wedgwood was the great grandfather of the first Josiah Wedgwood and he, along with two of his brothers, Aaron and Moses, later described themselves in their wills as potters.

I had wondered if the name "Wedgwood" came from the trade of wood cutting and splitting it with iron wedges placed in the length-wise cracks of the felled trees which were made with a sharp ax wielded by the woodsmen. But when I later read Eliza Meteyard's *Life of Josiah Wedgwood*, I found she had recorded in 1878:

> The name of Wedgwood, originally spelt Weggowode was derived from a very small rural hamlet or township of four hundred thirty-one acres in the parish of Walstanton, Newcastle, and was probably so called at some remote period from its situation in a densely wooded district.‡

From the 1670 Tunstall-Burslem Court rolls many other names will be familiar to us later on in our Tea Leaf story:

Ric. Edge	Ralph Shaw
Joseph Malkin	Wm. Edge
Moses Wedgwood	Wm. Taylor
Thomas Adams	Richard Wedgwood

† Simeon Shaw, *History of the Staffordshire Potteries* (New York: Praeger Publishers, Inc., 1972 reprint of 1829 original).

‡ Eliza Meteyard, *The Life of Josiah Wedgwood*, Vol. I (London: Hurst & Blackett, 1865).

By 1710–1715 there were over forty potteries in Burslem alone, with very few anywhere else.

Descendants of these men were potters in the nineteenth century and some are still in business today — 1980.

Because of the location on top of Moorland Ridge, Burslemites were spared many hours of discomfort from these "dense clouds of vapour from the ovens, when Salt was used for glazing, or the coal smoke when the ovens were fired on Thursday."§ These pot-ovens were vividly described by Dr. Plot in 1677 which Wedgwood repeated in 1913.

.The pot-oven described by Plot would be surrounded by a wall of clods of turf to keep in the heat, or by a "hovel" with walls of broken saggers, roofed with boughs and clods of earth. Each pot-work consisted of a "hovel" such as this: some thatched open sheds for drying the ware, and an open tank or sun-pan in which the clay mixed with water was evaporated. These sun-pans or sun-kilns were about twelve feet wide by twenty feet long and about eighteen inches deep. One portion partitioned off, deeper, and lined with flagstones, was used for mixing. Here the clay was "blunged" by a man with a long pole or paddle, and thoroughly mixed with water. The mixture was then poured through a sieve from the blunging vat into the sun-pan. A pot-works of almost exactly this description can be seen today at Gorshall Green near Stone and is used for making flower pots.

History is replete with references to Wedgwood beginning at Burslem, but we must note here that the great Josiah Wedgwood moved a couple of miles away to Stoke-on-Trent in 1769 and built his beloved Etruria on the original Ridge House estate grounds which encompassed about one hundred fifty acres. At his death in 1795 his holdings had increased to over three hundred fifty acres in Stoke and Hanley, quite a sizeable estate. Most pot-works were on an acre or less.

However, it is another Wedgwood, Enoch, who operated the Unicorn and Pinnox works in Tunstall from 1860 to the present time, who stars in our Tea Leaf story. There is no tie whatsoever between the two firms and so far I have found no evidence of family relationships.

Samuel Alcock operated the Hill Pottery in Burslem but most of the Alcocks were from Cobridge. Edge, Malkin and Co., an old potting company which was located here, made some of our pattern, as did Henry Burgess; W. & E. Corn; Mellor, Taylor & Company; Arthur J. Wilkinson; Bridgwood & Son; Thomas Hughes; and John Maddock; but many of us appreciated most of all the Tea Leaf made here by Anthony Shaw. Yes, Burslem was the home of many potters who have given us so much pleasure.

Longport was formerly Long Bridge because of the floodwaters in the valley, and the long bridge over them which originally consisted of one hundred yards of heavy planks anchored down with huge stones, to span the water course which in rainy times was quite deep and rapid. It was the home of John Davenport and his potteries which later were also owned/operated by W. & E. Corn as well as Thomas Hughes.

Cobridge lies between Burslem and Hanley and was the location of one of the Wm. Adam's pot-works, as well as several operated by Samuel Alcock along with other family members. It was the only home of the J. & R. Clews Pottery that made so much of Staffordshire Blue ware. Thomas Furnival had one pot-works here and one in Hanley; Edward Walley was in business from 1845 and made our Pre-Tea Leaf variant here.

Hanley and Shelton are considered together and are each about two miles northeast of Newcastle-under-Lyme which was not connected with

‡ Eliza Meteyard, *The Life of Josiah Wedgwood*, Vol. I (London: Hurst & Blackett, 1865).

the Potteries but was content with the prestige of being one of the oldest boroughs in England. Newcastle was also the closest market to Burslem, but all the roads were in such bad repair and infested with highway robbers, that a journey between any two cities was treacherous at best. This is possibly where the term "highway robbery" originated, but it could have come from the story of the Good Samaritan as recorded in the Gospels. One account given indicated that a traveller needed to be a boxer, as well as a peddlar or a potter, in order to adequately defend himself while on the road.

In 1715 there were only two potteries at Hanley: Ward's (the historian) and Paulson's, who was later associated with Minton. There were only one horse and one mule and very few carts in the country. Coal was carried by men, in sacks on their backs. Hanley, claiming to be the metropolis because of its "progressiveness," was named for William de Hanley of Norman Conquest times who was lord of the manor — rather like our mayor, and it is near the geographical center of this long, narrow community of potters.

Probably the most familiar name to us from the Hanley-Shelton area is Joseph Clementson, one of the best and most prolific producers of Tea Leaf. Another is Powell and Bishop who made our overglaze gold decorated variants, as well as J. & G. Meakin and several Alcock potters. The Thomas Furnivals had a pot-bank here as well as at Cobridge, and the Johnson Bros. also operated here. Another famous name long heard in Hanley was Elijah Mayer, and later his son Joseph Esq., a well known linguist, historian, and philanthropist, as well as an excellent potter. Their descendents, Joseph and Earnest, made the finest Tea Leaf in the United States from 1881.

Others, not Tea Leaf producers, but important to the potting industry were Job Meigh, who gave us the first lead-free glaze. After one enterprising pioneer built an oven so large it collapsed, another Shelton company, R. & J. Baddeley, built four ovens instead of the usual one, behind their manufactory, with the end result that they became one of the largest exporters of earthenware in a few years. Last but not least, Shelton was the site of John Atsbury's pot-bank. He will be remembered as one of two men who feigned idiocy in order to learn the secrets of the Elers brothers, first potters in Staffordshire to make red-ware and salt-glazed stoneware.

Hanley and Shelton were united in 1856 into one borough and John Ridgway was the first mayor.

Stoke-on-Trent, slightly below the middle of the Potteries area, has always been a parish town because it was the hub of an eight church circuit, according to Shaw. Even though there were few houses in Stoke proper, there were excellent school facilities for that day and time, sponsored by the church.

The Trent-Mersey Canal connected Stoke with the outside world from 1790 on, and the rail facilities after 1830 were considered the best, and newcomers assumed Stoke to be the center of activity. Today it is the seat of government for the entire Pottery district. It is a city, county, and parliamentary borough of Staffordshire. In 1910 the pottery towns of Fenton, Tunstall, Burslem, Hanley, Stoke, and Longton were federated; enlarged in 1922; became a city in 1925, and five years later it was enlarged again to a present area of slightly over thirty-three square miles.

Potting is still the chief industry, but coal mining and other allied industries are carried on to great benefit for all. Very little, if any, Tea Leaf was made in Stoke. Henry Alcock is the only maker of Tea Leaf with a pot-bank in Stoke to the best of my knowledge, but new information may come tomorrow.

Company Histories

I stand in awe of the histories of the potters who march through the pages of this book and wish to pay tribute to all potters — past and present — for preserving in clay their:

Ability to overcome insurmountable obstacles
Maintenance of high standards of business integrity
Fair and honest treatment of employees
Contributions to good and the progress of the entire industry

They have kept their spirit high, their art free, and have given us beauty with utility in this lovely ironstone Tea Leaf Lustre ware.

William Adams & Sons (Potters) Ltd.

1657 to present

Adams is an old name in the Staffordshire pottery industry; it was first mentioned in the Tunstall Manor Rolls of 1448 when two brothers, William and Richard Adams, were fined for digging clay in the road, as recorded by numerous early historians.

In 1657 John Adams converted the old Brickhouse in Burslem to a pottery. This was the beginning of their important impact on the entire industry which is still felt today. They became part of the Josiah Wedgwood & Sons (Ltd.) Group in 1966. John Adams and his descendants controlled the Brickhouse works for the next century, when in 1762, they were leased to young Josiah Wedgwood for a mere pittance of £20 per year!

Confusion rules the Adams' family history because there were three William Adams — all potters, but the well known one whose direct family line continues today in the Wedgwood Group is William Adams of Greengates, 1746–1805. This is still the business location. He was a contemporary, friend, and competitor of Josiah Wedgwood and some collectors prefer his Jasper ware colors.

Another of these three Williams is credited with being the first to use the copper plate transfer printing method of decorating — a secret so jealously guarded that two transferrers worked behind locked doors.

All Adams designs now, whether hand painted or printed, are underglaze; therefore they are completely safe from detergent damage. This was the reason they discontinued the Tea Leaf production in 1972 — they were unable to put the copper luster under the glaze so it was dishwasher safe. This information was supplied to me by Mr. E. H. Edge.

Our interest in the William Adams Company is two-fold. The Cloverleaf variant is the old pattern under first consideration. The following is part of a letter I received from Mr. E. H. Edge:

Adams Clover Leaf variant on a 10" plate.
AD-1

Dear Madam,

Thank you for your letter of the 28th November, giving me the background of your interest in the pattern Tea Leaf.

The decoration illustrated on the plate is not, strictly speaking, Tea Leaf, but was a traditional gold clover leaf type spray used by many potteries both in the last century and this.

As regards the backstamp the registration mark in the centre of the wreath is of the type used from 1868 to 1883. The day of the month is shown in the top segment of the diamond, the year in the right-hand segment, and the month in the lower segment.

The day of the month was the 15th, the letter H is for 1869 and the letter C is for January. The pattern in question was therefore registered on the 15th January, 1869.

On the other hand the trademark bears the established date of 1657. This was first applied in 1896, which indicated therefore, that although the pattern was registered much earlier, bearing as it does a backstamp only used after 1896, the piece must have been made after that date. . .

Yours faithfully,
E. H. Edge
Assistant Manager

Reproductions to Tea Leaf. Two cups and saucers only ½" difference in size.   (69)
AD-2

These four plates are prize possessions because until I found these in Arizona, I was under the impression all the Cloverleaf design was of Bridgwood or Bridgwood & Son origin. These are an off-white color, finely crazed, with gold in an overglaze application which shows very little wear. The shape is quite pleasing, and the body is lighter weight

Dazzling! This Empress-shape soup tureen, lid, ladle, and service tray is about 10½" high x 12" long. This shape was first used by them during most of the nineteenth century and is still very popular today. (12)
AD-3

AD-4

All trademarks found on the new Tea Leaf made 1960-1972
AD-5

than most ironstone. There is a dainty, embossed, scalloped design around the edge of these ten-inch plates.

Our second and current interest is due to the fine reproductions of Tea Leaf made by the Adams Company in the 1960s and which have now disappeared from the American market. If any of our readers is fortunate enough to find Tea Leaf by Adams, buy it and use it proudly with your original dinnerware. The cups should be especially welcomed. Reproductions are on a thinner, lighter body, creamy white in color. The flat soup is somewhat smaller than the original one; therefore, it is more practical on our smaller, modern tables. The tureens are especially lovely and if you are fortunate enough to find salt and pepper shakers by all means do not pass them up! I have seen only two sets. Evidently, no other Tea Leaf maker felt they were important.

Keep in mind these are now collectors' items as production has altogether ceased.

The following letter, also from Mr. Edge, should be of interest to all owners of these fine reproductions.

Dear Madam,

Adams — Copper Tea Leaf

Thank you for your letter of the 4th October from which I was very interested to learn that you are writing a book on the Tea Leaf pattern.

We know that the Tea Leaf decoration was popular from about 1850 to the early years of this century but we have no evidence that this was produced by the Adams family or the Adams potteries during that period. On the other hand, it was a typical ironstone decoration and Adams as manufacturers and exporters of this type of earthenware, would almost certainly have produced a common decoration of this type.

In recent years William Adams introduced Copper Tea Leaf of Empress shape in about 1960. The centre decoration of the spray was applied by a copper coloured print to the biscuit piece which was then glazed. The copper lustre of the tea leaf decoration itself was then hand painted on glaze over the underglaze print. The piece was then finished with a lustre band at the edge.

William Adams ceased to manufacture Copper Tea Leaf in 1972 . . .

We believe that some years ago attempts were made in the United States to register Tea Leaf as a new pattern! . . .

The spray shown on your letter is slightly different from the one used by Adams, an illustration of which is enclosed.

Yours faithfully,
E. H. Edge
Assistant Manager

N. Hudson Moore in *The Old China Book* included some interesting and unique quotations from Downman's *English Pottery and Porcelaine*: "William Adams was one of Wedgwood's favorite people and . . . he was initiated into all the mysteries of Etruria . . . It was his experiments which led to the improvements in the blue Jasper body by adding gold filings to its chief ingredient, the sulphate of bayta. After Josiah's death Adams settled in Tunstall and produced many fine specimens of ornamental Jasper and Basalt ware . . . Most of Adams ware was marked with his name, impressed, or by a peculiar border of interlaced circles."

This *Old China Book* was written in 1903 and in it, the author also comments: "In the early days of rummage sales (three or four years ago)

---

* N. Hudson Moore, *The Old China Book* (New York: Tudor Publishing Company, 1936 reprint).

AD-6

there were great opportunities to pick up old china which had lain neglected scores of years and which housekeepers were glad to clear out." She also agrees with Lowell in voicing the sentiments of so many of us: "I stand by the old thought; the old thing; the old place, and the old friend. It seems we do not give anything time to grow old, to get that dignity which a hundred years bestows. We are too anxious to renew, rebuild, or pull down and put up something larger. I feel one of the reasons why this old china is so eagerly sought is because it stands for a measure of Antiquity; it has the hall-mark of age and we love to have it to sober down our newness of yesterday . . ." Written in 1903 but it sounds like 1980!

Alcock Potters
1875-1935

Gravy boat, very neat and sturdy. Note the fine Blanket Stitch design around the middle; this is an Alcock trademark design.
AL-1

Water ewer. Blanket Stitch is much more distinct in this photo. None of the Alcock pieces I have seen is crazed.
AL-2

Samuel Alcock's name was listed as early as 1828 as a Cobridge potter. He had been a china painter for Copeland's and began potting on his own in 1830 when he took the Hilltop Pottery at Burslem. He operated three pot-works in the Burslem-Cobridge-Hanley area, and much of his ware was made for the American market. Even though his widow, Elizabeth, and two sons, Samuel and Thomas, were operating the pot-works in 1851, employing over seven hundred workers, some of the company wares were exhibited at the London Exhibition and received much favorable comment. The company failed in 1859 and all their moulds and models were dispersed. After that the various works were operated by several different men including Sir James Duke and Nephews; later Diggory, Bodley, Burgess and Leigh; H. Burgess; and finally a part of the holdings reverted back to one Richard Alcock.

John and George (J&G) Alcock — Cobridge Pottery was established in 1843 and was one of the branches of the Alcock family which catered to the American trade with ironstone as an early specialty. After 1850 they were known as John Alcock and Company, who can be recalled as having been the first to use the same shape ware with several styles of decoration. So often, an item had two names — the shape and the decoration; others copied this system later in the century. (It was common to see Tea Leaf or Moss Rose on the same shape.) In 1875 the change was made to Henry Alcock and Company. He was a son of John at the Elder Pottery in Cobridge. He became a leader in the manufacture of earthenware made exclusively for the American trade. He used the names "Ironstone China" and "Parisian Porcelain" to attract attention; but he also made semi-porcelain in striking colors and original designs. Careful workmanship made mechanically produced ware very artistic and much in demand.

Henry Alcock and Company was doing business in 1900 at the Waterloo Road Works in Burslem, which had been founded in 1820 by Thomas Hughes; and Alcocks were still in business from 1910 to 1935 at the Clarence Works in Stoke, using a variety of trademarks. Henry Alcock made quite a lot of Tea Leaf — most of it on a lighter weight body, with numerous trademarks.

It is significant to me that Richard Alcock, whose relationship to the other Alcocks has been obscured by time, took charge of one of the works which many years before had been under the control of Samuel Alcock, but more recently under Burgess and Leigh. He made white granite ware from 1878 at the Central Pottery which he rebuilt, remodeled, and enlarged. At his death in 1881, the works passed to Arthur J. Wilkinson who, for a few years used "late R. Alcock" as part of his trademark. Richard Alcock was one of many who made and improved the ironstone type wares which met ever-increasing demands for a cross between

Trademark used 1891-1910, Elder pottery, Cobridge (61)
AL-3

porcelain and earthenware — beautiful yet durable. It has been one of the most dependable types made by ever so many pot-works, large and small, throughout the 170 years since Spode's first patent.

So often ceramic historians are enamored with the potters of fancy ornamental ware or the expensive one-of-a-kind items. Therefore the common, simpler articles for everyday use for which there was a constant demand were often overlooked or dismissed as being of no interest or importance to the collector. These were the bread and butter lines of many pot-banks and were produced to sell at comparatively low prices. Those are some of the potters this book presents in all possible detail.

5" nappy, gravy boat, and relish dish; the latter in a shape I have heard called "Mitten."
AL-4

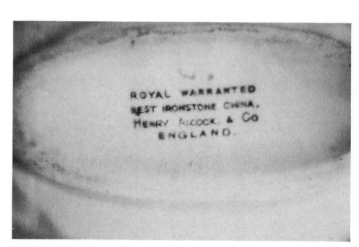

Trademarks — only Alcock marks I have seen.
AL-5

Baker & Chetwynd Co.

1869-1875

Another class consists of firms who have come into existence in recent years, whose products are known in the market, and a few details concerning them may be of interest and possibly in some cases, probably furnish data to some future historian.

W. P. Jervis: *A Pottery Primer*, 1911.

This describes perfectly the dilemma surrounding my search for the history of the old Baker & Chetwynd Company of Burslem. There was such a dearth of printed information, I was forced to turn again to Arnold Mountford of Hanley, England for help. One of the two bits of news he could find was this entry in Harrod's Directory of Staffordshire for 1870:

"Baker & Chetwynd, manufacturers of ironstone china, earthenware, for foreign markets only. Sylvester Pottery, Burslem." This entry was repeated in 1873-1874 but when the 1875-1876 data was recorded, this was the last entry:

"Charles G. Baker, earthenware manufacturer, Sylvester Pottery, Burslem."

Evidently, the Baker & Chetwynd Company was in existence only from 1869-1875. An oval vegetable dish (not Tea Leaf) which was sent to me from Ohio bears the Baker & Chetwynd trademark, as well as the British Registry diamond mark dated April 6, 1869, the date of a patent number registration #228430 which was also found by my English friend.

Lone specimen by Baker & Chetwynd   (8)
BC-1

Trademark on the sugar bowl
BC-2

Jewitt recorded in 1878 that this old Sylvester Pottery on Nile Street had been purchased in 1876 by Holmes, Plant and Madew, who made ironstone, French porcelain, door furniture, and other china sundries. Godden indicated Holmes, Plant and Maydew were successors to Holmes, Plant and Whitehurst, who very possibly were the purchasers from Baker.*

There was also a Globe pottery works (1867–1875) in Cobridge which adjoins Burslem. Those partners were Cockson & Chetwynd, who also made earthenware. Their style later was Cockson & Sneddon.

At the New Hall Works, Shelton, there was a pot-bank known as Cockson & Harding (1856-1862). One of their trademarks was an oval garter mark with the word "Imperial" as part of the logo. Since "Imperial" is part of our Baker & Chetwynd trademark, I am inclined to think there was a close relationship of some kind between Cockson & Harding, Cockson & Sneddon, Cockson & Chetwynd, and Baker & Chetwynd.

Godden records less than half a dozen other trademarks using the word "Imperial" for *all* the other 4,500-plus listings in his book. This verifies the fact that it was *not* a common descriptive term; therefore, it appears logical that it was used by men/partners in a few selected families. Very possibly *all* those before named were of the same family. Only two Chetwynds were named—Elijah and David—both in the Cockson & Chetwynd works.

It is also interesting to note that all these companies made goods primarily for export.

Through further research I was able to verify that the Chetwynd of Wallace & Chetwynd (1881-1903) of East Liverpool, Ohio was part of this same family. Barber† states Mr. Joseph Chetwynd of that firm learned the art of potting in his father's enterprise in England and was employed by Cockson & Chetwynd as a manager and a modeller. Evidently, he came directly to America, as the Wallace-Chetwynd partnership was in effect from 1881-1903 at the Colonial Pottery. Later they became part of a conglomerate operating the Colonial as part of the East Liverpool, Ohio Potteries.

There is nothing about my lone sugar bowl to recommend it as an outstanding sample of excellent ware, but perhaps when the whole set was displayed together, it delighted the new pioneer owner and her family.

Many of us today would be overjoyed to find a "set" still intact on one of our happy junking forays. Who knows—we may even find some Tea Leaf made by our Americanized Chetwynd friend; or by other Chetwynds in Staffordshire; or one of the companies with which he was associated in East Liverpool.

Bishop & Stonier —
See Powell & Bishop

* Geoffrey A. Godden, *British Pottery and Porcelain Marks* (A.S. Barnes and Company, Inc., 1963).

† Barber, Edwin A. *The Pottery and Porcelain of the United States*, 2nd edition (New York: Knickerbocker Press, 1902), p. 233.

Bridgwood (& Son)

1805 to present

A serving plate (or possibly remnant of a tea set) and a tea pot in their variant Clover Leaf design. The plate motif resembles James F. Wileman's design somewhat but it is on the same quality procelain as the tea pot. Both are decorated overglaze in gold, part of which has disappeared. Both unmarked, but compare with Kamm's OLD CHINA, pages 80, 82, and 196. (3) BW-1

Samuel Bridgwood did not make our Tea Leaf pattern but he did produce a variant which I feel is worthy of our consideration, the Clover Leaf design. It evidently was on the market before the hey-day of our favorite pattern so it might be considered as a forerunner just as Edward Walley's design is termed "Pre-Tea Leaf"! The clover leaf is also a design made by William Adams and Company.

The manufactory at Lane End of Sampson Bridgwood in 1802 was built in 1757 by Roger Wood of the Ash Works and used by a Mr. Ford for making stone and brown ware. Later Jewitt reported Sampson Bridgwood and Son as extensive manufacturers for many years, first in the Market Street Works, and later at works on Stafford Street which was torn down to make room for new market buildings. They then began potting at the Anchor Pottery where they made both china and earthenware. After Mr. Bridgwood's death the business was continued by his son-in-law and grandson, J. H. and George Walker. Most of their production was earthenware, white granite which they called "Parisian granite," and stamped "Limoges" or "Porcelaine Opaque." These tea, breakfast, and dessert services were beautiful, with a fine, hard, durable body and excellent glaze. If the ware was marked either of two terms was used: S. Bridgwood & Son or Bridgwood & Son. However, the items I found and identified as having been made by them were unmarked, almost transluscent, and very white. Bridgwood also made "Moss Rose" and used the cable-shape body—both of which were popular at the time Tea Leaf was so much in demand.

Henry Burgess

1864-1892

Creamer — Cable style, 4½" high. Same style made in graduated sizes to 13" tall (water pitcher for bedroom set). (84) BU-1

"It would be interesting, as someday it will be important, to trace the development in Europe during the latter half of the ninteenth century of stoneware—to detail the variety of forms that the earthenwares have assumed in the hands of the Mintons, Copelands, Wedgwoods, and Ridgways, and to discuss the white wares of the present day manufacturing as perfected by the Meakins, the Johnsons, and the Grindleys—. All these later developments are too near to us to be correctly and impartially appreciated so that, much as one would like to essay the task it cannot be attempted here. It must suffice—if we describe some of the 'English potters who converted the rude and inconsiderable manufacture into an elegant art and an important part of national commerce'."

Taken from William Burton's *A History and Description of English Earthenware and Stoneware.*

It is too bad Mr. Burton, or some other historian, did not record in greater detail **all** the histories of the smaller potteries in England 1875–1915. Henry Burgess is only one of many about whom very little is recorded. About all we know is that the name Burgess was first listed in Burslem in 1802 — then silence until some sixty years later, when Burgess and Leigh took over part of the old Samuel Alcock Works (the Hilltop Pottery), making common, ordinary wares, as well as some higher type goods for home and export. Some of their lines were ornamental, but most of their production was all the usual services; this included not only plates, platters, cups, and saucers, tureens and soup plates, but may also have meant any, or all, of the following:

1. Artichoke cups
2. Asparagus trays
3. Broth bowls
4. Butter tubs
5. Candlesticks
6. Card racks
7. Cheese dishes
8. Chestnut vases
9. Chicken tureens
10. Custard cups

A tea pot with a Cable style lid; sugar with another common Burgess finial, and a deep, round baker, beautifully panelled outside — all in heavy hotel-type ware. The sugar trademark was dated November 5, 1878. This is when the body style was registered not when the piece was made. The rope-like thumb-piece at the top of the tea pot handle is part of the "cable" body shape.
BU-2 (35)

Trademark on above Nov. 5, 1878.
BU-3

Milk jug 6½" x 8½" x 12" high. Very unusual style and shape but it is part of a complete line as seen in next photos. Probably also made in graduated sizes. (35)
BU-4

11. Ice pails
12. Ink stands
13. Match pots
14. Mugs
15. Pin cases/lid
16. Pen trays
17. Punch or Toddy bowls
18. Relish trays
19. Roll trays
20. Root dishes
21. Steak dishes
22. Strawberry baskets
23. Sugar boxes
24. Syrup pots
25. Toast racks
26. Turtle pans
27. Violet baskets
28. Wafer boxes

Besides the above list, any of these large ironstone pieces may have been crafted also:

1. Bed posts
2. Fireplaces
3. Goldfish bowls
4. Twelve sizes of jugs in same pattern
5. Vases — three feet tall
6. Wine coolers
7. Figurines — sometimes called toys — all sizes, shapes and qualities from Staffordshire dogs to grasshoppers; Queens to shepherd fairings (small cheap figurines sold at fairs); copies of the Wedgwood Portland vase; Thatched cottages, or bull-baiting dogs.

I have found no record that Burgess and Leigh made any Tea Leaf, or that Henry Burgess was connected with that company in any capacity. Burgess and Leigh were also doing business at the Middleport Pottery, Burslem from 1867 until at least 1964.

Henry Burgess was working the Kiln Craft works, Burslem from 1864 — where he made a superior grade of ironstone (Tea Leaf included) all dated before 1891 when the firm was sold to Thomas Hulme, and soon to Arthur J. Wilkinson, another Tea Leaf potter. Almost all of the H. Burgess Tea Leaf was made for the markets of the United States and Canada, just as was the total output of so many other small companies.

There was a Thomas Burgess at the Mount Pleasant works in Hanley 1903–1917, which previously had been known as Horrap and Burgess 1894–1903. We also have meager information concerning a Thomas Burgess at the Carlisle works in Longton 1922–1939, but no record of where they originated.

Many years before, Burgess and Goddard had been potters in Longton and possibly Burslem; as well as having carried on an extensive import business in the United States in the 1870's–1880's. An advertisement from the Pottery and Glassware Reporter, dated 1884, indicated they had offices and/or warehouse space at several locations in New York, Boston, Philadelphia, Baltimore, and Longton, Staffordshire. This pottery (at Longton) made white granite ware and earthenware so there is a possibility they made Tea Leaf, but up to now I have not seen it.

In our own country John W. Burgess was an original partner in the International Pottery company of Trenton, New Jersey from 1879. This was the first of four partnership and included James and John Moses and Edward and Thomas Clark, who had been operating as the Mercer Pottery Company in Trenton from 1869. Later, in 1879, John and William Burgess with a John A. Campbell operated under the name Burgess and Campbell; in 1895 Campbell withdrew. They made a fine durable earthenware and possibly introduced flow-blue to this country. William Burgess was born 1857 in Brooklyn and his father was the founder of the Burgess and Goddard pot-works in Longton, Staffordshire mentioned in the preceeding paragraph.

William was at one time the consul at Tunstall, and performed meritorious service for the potters and the government in that capacity, because of his business sense and integrity—knowing many potters on both sides of the Atlantic did not hurt either. After his term was com-

Tureen and lid — no ladle. Beautiful 7½" x 12¾" includes handles and 9" high with lid. Matches below.
BU-5   (69)

Butter dish, lid, drainer in same style as milk jug. 4½" x 5½".
BU-6   (60)

Tureen, lid, ladle, underplate. Yet another body style and larger — 10" x 16" includes handles. Finial and handles unique. Since ladles are never marked there is no way to tell if it is original. With such showy underplate, handles, and finial, we would expect larger Tea Leaf designs. Too bad the lid was cracked but it is still a show piece. (39)
BU-7

pleted he returned to active participation in the International Pottery until 1902. Since Mercer and International Potteries had so many close ties as well as nearly identical trademarks there may be Tea Leaf in existence with either name as part of the trademark. It should be a challenge to avid collectors.

Another American Company was Burgess and Company 1867 — stoneware potters, who were the predecessors of the West End Pottery in East Liverpool, Ohio. The plant was built on the site of the first gristmill built by Thomas Fawcett, founder of East Liverpool, and his sons. In 1869 operation as the Star Pottery was begun there by Thomas Starkey, a native of Staffordshire, and Samuel P. Curby, who was a practical potter. They made rockingham and yellow ware until 1872, when Sam Worcester and his son Thomas, made the same thing there for ten years. After another owner and much deterioration it closed in 1886, and later burned; then William Burgess and his son-in-law, Willis Cunning bought the site in 1889 and built a two kiln plant to make bone china. However there was no market for this "Made in America" ware, consequently they quit in 1893. Mr. Burgess, along with Cunning and four or five other partners, continued as the West End Pottery until at least 1925. They too, **could** have made our pattern, but it should not be confused with any of the other Burgess works. With the exception of the one reference to William Burgess, as the son of the founder of Burgess and Goddard — I found nothing to indicate family relationships, or lack of them — but it is probable they were like the Alcocks and Mayers — families of fine workmen, dedicated to improving the pottery industry.

Round butter dish with drainer. Burgess made at least two round, two rectangle, and one oval body styles. (11)
BU-8

Tureen (no lid or ladle) — another Burgess style similar to Mellor-Taylor or Wedgwood & Co. shapes. This has had a lid and ladle. 8½" x 13" includes handles. Notice the huge design on this piece. Trademark was usual Burgess with Registration date #54421 (1896) so it is somewhat newer style. (89)
BU-9

Underplate for tureen. Many seen in various shapes and sizes; often used for cake or sandwich plates. (39)
BU-10

Burgess trademark is Royal Arms mark which may or may not be included with impressed "H.BURGESS"; a diamond shape registration emblem or, as in below, a raised line of numbers beginning R^d No.
BU-11

Trademark R-No. 54421 (1896).
BU-12

E. & C. Challinor
1819-1880

Saucer 6½" in diameter, very deep — to drink coffee from instead of the cup. (89)
CH-1

The Challinor men, it would appear, owned or operated potteries in Burslem, Tunstall, and Fenton and the name has been very familiar since at least 1819 when Edward Challinor purchased and began business at the famous Overhouse Works in Burslem.

I found no definite statement as to whether they were brothers or father and son, nor pedigree charts of ancestors, such as were found for some potters.

The Overhouse Works had been in the Wedgwood family for over two hundred years until the last one in that particular family line passed on and the property was sold first in 1809, and finally in 1819 to Edward Challinor and Company. He continued there in various capacities for many years.

In 1868 the old works were razed and a much larger manufactory was erected. Challinor had all the very latest improvements in appliances and machinery installed, including steam-powered jiggers and drying-room stoves heated by exhaust steam. As a final touch of accomplishment, over the door he had placed a stonework scroll with this inscription:

Edward Challinor commenced business here
A.D. 1819, and rebuilt the premises 1869.

They produced the ordinary useful earthenware for foreign and home markets, along with some stoneware jugs. These ordinary wares included milk pans, jugs, ale containers, crocks, baking dishes, and plain heavy table services for use on board ship. Up to the advent of ironstone, nothing had been available that was cheap enough and durable enough to replace pewter.

Tea pot, Cable-shape. Notice huge handles. Challinor's leaves on the emblem were more elongated yet very distinctive. (75)
CH-2

Trademark on both pieces. (75)
CH-3

There were two types of granite ware made from 1850 to 1875: pure white and light-weight for the "city trade"; and a bluish-tinged, heavier ware for the "country trade." There were enormous amounts of this white ware in both heavy and light weights sold with dipped, sponged, or transfer printed decorations. Many were embossed with patterns like Ceres (Wheat), Garland, Paris, Lily, Lotus; many distinctive octagonal, or many-sided, shapes were popular around 1869. The Cable and Grape Leaf patterns were also used in making their breakfast, dinner, tea ware or their coffee sets and toilet wares, as well as many other useful articles.

In addition, by this time ironstone was much in demand for table services in hotels, clubs, colleges — anywhere hard usage was inevitable. The more elaborately decorated styles suited some affluent customers, and Flow Blue was one of these popular variations in ironstone that had world appeal because no changes of climate or temperature affected this wonder ware. Much of their ware was unmarked, but Challinor's trademarks when used included initials E.C. or E. & C.C. & Co., or sometimes the names were used.

Jewitt tells us that in the early 1800s Edward Challinor also occupied the Pinnox and Unicorn Works in Tunstall. It was a large plant where a general line of earthenware was made. It was located at Amicable Street and Great Woodland Street; the trademark was Edward Challinor. In 1825 this works passed to Podmore, Walker and Company and, in 1860 that name was changed to Wedgwood and Company. See the Enoch Wedgwood (Tunstall) Ltd. company story.

Also, according to Jewitt, around 1843 E. & C. Challinor acquired the Fenton Pottery which had been established about 1825 by Charles J. and George Miles Mason, in which some of Mason's Patented Ironstone had been produced. This Fenton Pottery was described by Ward in 1843 as:

> . . . standing obliquely to two turn-pike roads and on the line of the canal company's railway; (they) present an extensive front of four stories in height with the logo Patent Iron Stone Manufactory.

Even though this new ware was immediately accepted by the public, Mason's were soon succeeded by Samuel Boyle; then E. & C. Challinor (formerly of Lion Works, Sandyford in Tunstall), who were still there when Jewitt wrote in 1883. They continued with white granite (ironstone) in printed, common, and sponged wares for American, Australian, and other foreign, as well as colonial, markets. They made jugs in all the earlier-mentioned patterns; all their goods were specially designed and well adapted to various markets which Challinor supplied. As before, the pattern name was sometimes included with combinations of names and initials as their trademark, and here at Fenton Works, the word Fenton was also part of the mark.

Jewitt also recorded that the Lion Works in Sandyford, Tunstall had been established in 1838 by James Beach, passed through several owners, then to Ford and Challinor in 1862. They continued to manufacture a general line of earthenware for home and export. This pottery later passed to other owners (1880) and was finally closed in 1883.

These are but a few of the many enterprises these men were involved in. Therefore, it is an impossibility to say where our Challinor Tea Leaf was made. But who cares? It has a beautiful, slightly different elongated leaf in very dark lustre. I have seen only two pieces — a dazzling white tea pot and a very deep saucer. We wonder where it is. Be very proud if you own any made by this famous old company.

"It has always been the solid American trade which has made the fortunes of the Staffordshire potters." So wrote Josiah C. Wedgwood in 1914. The Masons, Grindleys, Alcocks, Johnsons, Clementsons, Meakins, and Furnivals, along with Enoch Wedgwood, Davenports, Wilkinsons, Mellor & Taylors, Shaws, and Adams were some of the largest exporters of ironstone to the United States and Canada. And they all made Tea Leaf!

Each potter had his own tricks to attract attention to his line of dishes; the use of fancy names was just one. Some are listed below, but there are likely others I have not heard!

Amherst Japan	Porcelain de Terre
English Porcelain	Real Ironstone
Flint China	Real Ironstone China
Granite Ware	Royal Ironstone China
Hotel China	Royal Semi Porcelain
Imperial Ironstone China	Royal Stone Ware
India Temple Stone China	Royal Vitreous China
Improved Stone China	Semi-China
Ironstone	Semi-Porcelain
Mason's Ironstone China	Semi-Stone
Newstone	Stone China
Opaque China	Stone Ware
Opaque Porcelain	Thrasher's China
Opaque Ware	Warrented Ironstone China
Parisian Granite	White Granite
Pearl Stoneware	White Stone-China
Porcelaine Opaque	White Ware
Porcelain Royal	

Clementson Bros.
1832-1916

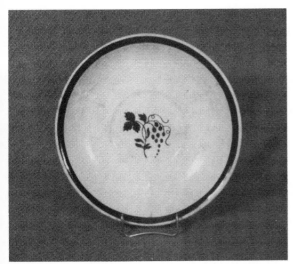

The first piece of "black" Tea Leaf which did not say "Clementston" on it. (31)

CL-1

Dishes from this company have had a special place in my heart since the night I was dazzled by a large collection I was privileged to photograph in an antebellum home on the bank of the Missouri River. Up to that time most of the Tea Leaf that had come to my attention was by Meakin, Shaw, or Wilkinson; so these sturdy pieces with the wide bands of dark copper lustre, the unusual shaped leaves, and the dangling berries really caught my eye.

The owner of these beauties had always lived in or near her present home; there had been Tea Leaf in her parents' home from her childhood, so it was natural for her to collect it; however, few, if any, of her 150 pieces were originals of her family dishes. The Tea Leaf she ate from as a child, and what she had collected, probably came up the Missouri River by boat to Arrow Rock, Glasgow, or Miami, along with numerous other stops from St. Louis to Parkville, the hemp capital of the world. Although I have nothing just now to verify this, I am confident that barrels of these pretty dishes were bartered for bales of hemp at that pioneer Platte County market.

This visit was also the first time I had seen black Tea Leaf. As with all rarities, legend had grown about it to the effect it had been made to commemorate (mourn) the death of a famous person — in this case, Abraham Lincoln. However, I learned this was not the correct answer after correspondence with Mr. Arnold R. Mountford, Director of the City Museum and Art Gallery, Stoke-on-Trent, who wrote:

Too high a temperature could indeed darken a lustre but some of the irridescence usually remains. Black banding does not signify the death of a monarch . . . on the death of a sovereign, wares were made especially to record the fact, usually giving the date of accession, coronation, etc.

Row 1: *Clemenston, Embossed Wheat, 8" dia. 12 berries, green, Nov. 15, 1861. Clemenston, Embossed Wheat, 8" dia. 12 berries, black, Nov. 15, 1861.* **Row 2:** *Shaw, Plain, 9½" dia. green underglaze. Wileman, Plain, 8" dia. another variant, good copper lustre. Unmarked, 12 panels, 9" dia. good copper lustre.* **Row 3:** *Clemenston, 14 panels, 7½" dia. 18 berries, good copper lustre. Clemenston, 10 panels, 9½" dia. 17 berries, green underglaze. Elsmore & Forrester, 12 panels, 9½" dia. 12 berries, green underglaze.*

CL-2

Phoenix shape sugar — no lid — blue white, no crazing — heavy. Trademark Dec. 8, 1858.
CL-3

Beautiful old Phoenix shape tea pot. Mark is same as above, impressed in wet clay and filled with glaze, impossible to photograph. This body style was sold as plain white ironstone before the advent of Tea Leaf.
CL-4

In essence, black and green Tea Leaf seem to be mistakes; but because this was such cheap ware, the potters could not afford to discard any but the most defective, and the decoration color was no serious fault.

I have no explanation why the underglaze design was done in green or black by this and other companies such as Anthony Shaw or Powell and Bishop. In my collection are two plates by Joseph Clementson with the diamond British Registry marks dated November 15, 1861. One is green underglaze with almost no lustre; the other is identical in black underglaze with half the lustre intact. I have another variant design, by Clementson, on a beautiful sugar bowl and tea pot of earlier vintage in the Phoenix-style body. These both carry the same British Registry marks but dated December 8, 1858. These four pieces are all much thinner and lighter weight than later wares from the company made under Clementson Brothers after 1872. Among other Clementson items on my shelves are two very heavy cups, one with and one without handles, both with black underglaze design. The handleless one has absolutely no crazing but the glaze is badly worn and, because the body is dark and has numerous black specks, the cup is unsightly. This was the first piece of black Tea Leaf I had purchased (and for just three dollars!). The last cup has some crazing but is very white. About half the lustre is gone from both pieces. We learn to expect and accept such diversities.

It seems that after 1872 the Clementson Brothers' ware was on much heavier weight plain bodies, as the craze for the white embossed ware was passing. I suspect some of the Tea Leaf or variant decorations were applied to left-over stocks of the thin biscuit ware when the popular demand changed to Tea Leaf decorations. Another possibility was that smaller potteries could not afford new molds and had to make do with what they had as long as the molds were serviceable.

Clementson's designs varied: Some had as few as eleven little berries and very sharply serrated leaves while others had as many as eighteen hanging berries and rounded leaf edges.

Several marks were used in addition to those previously mentioned. Most of them included some combination of names or initials, often along with the British Registry mark; Royal Arms; a Phoenix bird atop a circle; a globe; or a crown. Some ware was unmarked but it was all distinctive. The marks shown here are all I have seen on the Clementson Coffeeberry.

*Octagonal jug — same variant. Handle repaired. 8"
high.   (11)*
CL-5

*Different style with embossed Wheat design. Heavy but
fancier than regular hotel-type — very attractive. (74)*
CL-6

Hotel-type creamer, 7¼" high — most unusual handle.
CL-7

Several of my friends prefer these "odd" dishes to the original design and have told me of children's tea set collections on display in St. Louis. I have received photos from Texas of a partial set; these are shown in the Children's Tea Sets section. I have not seen any complete Clementson Coffee-berry tea sets for children as yet, but I am still looking.

Some refer to this pattern as Tea Leaf with Berries, or Teaberry, both of which seem rather confusing. The small tea tree has no berries of consequence; only the smallest leaves are used for the dried tea. The coffee berries of which our ground coffee is made do, sometimes, hang in small clusters which are harvested when the berries are red ripe. These coffee berries come from trees which would grow 30 feet tall if not pruned. The teaberry (or checkerberry) is an entirely different plant; it is a low bush and the leaves were used as a poor substitute beverage by the colonists just before the Boston Tea Party.

A gentleman writing in 1957 for the *Drovers Journal* noted:

The little covered dish, decorated with "coffee-berry" (mine) leaves, served as a soap dish in the bathroom of my grandmother's home.

The late Thelma Shull recorded in 1963 in *Victorian Antiques:*

One novel idea often used in painting cups many years ago was the decorating of the teacup with sprays of leaves and blossoms of the tea plant, and the coffee cup with the berries and leaves of the coffee plant.

Advertisements appeared in *Spinning Wheel* magazine in the 1950s several times where "Coffeeberry" was used to signify this variant. In reading I have seen numerous other references to this ware by the name "Coffeeberry."

Perhaps some will disagree with me, but until written records are found of orders for this ware by a specific name, I prefer and will use Coffeeberry when Clementson ware is the subject. I found no "regular" Tea Leaf bearing this trademark.

Who was Joseph Clementson?

In my estimation he was a fascinating, hard-working, master potter who "had a mind of his own" and a flair for pleasing people. The very fact that his answer to the Tea Leaf craze was original is evidence to me that he had an eye for turning a pretty plate without pilfering the designs of fellow potters. Or perhaps it was his tribute to those who preferred coffee as a beverage rather than the highly touted tea from China. After all, coffee had been the favorite drink (next to ale or beer) long before tea was brought to England in the 1650s.

Historians tell us that Joseph Clementson was born in 1794, just a year before Josiah Wedgwood died. His first attempt on his own, at age 26, was a short-lived partnership with Jonah Read in 1832. Just before, or shortly after, the start of this business venture, he made a trip by sailing ship to North America looking for business.* As a result of that trip, his oldest son, Francis, later spent 25 prosperous years as the company goodwill ambassador — sales representative in Canada. The end result was that their Staffordshire Company was handsomely rewarded with lucrative orders for their many products. Francis finally returned to England to retire in his late father's home while the Canadian business continued for almost another quarter century. The Clementsons, Canada, and the United States were all far richer because of this close association for so many years.

---

* Elizabeth Collard, *Nineteenth Century Pottery and Porcelain in Canada* (Montreal: McGill University, Press, 1967), pg. 81-83.

Three pieces with black underglaze. Until part of the glaze wears off it is impossible to tell what color the underglaze design is. All are heavy hotel-type ware common after 1872. Cups are found with and without handles or panels.
CL-8

The Bell Works, before 1750, were carried on by Werner Edwards until his death in Hanley in 1753. He was the originator of painting on biscuit ware to make underglaze decorations, as well as an ancestor of John Edwards, another Tea Leaf potter. Later the Ridgways were there from 1790-1854.

In 1856 Joseph Clementson bought those former Ridgway Bell Works where he, as they had, continued catering to the American markets. They had been closed a short time when Clementson took the Works and operated in conjunction with his nearby Phoenix Works.

In 1867 he turned the responsibilities over to his four sons who carried on as Clementson Brothers from 1872.

He was 77 at his death in 1871, but his name meant much in pottery history for many years. The business was disposed of in 1916. The works now belong to G. L. Ashworth and Brothers who operate as Mason's Ironstone China, Ltd., using Mason's moulds and patents.

As long as there is Clementson Coffeeberry around, there will be people asking: "Who was Joseph Clementson?"

Milk jug — 8½" high. A real beauty.   (35)
CL-9

Relish dish and gravy boat in the older style   (35)
CL-10

Trademark for above R.ᵈ No. 19886 (1884). They used this particular mark 1891-1910 at their Bell and Phoenix Works.   (61)
CL-11

Sauce tureen, lid, ladle, underplate. Fit for a museum! Only 5" x 8½". Ladle 8" long. Same style was made in large soup tureen, a covered vegetable and round high-domed butter along with countless other pieces.   (11)
CL-12

Unusual toothbrush holder — part of a 10-12 piece set. (1)
CL-13

Six pieces — a study in variations of a variant! Cups and saucers vary slightly; platter most unusual with twisted handles and matches tea pot on page 54, while the stunning tea pot here is a mate to the jug on page 56. All have illegible British R.ᵈ marks.
CL-14 (54)

Oval relish dish — definitely brown underglaze (82)
CL-15

Wash bowl and ewer set shown on a marble topped walnut table that has been in the same house since the 1870s. The only Coffeeberry wash set I have seen. (80)
CL-16

One more variant! Creamer 6" high.
CL-17

CL-18

Two most common backstamps found on Clemenston ware.

CL-19

W & E Corn
1864-1904

Here is another outstanding example of a pottery which made fine wares, being shunted into oblivion because no one cared enough to record their history.

From meager information available to me it seems the Top Bridge Works, Longport, was operated by William and Edward Corn, 1864-1904. They may have purchased it from the Davenports, who were beginning to come into hard times about 1864 and had started to dispose of some of their property. This Top Bridge Pottery had been one of the early ones acquired by John Davenport.

Corns also were operating in Burslem in 1864-1891. There was mention of Edward Corn on Navigation Road in Burslem who had built a pot-works where, at one time, there had been a lumberyard. It was later carried on as W. and E. Corn and their entire production was white granite ware for the American and other foreign markets. The pattern name was often part of their trademark but much of their ware was unmarked.

Their white granite (porcelaine royale) with the Wheat and the Lily-of-the-Valley designs on plain white ironstone was a very popular item on the American market. According to Elizabeth Collard* some of their plain white ironstone received in Canada was decorated there and most often carried the mark or name of the decorator as well as the potter.

One of Corn's wheat patterns had a scalloped plate well which was very attractive, but most were on plain bodies. However, some tea pots had vertical ribbing around the base similar to that of Enoch Wedgwood (Tunstall) Ltd. Company.

The handle on the one pictured was a generous size, affording a good grip; and even though the finial was broken, I am sure it would have been easy to hold. I wonder why they did not make a corn pattern.

Each of the four examples I have seen are slightly gray-white with no sign of crazing which indicates very good potting knowledge. The plate in the photo is prized by the owner because of a minute slip of the brush on the edge-line. As an artist and a ceramist of some years, she bought the plate just for that reason, even though it had a hair-line crack. She knew how difficult it is to make perfect lines all of the time; this plate bears the human touch of imperfection.

The tureen has a comfortable "feel" with good balance when picked up to carry, and it is in mint condition.

How I wish someone would come forward with more details on this company.

This 8" plate is precious to the owner because of the slip of the brush on the outside line. She, as a ceramist, appreciates the skill it took to make millions of perfect lines. For years this was the only item by Corn I had seen. Finally other pieces have shown up. (88)
CO-1

A rare tea pot in a shape similar to Mellor & Taylor or Wedgwood & Co. styles. The handle is almost too large. Too bad the lid finial is broken. (85)
CO-2

Toothbrush holder — over 6¼" tall. It looks as if it had been made in two pieces. (35)
CO-3

The only trademark found on all these Corn pieces. This was used at the Top Bridge Works, Longport, 1891-1904. (61)
CO-4

---

* Collard, p. 314.

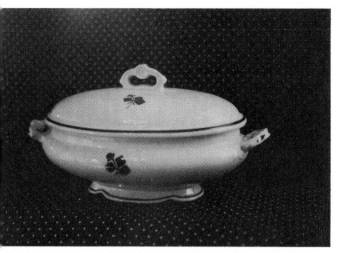

Oval covered casserole 7" x 11½" x 6" high. The quiet elegance bespeaks quality. (35)
CO-5

Oval milk jug and squat sugar bowl in the same body style. The tiny indented circle at top of handle is a six-petaled flower — a Corn trademark design.
CO-6

Davenports
1794-1887

Davenport made them all — from the tiny 3½" cup plate to the 10" dinner plate. The double hand was a common sight on their wares. (60)
DA-1

The Davenport Company was in operation at Longport in Staffordshire from 1794-1887, and used the same formula for some of their china ware for almost 80 years—because it was good enough that it needed no improvement. There were changes in decorations, but the formula for the body was preserved and used by three generations of the Davenport family. This record has never been excelled; so states W. P. Jervis in his *Encyclopedia of Ceramics* and his *Pottery Primer*.

John Davenport's father was Jonathan of Leek, and the family records date back to 1585. John was born in October 1765, in Leek; but his father died when he was only six years old. Little John was put to work; finally he was placed in a pottery in Newcastle as an apprentice—according to T. A. Lockett in his captivating book, *Davenport Pottery and Porcelain 1794-1887*. (Much of the information used in this chapter is found in this book and is used with proper permission.) Young John remained there until he was 20 when he became a partner of Thomas Wolf, whose small works was next to Mintons at Stoke. Those early-day hardships left their mark on the man as we shall observe later.

In 1794 he had enough money, experience, and ambition to go into business on his own, so he bought the first of the three oldest potteries in Longport—the Unicorn Bank which belonged to John Brindley, a brother of James Brindley, who had built the Trent-Mersey Canal under the watchful eye of Josiah Wedgwood. The acquisition of the other two of these old potteries was to come later.

Shortly after acquiring the Longport Works, Davenport found the English porcelain much inferior to that made in France; he went to France to learn the secrets of their fine ware. He learned all he could, then came home to adapt the French ideas to the English requirements and soon he turned out a superior ware of remarkable transparency to satisfy the growing English market. He also learned much about the continental markets which was to be vital to him in a short time.

His restlessness and boundless energy were good attributes to help bring success to the manufacture of glass which he began in 1801—something no other potter had done before. It remained an important part of the Davenport Works to the end, almost 90 years later. By 1804 he had purchased Cliff Bank Pottery at Stoke which was leased to William Adams.

This simple creamer is 6" tall and matches the most common style of Tea Leaf we see by this company. Has a registration date of April 1880. (35)
DA-2

Collection of some very unusual items: handled cups that vary less than ½". Notice how the right cup-plate hugs the cup. The matching bowl and pitcher set is rare also. Oh, for a lid for the sugar with the pretty pink lustre. (33)
DA-3

Royal Arms mark — Wm. Davenport Co. 480 (April 1880) (33)
DA-4

Evidence that Davenport prospered from the beginning is found in the range of goods he produced: drug jars, syrup jars, infant feeders, food warmers, all kinds of toilet and bedroom necessities, as well as tea, dinner, and dessert sets decorated in all manners—made to sell at all prices—Davenport made them all. Although ornamental ware was made, the emphasis was on table ware. Perhaps his early life had impressed on him the importance of providing actual necessities rather than spending time, money, and effort on luxuries.

His purchase of the Longport Works came only about a year before Josiah Wedgwood passed on, but there is no doubt that Davenport had copied Wedgwood's Jasper and cream-colored ware, even though it was old-fashioned by 1795. Davenport, a master imitator, was not distinguished as an innovator or originator of new trends in types or colors, but the workmanship of the company was above reproach. Some of his wares were copies of Oriental styles, and a casual observer could easily mistake Davenport stoneware for Oriental hard porcelain.

In North America, Davenport was a household word. The firm had evolved into a major exporter as there was so much variety to choose from and his wares were both practical and popular—there was something for everyone.

His shining hour came in 1806 when the Prince of Wales (later George IV) and his brother, the Duke of Clarence (later William IV), came to see the Davenport Works. The royal callers were quite impressed and commented that Davenport's ware was equal to that of Sevre's and that France should quit boasting—Staffordshire had surpassed them! To prove his sincerity, the prince ordered several services of the very finest, most expensive ware Davenport had to offer.

In a magnanimous gesture, after the royal visit, Davenport added a group of cottages, each with a small garden, for some of his employees.

About 1814 he purchased and maintained a home, Westwood Estates, in Leek, for which it is said he paid £15,500—quite an accomplishment for a poor, uneducated farm boy in less than 30 years! He died at the palatial home in Leek in 1848; but seemingly his days there were not as happy as he had anticipated.

John Davenport had married in 1795, shortly after he purchased the first Longport Pottery, and five children were born before his wife, the former Diane Smart Ward, died in 1811. The oldest was a girl who married a Liverpool gentleman, Sir John Bent. The oldest son, John II, did not take an important part in the family business but studied law. The other two sons, Henry and William, were working potters who took active part in the family enterprises. The baby, Mary, became the wife of a silk manufacturer at Leek.

Just after the turn of the century, in the war with France, John Davenport proved his loyalty to Great Britain by his offer to raise, clothe, and equip a volunteer corps. His offer was accepted and, as major, he trained four units of eighty men each to a high level of discipline.

The end of the war was commemorated with a parade and celebration by and for his employees. The parade route was from Longport to Burslem (about two miles); they marched to the music supplied by a band composed of company employees. Davenport and the plant manager were parade marshalls. Both wore glass hats and carried glass walking sticks, all made specially for the occasion. That must have been some parade!

The end of the war also brought more opportunities to expand the foreign markets, and expand he did—in spite of competition. He established a china house at Hamburg, among other places, because a family member who lived there was willing to look after his interests.

A superb group of Davenport items — all with pink lustre trim on the flowers along with rich copper lustre banding and Tea Leaves. The pieces vary in height from 5¼" for the creamer to 10½" on the water ewer. Only the sugar lid finial is missing. (1)

DA-5

Seal with anchor and 12
DA-6

Below, left: Royal arms with "ironstone" printed below, then Davenport and the seal/anchor. Below, right: same Royal arms with impressed ? Davenport & Co. and 381 (March 1881). Any combination of these items may be found or some ware may be unmarked.

DA-7

DA-8

Along with the purchase of the Newport Pottery in 1810, where most of the earthenware was made thereafter, he opened showrooms and a warehouse in Liverpool to speed up the shipping routine emanating at this port, the nearest one to Longport.

From available records, *it seems* John Davenport enjoyed keeping an eye on the warehouse at Liverpool when he was able to leave the day-to-day operation at Longport to Henry—beginning about 1822. But a man who was so very knowledgable of all facets of the trade was not content for long to let others run his show.

In 1830, at age 65, he was given a commission to make an elaborate service to be used at the coronation banquet of William IV, the former Duke of Clarence. This was welcome publicity for the pottery and John Davenport personally, as further recognition of his high-quality work. After this honor he added a crown above his name on the trademark.

A year later, when many men think of retirement, John D. entered politics because he realized the potteries needed representation in the House of Commons and the House of Lords. Josiah Wedgwood II and Davenport won in a surprising victory, as many in the potteries were not too pleased with the Davenports.

By then as a member of Parliament, he was able to keep in close contact with the London showrooms, which was much to his liking. He served until 1838 when he permanently retired to Westwood.

With age he became more difficult to get along with; he was stubborn, self-righteous, and his own sons seemed to have problems pleasing him. But Henry apparently was strong enough to refuse to be dominated by his father. One historian referred to Mr. Davenport as "an old curmudgeon."*

Henry was a more warm, likeable fellow, less arrogant and ruthless; and with less drive than his father. Old Mr. Davenport had come up the hard way; he had to scramble and make every minute and every penny count. Because he was forced to be old before his time, he seemingly had built a wall around his heart and presented a cold, harsh, foreboding image to his fellow men that was rarely penetrated. Henry, on the other hand, had been born with the proverbial "silver spoon in his mouth," and had enjoyed a comfortable, care-free life; consequently he was a much more relaxed, lovable person.

---

* T. A. Lockett, *Davenport Pottery and Porcelain – 1794-1887* (Rutland, Vermont: Charles E. Tuttle, Inc., 1972), p. 16.

Henry changed the name to Henry and William Davenport and Company in 1834, and added yet another pot-works to their holdings the second of the three original old works of Longport, namely that of the Robert Williamson Company. With this works, the Davenports were the largest operators in Staffordshire. Henry was killed in a fall from a horse in 1835.

When William was forced to take charge of the family's affairs, he never put that responsibility first as had his father and brother. He maintained his lifestyle of a country gentleman.

An occasional walk through the potteries, properly attired and wearing a tall black silk hat and shining boots, was about the extent of contact with the workmen who toiled to help him amass and keep his wealth. He was not the shrewd, hard-nosed, ambitious businessman his father had been, nor was he the kind, benevolent type Henry was. There is ample reason to believe he was, on occasion, cruel and heartless in dealing with his employees, especially if they displeased him.

His expensive tastes or habits were more important to him than the foreign sales offices which were already established around the world: Brussels, Liibeck, Messina, and Hamburg in Europe; St. Petersburg in Russia; Montreal in Canada; New York and New Orleans in the United States; Mexican ports; Buenos Aires, Rio De Janeiro and Lima in South America; Bombay, Calcutta, Madras in the Far East—all seemed to be unworthy of his attention. At best, the operation of the Davenport empire was left to trusted friends or underlings. It would appear his interest ceased at the monotony of the day-to-day operation.

By 1840, the purchase of yet another pot-works, that of Edward Bourne—built in 1775—completed the family ownership of the first three potteries built in Longport.

In 1843 he bought the Maer place which had been the home of Josiah Wedgwood II from 1803 until his death that year. The price was reported to have been £200,000. But times were so bad in his potteries, he had to reduce the wages of some of the workers! In 1848 their pottery inventory was around £100,000. One hogshead held a service for twenty-four—222 pieces, and was priced for export to India at less than £16, less ten percent. We can see this was a lot of dishes! (A regular barrel holds a service for twelve—100 pieces.)

For some unexplained reason, the Newport Pottery, purchased in 1810, was sold in 1846 to Cork and Edge (later Edge, Malkin and Company).

In spite of all his weaknesses, William was for all intents and purposes a most successful and affluent pottery tycoon. He was high in the social realm of Staffordshire; he laid the cornerstone for the present Burslem Town Hall in 1854 and had a new organ installed there ten years later, at his own expense. He was named High Sheriff in 1859.

No one seemed to know what went on in the business, as there were no records available to historians; but at his death in 1869, his only son, Henry, inherited a real headache and a heartache as well.

William's wife was the daughter of John Wood of Brownhills and their children included Henry, the oldest, then eight girls. To provide a dowry for eight daughters was quite a responsibility, even for a wealthy gentleman. It seems the youngest three remained spinsters for lack of money to marry them off properly.

It is possible William secretly mortgaged property in order to keep his family living in the manner to which they had been accustomed, hoping the girls would be married before the day of reckoning. But it was not to be.

At his father's death in 1869, young Henry was charged with the responsibility, at age 29, of administering his father's will and found it impossible to make the available money stretch far enough. This would have been a task to challenge a mature, astute man with many years of business experience. It was overwhelming for a young fellow.

Communications between the home offices were carried on by managers and people of lesser authority, and were poor, at best. Moneys were not always collected, goods not shipped, and improper merchandise shipped to impatient customers. All made for a hectic situation and eventual loss of business. Young Henry seemed to refuse to face the fact they were going under. An uncle from the Wood family, along with others, handled most of the dispersal and a new, much diminished company—Davenports, Ltd.—was formed. It was the original works John Davenport began with eighty years before—the Unicorn Bank of Longport and the Glass Works. This was a profitable venture at first, but a depressed economy and a fire in 1883 caused further decline.

Even though Henry tried to live on a limited income, his father's debts, along with his own, hung like an albatross around his neck. The forced sale of their beloved Maer Estate seemed to bring home to each of the heirs their further defeat until the year 1887 closed with the December sale of the equipment and materials at the Unicorn Bank and Glass Works. Early in 1888 Thomas Hughes, who earlier had bought the Top Bridge Works, purchased the Longport properties; he moved into the property and leased the glass works. It was operated as Thomas Hughes and Son until 1957; then sold to Arthur Wood and Sons, and finally torn down in 1961.

All through the long history of the Davenport pottery their products were consistently good quality. Each line of cream-colored ware, white stone ware, various earthenwares, ironstone, porcelain, ornamental wares, and the numerous other goods were always modeled in conservative good taste, usually along classical lines. In 1980 they are in great demand by collectors.

The Tea Leaf which was a minor line with them was produced in copper and pink lustre and is some of the most beautiful ware we could ever wish to own.

(Cork) Edge, Malkin & Company
1860-1903

As I began research for this book, two names came to my attention: Edge and Malkin, both of which appeared on a cup and saucer then in my possession. Since the design resembled a clover bloom more than anything else, I soon traded it—greenhorn that I was—for a specimen with the traditional motif, never dreaming I had a rare example of fine ware by two with such illustrious backgrounds. Very little more of this company's Tea Leaf has come to my attention since then, so if you are fortunate enough to own a piece by Edge, Malkin and Company, cherish it and exhibit it with a great deal of pride.

As we have no way of knowing the exact family relationship of each person listed, we can only assume they were all from the same family groups. Remember, the Staffordshire District is only three miles wide and nine miles long; so the same last name almost surely denoted some family tie. This is my assumption for *all* of the family histories which are given in detail in any of the other chapters.

A rare piece even without the lid! 8" in dia. The embossed Corn and Wheat design is quite pronounced yet blends quite well with the base. This originally had handles but they are gone and the places have been smoothed over. (60)
CEM-1

Trademark for above. (60)
CEM-2

Both names were in the very earliest published lists of Staffordshire potters. From the Tunstall Court Rolls, as well as writings of various historians since then, we find:

1670   Ric. Edge (Burslem) potter

1670   William Edge (Burslem) potter

1710-1715 Samuel Edge (Fenton) was an apprentice to Thomas Wheildon, a foremost potter at Fenton, who later was a partner of Josiah Wedgwood. Edge was in good company, and he had learned his trade well because, in a few years, he was one of the five largest producers of stoneware in Burslem.

1752   John Gretton and John Edge (Lane Delph, Fenton) leased the Whiteware Works and the Dipware Workhouse from John Peat

1828-1830 Daniel Edge (Waterloo Road, Burslem) was a partner with Mr. Grocett (Liverpool Road, Tunstall) for a short time around 1830. They produced average quality decorated earthenware and ironstone, but no examples are known.

1834-1842 Daniel Edge (Waterloo Road, Burslem) still in business. See later entry.

1835-1836 Edge, Barker and Company (Lane End, Fenton). They often used the pattern name as part of their trademark.

1841-1848 William Edge and Samuel Edge (Market Street, Lane Delph). Probably sons or grandsons of the first William or Samuel Edge.

1843   Daniel Edge (Waterloo Road, Burslem), same as mentioned
1846-1860 earlier; later a partner in Cork and Edge (Newport Pottery, Burslem). Their wares were beautiful and executed in good taste. This was one of four Burslem potters to attend the Great Exhibition in London, 1851.

1860-1871 Cork, Edge and Malkin (Newport Pottery, Burslem) is a continuation of the same works with a Malkin added to the roster, the first mention of the two names linked in a business venture.

1871-1903 Edge, Malkin and Company (Newport Pottery, Burslem)

Daniel Edge must have been quite an old man, so perhaps he had played the role of the banker while younger men did the work; this may account for "Edge" being the first name in the title.

In addition to mocha ware, they made jet, enameled, and lustre wares and other fancy goods, along with all ordinary wares including ironstone, a staple item which they produced in huge quantities for home and foreign markets. Tea Leaf was just one of their many patterns. A tea set in my collection is on a rich cream colored earthenware, light in weight, but dazzling in color with the dark burnished copper lustre!

The Newport Pottery had originally been established in 1790 by

Brush holder has a divider in the top which extends down into the holder about 1½ ". The top handle is something different also. Same cream-rich color. (90)
EM-1

Trademark for this company may or may not have name embossed as this does. The greyhound emblem is peculiar to this firm.
EM-2

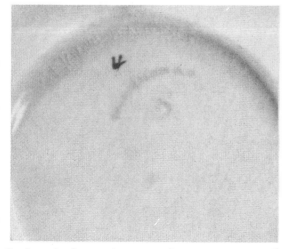

Trademark frequently seen alone — very small, impressed, hard to read. Mr. Mountford noted this was used at Newport and Middleport Potteries, Burslem, Stoke-on-Trent 1871-1903. "Ltd." may have been added from 1899 (that is, a limited company). (61)
EM-3

Walter Daniel and had passed, in 1810, to John Davenport of Longport; later to Cork and Edge; then, as stated earlier, to Edge, Malkin and Company which was liquidated in 1903.

1874   J. Edge and others were at the Queen Street Pottery in Burslem until 1874 when it was taken by Mr. Tinsley and Mr. Bourne who were succeeded by W. H. Adams in 1882.

1882   Whittaker, Edge and Company (Hanley) established the Hallfield Pottery in 1882 where they made fine quality general wares for all markets.

Arnold Mountford, F.M.A., writing in his fine 1971 book *The Illustrated Guide to Staffordshire Salt-Glazed Stoneware** remarks that:

> The Burslem families of Wedgwood and Wood are inseparably linked with the history and development of Staffordshire salt-glazed stoneware from the 17th Century onwards. Above all others, they provide a succession of master-potters who were instrumental in maintaining the Potteries as the center of English ceramic manufacture. Inherent skill in the effective manipulation of the plastic clay, coupled with the ability to adapt to new ideas and methods of production kept the Wedgwoods and the Woods ahead of their contemporaries. Intermarriage over the years with such as the Adams; the Malkins; the Littlers; and the Wheildon families established a potters elite which, through its new-found relationships, achieved an interdependence that in most cases was to prove invaluable.

He went on later to recount that Jonah Malkin, brother-in-law of Thomas and John Wedgwood, made salt-glazed stoneware and records some of his purchases of flint for the year 1749, which totaled 184 pecks. Malkin bought from six to twenty-four pecks at a time—usually about twelve. This may not seem like much to us now, but we must remember this was brought into Staffordshire by horse-pack from various parts of England. No prices were given, and no comment, as to whether the flint was already ground to a fine powder.

From a sales book of this same account, Malkin indicated he sold, in 1747, the first oven-full of dipped white (ware) at eight pence per dozen; and five crates packed with 25 dozen pieces in each crate for £4:3:4 for each crate. An oven-full (five times 25 dozen) would be 1500 pieces.

This represented at least two weeks' work from the grinding of the clay, mixing, moulding, stauking, firing, and packing those 1500 pieces! This is just a small insight into life in the Potteries 225 years ago.

Now let us see what other Malkins were potters:

1670   Joseph Malkin (Burslem) potter

1676   Thomas Malkin leased a farm and other outbuildings to his brother, John, for 1000 years for the sum of five shillings plus one peppercorn per year if it was demanded

1681   Thomas Malkin, the same, (Sneyd Hamlet, Burslem) fined for digging clay by the road near Dale Hall and not filling up the holes

1710   Samuel Malkin (Knowle Works, Burslem) 1668-1741. One of the early slip-ware potters who used moulds for faster

---

*Arnold Mountford, *The Illustrated Guide to Staffordshire Salt-Glazed Stoneware* (New York: Praeger Publishers, New York).

A pancake plate and cover! One of the rarest items in the book. It is 10" in diameter and matches the previous items. See Odds and Ends Chapter for mustache cup in this same line. (42)
EM-4

An exquisite tea service for nine in a rich, buttery yellow earthenware. All pieces are mint except two cups. For a gal who earlier sold the only cup she had seen which has this distinctive tiny cloverlike "tea leaf" on it, this is quite a collection.
EM-5

production. His large plates and bowls are to be seen in several museums including the Victoria and Albert Museum in London; City Museum and Art Gallery, Stoke-on-Trent; Fitzwilliam Museum, Cambridge, England; Royal Scottish Museum, Edinburgh, Scotland; and the Nelson-Atkins Art Galleries in Kansas City, Missouri. His humor was apparent, especially when he depicted Prince Charles hiding up in a huge tree from his pursuers, the Roundheads. It was exceeded only by his religious expression, subject of many pictures on the specimens he created. He was a member of the Burslem Parish Vestry and, at his death, he was referred to as "the Old Parish Clerk of Burslem." His wares were well marked; usually his name was part of the decoration. Often they were dated, as proved by six plates dated from 1712-1734.

1710-1716   Thomas Malkin (Sneyd Hamlet, Burslem). Black mottled ware.

1710-1715   Richard Malkin (Knowle Works, Burslem). Black mottled ware.

1710-1715   Isaac Malkin (Green Head, Burslem). Black and mottled ware.

1750   Clark Malkin (Burslem) north of Samuel Malkin, potter

1786   Burnham Malkin (Burslem) potter

1786   Bourne and Malkin (Burslem) made china, glazed, blue, and cream-colored ware

1839-1846 William Edwards, a lawyer, and a Mr. Tunnicliffe established a pottery at Burton-on-Trent, using Staffordshire potters, one of whom was a Mr. Malkin, a clay mixer. Mr. Edwards ordered the wares dipped in skimmed milk to improve their appearance; but the packer said it "only made them turn mouldy."[†] However, Josiah Wedgwood had earlier used hot skimmed milk to dip his black Egyptian wares to make them look better.

1858-1864 Malkin, Walker and Hulse (British Anchor Pottery, Longton) earthenware. They were later Walker, Bateman and Company.

1863-1881 Ralph Malkin (Park Works, Fenton) earthenware

1882-1892 Ralph Malkin and Sons – same

1891-1905 Frederick Malkin (Bell Works, Burslem) earthenware. Malkin, Edge and Company is the same as Edge, Malkin and Company – see earlier entry.

To the best of my knowledge, none of the descendants of either family brought these names to the potting industry in the United States. I have never found either name in our list of potters; but they may turn up tomorrow, so keep looking for this fine old ware and descendants of the men who made it.

John Edwards (& Co.)
1847-1900

For a company which made such fine ironstone and other wares, it is too bad there is so little recorded history about them. Perhaps this attempt at further identification will bring more details to light.

The Edwards name was familiar in the Potteries since at least 1710 when Werner Edwards, the originator of painting on the biscuit ware (so the design was under the glaze), was listed at Shelton. His son, William, was at Lane Delph, 1757-1786, when he made very beautiful open lattice-work type (pierced) ware for local use.

Then silence until 1825 when James and Thomas were listed at the Kiln Craft Works in Burslem. A Mr. Handley had built that pot-bank about 1800 and operated there until he was succeeded by the Edwards brothers who were quite successful, especially with their issue of plates, platters, and the like commemorating the Cunard Company's "Boston Mail" venture. They also supplied a large variety of wares for use on board ships and for the American markets. Edwards were in turn succeeded at Kiln Craft by Willet and Marsh; T. and R. Boote; and in 1864 by Henry Burgess.

In 1843 the brothers went their separate ways. Thomas stayed on for awhile but later went to operate the Swan Bank Works in Burslem. This manufactory later passed to Pinder and Bourne; then to a series of other owners. Thomas was also at the Waterloo Pottery in Burslem during the 1840s. In 1850 it also passed to T. and R. Boote. It had been built before the turn of the century and held by several before Thomas took it over. This seemed to be a common procedure in many of the small or medium-sized works in England and the United States.

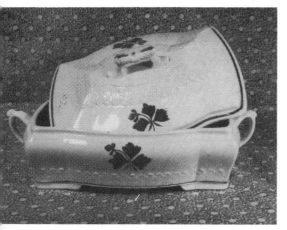

Feather design is repeated on this rectangle covered casserole with an 1887 registration date. See page 68 & 69. (35)

ED-1

[†] Chaffers, p. 839.

Water pitcher—Victory shape/Dolphin handle.
ED-2

Quite a flashy ewer with a huge motif. On a lighter weight body marked Porcelaine de Terre.
ED-3

This 5¼" pitcher has the feather design on the sides only. The huge motif and bulbous top are noteworthy.   *(1)*
ED-4

James Edwards went to Longport about 1840 and began a partnership with Thomas Cope on Market Street. They moved later (probably when his association with his brother, Thomas, was severed in 1843) to the newer Sheridan Works. At James' death in 1874 at age 79, his younger son, George, succeeded him and, at Jewitt's writing almost ten years later, he was still busy making all kinds of tableware in plain and decorated types, especially imitations of Japanese styles for foreign markets.

Jewitt also recorded that, when James and Thomas separated in 1842, James took over Dale Hall, the oldest works in that community. The comment repeated by numerous historians was to the effect that James was a well-respected, self-made man; fair, benevolent, and seemingly one who "planned his work then worked his plans" and was not easily deterred. Hughes* said he made the "most handsome of granite ware — in Burslem *his* standards of excellence in all wares became the aim of his competitors." Upon his purchase of Dale Hall he installed the most modern equipment, increasing the output six times without enlarging the premises. They made all types of table crockery and earthenware.

In 1861 his son, Richard, was taken in as a partner and, at the father's death, continued on as James Edwards and Son until in 1882. He was succeeded by Knapper and Blackhurst, but the works was closed in the early part of 1883.

The trademark James Edwards used about 1863 consisted of an anchor and a dolphin with the royal arms above the name, all surrounded by a garter with the words "Ironstone China" printed on it. There were other marks used too, some of which included the initials D. H. for Dale Hall; they used several combinations of initials, names, and motifs.

To us, the most important part of the Edwards story is that about John Edwards. Godden and Jewitt agree that John began business at Longton in 1847 (possibly with his father) and moved to the King Street Works, Fenton, in 1853. He operated as John Edwards until 1873 when "and Company" was added and used until 1879. From then two trademarks were used: the common one we see on our Tea Leaf, and the other with "Porcelaine de Terre" over a shield with the Edwards name below.

Jewitt gave more detail: The King Street Works was built by a Mr. Shelly late in the 1700s. He was succeeded by Mr. March; T. and J. Carey; then an unidentified company and, finally, in 1850 by John Edwards who made porcelain, semi-porcelain, and white granite (ironstone) for the foreign markets. Porcelain was discontinued about 1856—it may not have been a profitable line, or he may have been too busy with his inventions. He patented a process for making new type pins and stilts and other kiln furnishings to aid in better placing procedures in the kilns. This sounds complicated, but any help in keeping wares apart in the saggers and the prevention of marks on the surface of the goods was most welcome by all the potters.

For those who own John Edwards Tea Leaf—enjoy it and appreciate the beauty of the Peerless shape with the vertical feathered designs on the outside of the squarish-shaped pitchers, sugars, bowls, and the like. I enjoy dreaming that it may have been his personal tribute to the Prince of Wales who paid his pottery that memorable official visit, and gave his permission for the use of his insignia—the three-feathered plume—to be used in Edwards' trademark. This is a rather rare mark—not common like the use of the crown or the word "Royal," and denotes a real honor had been bestowed.

The other Tea Leaf shape I have seen—Victory—is much more

Open bakers like this, whether oval, square, or round all come in graduated sizes from 4" up to about 10" in diameter. Every pottery had its own styles but each made more than one shape. On this dish Edwards put the feather design on the inside around the top instead of around the outside base. (53)
ED-5

John Edwards exhibited his sense of humor in the dolphin handles and finials on this Victory shape sugar bowl and tea pot, along with the water jug on page 68.
ED-6 (35)

Trademark on some items. Both backstamps in use 1880-1900. (61)
ED-7

This typical feather design on outside of square baker of the Peerless body shape is peculiar to the John Edwards Company.
ED-8

Trademark common to most Edwards ware may have body style (Peerless, Victory, etc.) incised with an R^d No. Three plumes indicate a visit to the factory by the Prince of Wales . . . quite an honor.
ED-9

intriguing. Each hollowware piece has a smiling dolphin head on the handle or as part of the finial. Why? To me this was the final proof that John was indeed the son of James. Up until that time I had felt he may have been Thomas' son; I had read of James and his other sons, George and Richard, but I finally decided James *could* have had three sons and helped each one become established in his own pottery and had really worked with each one for a time.

It was common practice for a successful potter to operate several works simultaneously or to have some interest in more than one at the same time.

Edwards' Tea Leaf is rather scarce and hard to find, but the leaves are usually large and showy with excellent lustre; very little crazing is apparent, consequently there is a minimum of discoloration. The pieces are medium to lightweight, yet blend well with any other items you may have.

Buy it. Use it. You will enjoy it.

---

* G. Bernard Hughes, *Victorian Pottery and Porcelain* (New York: The McMillan Company, 1959), p. 51.

EF-2A

The Pepper Leaf variant shown on this page is one of the most eyecatching designs in this book. It is all on heavy ironstone, blue-white, with no crazing. Each piece is designed to be sturdy to use, comfortable to handle, and beautiful to behold. (7)

EF-3A

EF-4A

Photos by Robert Finney

Elsmore & Forster
later Elsmore & Son
1853-1887

Underplate which probably is the correct one to use with the large covered casserole in lieu of the plain one shown on page 70. (35)
EF-1

Footed compote — in this magnificent Pepper Leaf motif **EF-2**

It is sad, sad indeed, when virtually nothing is recorded about the potters (and even less about their pots) who made such beautiful plain white ironstone as Elsmore and Forster. Even the spelling of both names seems in doubt.

In early Staffordshire days when spelling, at best, was often wrong, we find Forster spelled Foster, Forester, Forrister, and Forrester.

Who knows why there were so many name spelling variations? Did men change their own names? Was it poor spelling by old writers? Was it carelessness in translation? Or was it typographical error?

The name may have originated with someone who lived or worked in or near a forest; there was a great deal of wooded land in Burslem in 1670, the first time the name is recorded in local history. Through 300 years there seem to have been numerous spellings by authors and dealers. Even though I have no written proof, I feel all the name variations refer to the same family.

Outside of the Elsmore & Forster partnership at the Clayhills Pottery, Tunstall, 1853-1871, I found no further tie to our story for anyone with a similar Forster name.

The occupancy of the Clayhills Works is the only place I found an Elsmore listed, so evidently this is where our beautiful Pepper Leaf variant was made. The 1871 closing date makes this ware well over 100 years old. They originated several beautiful body styles for the popular plain white ironstone. Wheat (or Ceres, the Roman goddess of agriculture) was registered August 5, 1859. Medeci was registered September 5, 1857; and Laurel Wreath, April 4, 1867, along with Morning Glory and others. These body shapes appeared occasionally in later years with other decorations on them. For instance, another variant with the green underglaze design is to be found on the old Portland shape ware.

Even though two of my Pepper Leaf plates have the impressed emblem of Elsmore & Forster, my beautiful jug says Elsmore & Foster, and a stunning footed compote is unmarked! They have the same body, glaze, and heavy copper lustre trim. Magnificent pieces, all of them. I hope you find the same measure of pleasure in your Elsmore & Forster ware.

EF-3

EF-4

Another variant (unnamed) by this pottery. It is very much like the James F. Wileman decorated ware and somewhat resembles Bridgwood's (& Son) Clover Leaf. This is on heavy, blue-white ironstone, with no hint of crazing. The lustre is quite dark and adequate but not overpowering in effect. Notice the extra decoration around the handles, under the lip of the creamer, and spout of the teapot. The finials are like a bell shaped flower, possibly a morning glory in full bloom. I feel sure this was one of the body styles which was so popular when plain white embossed ironstone was the rage; it may even be called Morning Glory body style. (90)

Tea pot variant. (90)
EF-5

Elsmore & Fisher was listed in *Homespun Ceramics* by Greaser as having made spongeware. Some of these rejects bearing E & F trademarks were used to teach beginners the art of china decorating. The name "Fisher" is probably misspelled and it should be Forster.

Thomas Elsmore and Sons continued operation in the same location from 1872 to 1887 and there are numerous examples of "regular" Tea Leaf ware made by them. Sometimes the name was impressed; a Royal Arms mark was used; and often the word England was included before it was required beginning in 1891. I found no record of the disposition of this company but the hope is always present that one of our readers can add to this chapter in Staffordshire ceramic history.

This variant has surfaced several times but this is the only time a marked piece has been identified. The shape is noted as Portland (incised on back). The wide outside band is green where lustre is gone. Center motif resembles a bunch of grapes! (1)
EF-6

Number 2 E & F, trademark.
EF-7

Elsmore & Foster, trademark — notice different spelling.
EF-8

Beautiful covered casserole by Thomas Elsmore & Son was a wedding gift to the owners (29)
EF-9

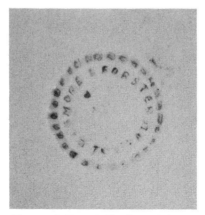

Elsmore & Forster Trademark.
EF-10

Thomas Elsmore & Son — 1872-1887 — use of **England** *indicates pre-1891 date; used at Clayhills Pottery, Tunstall.* (61)
EF-11

Thomas Furnival (& Sons)
1844 to present

Thos. Furnival 1844-6; "And Sons" added 1871. "Ltd."
from 1890 to present. (61)

Five pieces of Furnival ware with the rooster head finials. Sugar and creamer are each 6" high; large covered dish is 10" long, while sauce tureen (with ladle) is only 7½" long. Creamer carries an R^d No. 87911 (1887) which is legible but others are too blurred to read. (35)
FU-1

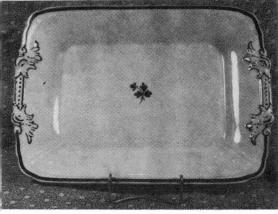

Platter 9½" x 13½" with "Rooster" molded handles.
FU-2 (35)

Gravy boat (Cable shape) and covered casserole in "Rooster" style. Note the four Tea Leaves on the lid. This style sports a curved footed base rather than the solid ring style of the cable shape of the gravy boat. (1)
FU-3

Thomas Furnival would fit into our 1980 society very nicely—he was an environmentalist. One of his outstanding achievements was the development of a non-lead glaze which was practical and cheap enough for all the potters to use. Lead poisoning, as mentioned earlier, was one of the plagues of the Potteries. Josiah C. Wedgwood, M.P., writing in 1914, confirmed that Mr. Furnival (and Mr. William Burton) had done the most to make these beautiful soft glazes with the use of borax in the formula, rather than the poisonous lead. This removed a double threat —to the pottery workmen who breathed the dust or fumes; and to the customers who ate regularly from these lead-glazed dishes. For this, if for no other reason, Thomas Furnival should be remembered.

His sense of humor is quite evident in the modeling of one line of ironstone decorated with Tea Leaf, where a rooster head is incorporated into the designs on the handles and finials. Sometime during his career, Thomas Furnival got hold of some very old moulds from a defunct Derby pottery that had been operated until 1848 by William Duesbury and others. These molds included patterns in an Oriental style with motifs of plants such as asparagus or cauliflower, and birds or animals such as swans, rabbits, or roosters. He included these moulds in his own production line, and this may have been where the rooster idea was born: thus with his sense of humor he provided us with a chuckle. Was he an "early bird" after the "worm" or was he "cock-of-the-walk"? Who knows?

We *do* know, however, that he and his sons were excellent potters and hired competent employees to maintain high-quality standards for their work. The company was reported to be small enough to be able to give personal attention to the individual orders from each patron—one sure key to success. Production was restricted to staple, utilitarian goods, especially dinner ware and toilet wares. Furnivals were highly respected by other Staffordshire potters because of their fine-quality production and their integrity. Most of their production was shipped to the Continent, Canada, or the United States.

Some of their plain goods were shipped to Canada to be decorated there by local decorating houses. Often the advertiser's name rather than the potter's name was shown. This was another example of making wares to please the country of acceptance. Because of their fine selection of Maple Leaf and Beaver designs, Furnival ware was readily a Canadian favorite, especially popular during the 1880s. Some of their old copper plates used in Canadian-designed productions, though badly worn, were not disposed of until 1963 or 1964.

Furnivals were also "copy cats," but good ones in a beautiful, useful way: In 1910 they presented their reproduction of the old Chinese Onion pattern on an outstanding dinner service which was distributed by George Hamilton of New York City. The company motto in this ad was "If you want an imitation why not buy a good one."

This was not the first time they had copied a popular idea. During the height of the Cable pattern demand, Furnivals made their share, beginning in 1867 or 1868. This design did not seem to be commemorative of the laying of the Atlantic cable which was in 1866, so I prefer to think it was to catch the attention of the sailors on board the ships who used and carried this beautiful ironstone (or white granite) to ports all over the world. Cable was one of the most-used body styles which was decorated with our special pattern.

Each potter who used this cable design added his own touch—some very bold and outstanding, such as Anthony Shaw; others very plain (such as Furnivals); and yet by other designers, the cable used was almost hidden in the remainder of the embossed designs. Many other potters

Gravy boat in "Rooster" style
FU-4

Wash bowl and ewer. Unusual extra long stemmed flower on this Furnival motif . . . one of their own variations. The bowl has three Tea Leaves around the inside. A platter, saucer, and a bowl have also been seen in this long stemmed change. (63)
FU-5

Trademark for above
FU-6

used the Cable idea including William Adams, E. and C. Challinor, John Maddock and Sons, Anthony Shaw, J. and G. Meakin, plus two or three American companies.

About 1840 Thomas Furnival (junior) succeeded Reuben Johnson (no relation to the Johnson Brothers of Tea Leaf interest) at the Stafford Street Works in Hanley. Shortly the name was changed to Furnival and Clark when a Mr. E. Clark of Longport was taken in as partner. That lasted until 1851 when the complete works there moved to Cobridge. Here they occupied two old manufactories, one of which had belonged to an Adams and the other to a Blackwell. They began at that time operating as Thomas Furnival and Sons and, in 1890, the style became Furnival's Ltd.

The Stafford works in Hanley was taken over after Furnival's departure, by Livesley and Powell and, in 1865, it became Powell and Bishop; finally in 1878, Powell, Bishop and Stonier. (See Powell and Bishop chapter.)

Jacob Furnival seems to be the mysterious J. F. of pottery history. He was a relative — possibly an uncle or a brother of Thomas.

They were in business together in Cobridge, 1845-1870; while Thomas also had a pot-bank at Hanley, 1844-1846, then at Cobridge, 1870-1890(?). Jacob made a fine line of old Staffordshire Blue wares for the American market, as well as white ironstone. Godden recorded Jacob and Thomas at Miles Bank, Shelton, 1843; later the style was Thomas Furnival and Company, 1844-1846; then Furnival and Clark for awhile; succeeded by Thomas Furnival and Sons, 1871-1890 on Elder Road, Cobridge, when Ltd. was added. They used a series of marks; but I show, as usual, only the ones I have photographed on Tea Leaf dishes.

Minnie Watson Kamm mused that the Tea Leaf design may have been inspired by motifs on the rice paper wrappings over the foil, which was also wrapped around the packages of tea shipped to England from China. That could have been copied from a leaf drawn by a forgotten Chinese artist. If this be true, then Thomas Furnival had plenty of time to adapt the design to his own use since he had been a potter from the 1840s. From all indications, his sons were also well-trained in the "art and mystery" of potting, as they carried on a very successful enterprise for a long time after his demise.

The leaves in their designs were more rounded on the serrated edges; usually the designs were smaller in size than those on most other wares. Quite often the underglaze was painted in a lighter shade of brown, so when the glaze wore off the contrast in design and body color was less. Some of their production was on better quality body than others; but usually the soup plates and plates were larger and deeper. Often crazed and/or brown-stained dishes were left sitting on a shelf, but most of their Tea Leaf is beautiful, desirable, and well worth buying if it can be found.

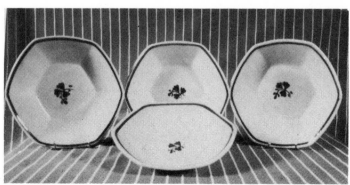

Four hexagon shaped berry dishes (nappies) 5" in diameter (11)
FU-7

Oval covered casserole, also cable body, has no cut in the lid for a ladle. (13)
FU-8

Huge soup tureen, lid, underplate, while ladle only is by Powell & Bishop. An ideal show piece which sold in 1979-80 for $500.00! Cable body style. Trademark on page 74. (90)
FU-9

"Mitten" shaped cable body style; relish dish or spoon rest 5¼" x 8¾". (82)
FU-10

Tea pot in cable body style; 9½" to top of finial. Notice again elongated flower peculiar to Furnival. Same as trademark on page 74, R^{d} No. 5458 — (1884). **FU-11** (21)

Oval milk jug also on cable body style, 9½" high. (85)
FU-12

Trademark changed slightly, also has R^{d} No. 30039 (1885). These two marks are the most common found on Tea Leaf by Furnival but others may be found as they have used quite a number through the years.
FU-13

One more cable style in a bulbous creamer, this one only 6" high, which came in various sizes up to 13". (74)
FU-14

Square 5" nappies — very popular 1885-1890; edge is slightly scalloped.
FU-15

10" plate — probably part of a tea set. Not an underplate for a casserole as it has no well. **FU-16** (90)

A most unusual covered 7½" square casserole with a striking finial, and two Tea Leaves on lid; 9" high. **FU-17** (59)

Two brush holders. The one on the right can easily be identified as Furnival by the motif, and gold, not copper, lustre; 5" high. Left one, by Shaw, is 5¼" high. Both these have drainage holes towards bottom, but not all holders had this added feature. (41)
FU-18

Quite a nice collectors' item . . . a chamber pot. (54)
FU-19

W. H. Grindley & Co.
1880 to present

Covered vegetable casserole; 6" x 11" x 6" high. The only example of one of these body styles I have found, but doubtless this style was also used for one of their full lines. Since we have no catalogs we can only guess that each body style was produced several years, then a new style chosen . . . a "newer model" of Tea Leaf so to speak. Notice the motif is much smaller on this piece than on later wares — particularly the next group shown, which has wide vertical ribbing around the base similar to Enoch Wedgwood (Tunstall) Ltd. The third body style shown is Bamboo, on the order of Alfred Meakin's line. (11)

GR-1

8¼" milk jug with distinctive rope handle, vertical ribbing, and enormous design. This entire body shape line showed quite a lot of crazing and discoloration but the lustre was superb.

GR-2

One reason there is so little written about this company is that they are so young. Sparse records show they have been in business only since 1880. I found no mention of the name in Staffordshire history prior to that time. However, they were "doers-movers" because in less than ten years they were considered one of the American "Big Four" — suppliers of pottery to the United States. The other three were A. Meakin, Johnson Bros., and John Maddock, according to the 1914 writings of Josiah C. Wedgwood. It is interesting to note that all four of these companies made Tea Leaf, and a chapter on each is included in this book. Maybe Grindleys were too busy making "pots" to advertise or call attention to themselves.

W. H. Grindley began as a tenant in the New Field Works in Tunstall which had been built way back in 1763 by Smith Child, Esquire. During that 117 years there had been a great many other tenants, among them one of the Adams family of potters (about 1857), also our good Tea Leaf friend, Anthony Shaw. From the very beginning, Grindley's reputation was based on the manufacture of a fine class of earthenware for home and export.

In 1887 he moved to the Woodland Works in Woodland Street at Brownhills, also, in Tunstall, where another of our Tea Leaf friends, Edward Challinor, had been in partnership with some of the famous Wood family of potters. There, Grindley began immediately to make white granite for the American market. This time Wedgwood observed that Grindley's wares were outstanding examples of up-to-date economical manufacture.

These Woodland Works had been built in 1831-35 by one John Wood so they were much newer (by 68-70 years) than Grindley's first place of business. We can well imagine he modernized the new home to the highest degree. Machinery of all kinds and assembly line production methods in every step of pottery manufacture had been or were rapidly put in use. The day of the "one-horse" operation was past. Grindley was contemporary with Alfred Meakin (1881) in England and J. & E. Mayer (1881) in Beaver Falls, Pennsylvania, along with several other Tea Leaf producers.

Even so William Burton* writing in 1904, preferred to withhold evaluation of the lasting effect of these new-breed potters on the entire industry. It is now evident that their use of new methods of manufacture and decoration along with newer formulas and firing techniques were successful beyond even Burton's wildest dreams—and *he* was a master potter as well as a fine journalist with many years of experience in both areas.

A little bit later (1907) the Rhead brothers, G. Wooliscroft and Frederick A., recorded that Grindley deserved notice not for the quantity of their exports—but for the durability and finish of their products.

The W.H. Grindley & Co. trademark is to be found on Moss Rose along with Daffodil and various brown printed decorated wares all so popular in the 1890s. Their use of the Bamboo shape makes it imperative to look at the back stamp to see if a piece was made by Grindley or A. Meakin.

Very little of the Grindley ware I have seen has been crazed or stained. It is adequately decorated with copper lustre and will add beauty to any table setting.

---

* William Burton, *A History and Description of English Earthenware and Stoneware* (London: Cassell and Company Limited, 1904).

Waste bowl, 5" in diameter, in same body style along with oblong open baker, platter, and butter chips, all Grindley. Only the waste bowl is discolored.
GR-3

Square butter dish, 4½" x 4¾" high. This Bamboo shape is so much like that of Alfred Meakin's line a look at the back stamp is a necessity.
GR-4

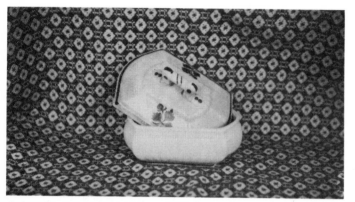

Covered soap dish to match Toothbrush holder, below. Soap dishes usually were oblong while butter dishes were square or round. Soap drainers had several holes, butter drainers only one large one. (77)
GR-5

Oblong covered vegetable casserole in Bamboo style, 5" x 10¾"
GR-6

Tooth brush holder 5¼" tall x 3½" diameter. Some would call this a spooner, but they were never shown in ironstone dinnerware in the old catalogs. A (tooth) brush holder was always part of the toilet set; however I would use this for a flower vase as it has no drain opening and is such a lovely shape. **GR-7** (12)

Their marks before 1891 may include the word Tunstall rather than England, which was used exclusively after that date. They became a limited liability company in 1925 and LTD. was added to the trademark. They were acquired by Alfred Clough in 1960.

Their name now (1980) is Grindley of Stoke and their United States distributor is Auslander Import, 225 Fifth Avenue, New York City. In an announcement in May, 1979, in the "China, Glass & Tableware" publication (pg. 59) it was reported that Grindley produced mugs and assorted giftware along with dinnerware.

Their "century of progress" from 1880 to 1980 has indeed been one of the most outstanding facets of our Tea Leaf story.

Teapots. Top: (left to right) Clemenston, Clemenston, Grindley. Botton: (left to right) Meakin, Wilkinson (Late R. Alcock, Burslem). (54)
GR-8

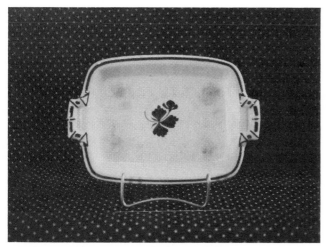

Oblong service tray for oblong sauce tureen
GR-9

Oblong sauce tureen, lid, and ladle. Should have a service tray (left). 5" x 8" x 4½" high. This same item was made in a much larger size which would hold about four quarts. It also had a service plate. (15)
GR-10

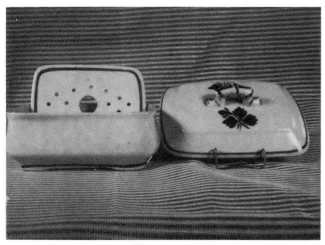

Soap dish, lid, drainer; 4½" x 6" x 4" high (12)
GR-11

Two Bamboo jugs. These also were made in graduated sizes from about one pint up to one gallon capacity. The motif on this body style is not quite as large as the previous style, and more of this line is seen with the copper lustre partially or completely worn off. **GR-12** (15)

Chamber pot with lid; 8½" diameter x 7" high   (69)
GR-13

' *W. H. Grindley & Co. trademark*
GR-14

Thomas Hughes
1860-1960(?)

Tea pot — bulbous type with acanthus leaves around the handle. Lid may not be original but it fits.   (56)
HU-1

If you had your morning coffee, lunch, and dinner served on English ironstone made by Thomas Hughes, you were in good company with a growing populace.

The first Thomas Hughes listed was in the 1818 Lane End directory but he had been preceded by Samuel Hughes (probably his father) who had built the Daisy Bank Works at Longton in the late 1700s. This first Thomas Hughes also built the Waterloo Road Works at Cobridge in 1820. That was a family affair as his son Stephen succeeded him until 1856. By then Thomas II was old enough to take over and continue the good work of his family.

Jewitt remarked that Hughes' entire output was for the American market. His goods were made in a limited number of styles but consistently acceptable to the American families who needed and wanted this sturdy ironstone ware. He was reputed to have made no changes in the formulas, only in the production and firing. There is little question that he kept up with the latest improvements as he completely renovated and enlarged the old Waterloo Works while he was there.

He moved in 1881 to the Top Bridge Works which had been in the John Davenport holdings for so many years, and continued until at least 1957 to please the public. Mellor, Taylor & Company later took the vacated Waterloo Road Works. We know of course there must have been succeeding family members to operate the Top Bridge Pottery for so long—sons, family—who knows? It was made a limited liability company in 1910.

Jervis had observed that in pottery a good hard body was less likely to craze, always on the assumption of perfect unity of body and the glaze. It was more expensive to make a dense, heavy body—but that seems to be what Thomas Hughes did best. The lone tea pot in my collection was *much* heavier than others the same size. There was no crazing; the glaze was exquisite and the lustre perfect. If I could have a second choice after Anthony Shaw, in a complete set by one potter, my Tea Leaf would all be by Thomas Hughes.

In 1886 Hughes bought the Unicorn Works also from Davenport as they were going out of business. The two plants are close together. It was later sold to Arthur Wood and Son.

Trademark used 1895–1910, Thomas Hughes & Son **HU-2** *(56)*

When Thomas Hughes II was a younger man, about 1868, he was active in conciliating labor disputes. Their system called for ten men from each side (potters and owners) to hear the grievances. Then an umpire helped to decide the issue—he was an umpire along with Henry Davenport and others. Hughes passed away in 1901.

It will be interesting to see where most of the Tea Leaf made by this fine old company is to be found today.

Johnson Bros.

1883 to present

Two jugs — left, Meakin's Chelsea shape; right, Johnson Bros. Both lighter weight with vertical fluting full height of each piece. Meakin's Chelsea shape was featured in plain white ironstone around turn of the century in Sears and Wards catalogs. *(74)*

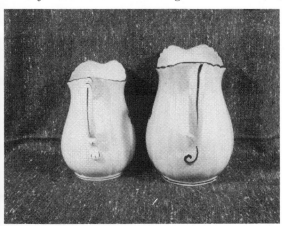

JO-1

In terms of Tea Leaf history we could, with tongue in cheek, refer to this company as the "Johnson Kids" — they were the "babies" of the Tea Leaf family of the early-day English potters, because they were the last to begin making it just before the turn of the century. But let us not sell them short for, just as is happening today, the "kids" are making greater progress and are now more successful than many of the "old timers." Where are the Cartwrights, the Davenports, John Edwards, or the Clemenstons, or the Anthony Shaws of the nineteenth century pottery fame? Gone — factories closed or out of business.

It is possible this twenty-five to thirty-year-old pattern looked to Johnsons like a perennial favorite such as Blue Willow; there was no way they could know it would be out of style in another twenty-five to thirty years. (It was not shown in catalogs after 1910.)

Let us get acquainted with this family and learn who they were and what they made. Even though Johnson was a rather common name in the Potteries, there was not a great number listed, and that is one reason I feel most of them may have been related. As I have done before, I have listed the Johnsons who may possibly have been part of this family, even though I found no adequate records for proof.

The first mention was of James Johnson on a 1691 list of Staffordshire potters who made slipware. Three years later, T. Johnson signed his name on a piece of old slipware. The next record was of Thomas and Joseph Johnson who, from 1725–1775, worked a pottery opposite the Church at Lane End making good salt glaze, crouch ware, and white stoneware. They were succeeded by Mayer-Newbold who greatly enlarged the works. There was a Johnson and Brough listed at Lane End in 1802 who may have been heirs of one of these men.

Another predecessor of these Johnsons and probably *not* a relative but an interesting fellow nevertheless, was Dr. Samuel Johnson. He was reported at Chelsea Works in Derby complaining about the price of china he had purchased and challenged that he could improve on the product. A pottery was put at his disposal to try his experiments, but they were foolish failures. Somewhere along the way he developed a weakness for tea pots; two outstanding ones in his collection were huge — one held two quarts, the other one three quarts which, in 1777, was a lot of tea. His doctorate degree was not in medicine, but it seems he was a historian along with his many other writings.

Ralph Johnson was listed in 1802 in the Staffordshire Pottery Directory as a modeller at the Mt. Pleasant Works in Longton, and, in 1818, Ralph Johnson was in business at the Church Street Work in Burslem. Sometime before 1878, at the Mt. Pleasant Works at Hallam, the Johnson Company made ordinary china. This may have been the same man but probably was a son. On High Street in Longton, about the same time, a J.L. Johnson made all the usual services and common class of china; while in Fenton, on Edensor Road, a new china works was built by Johnson and Poole about 1878.

Round butter dish, lid, drainer, one hole for drainage instead of several as for soap; 7" in diameter (84)

JO-2

Squared nappy similar to Grindley and Enoch Wedgwood (Tunstall) Ltd. wares. Very mottled and brown. (90)

JO-3

More of the Johnson story had to be written by other historians, as Llewellynn Jewitt's *Ceramic Art of Great Britain* (where much of the foregoing was recorded) was published in 1883 — hardly time for good news of the successful newcomers, the Johnson Brothers, to be mentioned, as they began business that same year.

The Charles Street Works of Hanley had been established by William Mellor in 1758 for the manufacture of black basalt and other wares of that day. The works were sold 125 years later at a receiver's sale in 1883, to the Johnson Brothers.

From the very beginning, Fredrick, Robert and Lewis Johnson had the right touch to put the business on a paying basis. They turned from making the heavy, cumbersome white ironstone to a lighter weight, yet more durable type, ware. With new body styles, fresh decorative ideas, and different shapes, their lines were an immediate hit with the American housewives. Johnson also began to sell to Montgomery Ward with its advantageous catalog mail-order system.

At the turn of the century, several other companies were catering to the same market, including: W.H. Grindley; Mellor, Taylor and Company (both graduates of the Meakin Works); Edward Challinor; as well as the Meakins and others.

Some of the Johnsons had taken over the Victoria and Albert Works in Tunstall in 1874. These boys were nephews of James Meakin,* whose wife was a Johnson. Within five or six years, they were strong competitors for the trade with the American buyers. By the time Josiah C. Wedgwood wrote in 1914, the Johnson Brothers had five factories in Hanley, Tunstall, and Burslem, all turning out goods to meet this demand.

Brown was the leading choice in decorating colors from 1870–1890, and square or rectangle shapes were the rage. Footed (rim) individual oyster bowls were one of the few round bowls made then, but the huge oblong tureens with lid, ladle, and service plates were very desirable then, as now, for serving oyster stew, potato soup, chili, or other cold-weather favorites after a sleighing party or a stay on the ice (or after a football game today).

One of the later favorite styles in Johnson Brothers dinnerware was the light weight body with the shallow, irregular scallops on the edges, and faint side panels radiating out from the plate well or up the sides of the hollow ware.

There is a notable similarity to the Meakin offering of this early twentieth century period. Toilet sets shown in catalogs included ten pieces, or possibly twelve if a tall slop jar and cover were added to the large pitcher (for cold water), the smaller pitcher for hot water, a huge bowl, a chamber pot and cover, a mug, a three-piece covered soap dish, and a brush holder. Occasionally a silencer was included. This silencer was placed in the bottom of the tall chamber (combinette) to lessen the noise when it was used. The word combinette is self-explanatory, but it was used by genteel ladies who felt it was a "nicer" word than "chamber." It really was a combined word for a combined use — the covered waste jar and chamber pot.

There are a few other Johnsons that should be included on our list. Jewitt listed Samual Johnson, Ltd., at the Hill Pottery in Burslem, 1837–1931; H. & R. Johnson (Ltd.) Crystal Tile Works, Cobridge and High Gate Tile Works, Tunstall — both in business in this century, and brothers to Fredrick, Robert, and Lewis. Leslie Johnson was a decorator, from 1900–1920.

* See chapter on J. & G. Meakin, and Meakin family tree in Alfred Meakin chapter.

Trademark Johnson Bros., 1891-1913
JO-4

Even Canada had one Johnson pottery man: William Johnson mentioned by Collard† in her Canadian pottery history provided passage to the great Northwest for crockery shipped from Staffordshire around 1819–1820. Cargo arrived in Canada packed in 300-pound crates or 400-pound hogsheads, and this William Johnson repacked them into smaller containers which weighed only about 100–150 pounds. There were many portage points where back-packing was the *only* means of transportation to reach the back woods of Canada. He was a very important link in this crockery chain which has fastened the entire world together in order to satisfy our love of tea and pretty dishes. He may have later chosen an easier way to earn a living as, in 1845, William Johnson & Son of Niagara were dealers in crockery, glass, and earthenware from *Staffordshire* — that was the magic word — the maker did not matter.

Grace M. Ellis, writing in a 1948 *Farm Journal* observed that:

> The Meakins and the Johnsons were the "Henry Fords" of the dish world. At a modest price, they turned out ironstone china. Their most popular patterns were Edge Line and Sprig, sometimes called Lustre Spray or Tea Leaf, and the charming Moss Rose.

The Johnson Brothers had a great deal of influence on the high quality of domestic wares which were created in much more pleasing style and decorations than had been made in by-gone years.

If Tea Leaf was "the curse of poverty" as it was called by some wag, then we should have been proud to be poor. Today that certainly is not true and the prices go up all the time as the supply goes down.

John Maddock
1855 to present

Truly the rubbish of one generation becomes the treasures of the next.

W. P. Jervis: *Encyclopedia of Ceramics*, 1902

Since Tea Leaf certainly was the "rubbish of one generation" and is now one of our most treasured collectibles, it seems most appropriate that the only photo I have of this treasured pattern by John Maddock and Sons came from no less prestigeous place than the Abraham Lincoln home in Springfield, Illinois.

The other photos in this chapter show a variety of pieces by several potters that well-wishers have donated through the years for use in the Lincoln house, and which were on display in 1974. This famous landmark is under the administration of the National Park Service. Mr. Albert Banton, Jr. who was in charge at that time, was most cooperative and knowledgable.

Many people had mentioned the Lincoln use of Tea Leaf in the White House and, even though it seemed (to me) rather unlikely, it was necessary to investigate that possibility. We should remember the Lincolns never lived in the Springfield house after their move to Washington in 1861. The earliest recorded date we have for Tea Leaf was 1856 for Anthony Shaw. That does *not* indicate the year the decorated ware was put on the market, but rather the year that particular body style was registered (or patented) by a pottery. That company could have used that body style for many years, with decorations other than Tea Leaf, before that design was finally applied and

---

† Collard, pp. 24, 35, 170.

*Sauce tureen, lid, ladle, and service plate. 5" x 8" x 5½" high. Mint! A show piece in the Lincoln Home in Springfield, Illinois and my only representation of this old company's Tea Leaf. This set was made **after** 1906 according to the backstamp.* (47)

MAD-1

Backstamp of above: John Maddock & Sons 1906 (47)

MAD-2

*Part of the collection of Tea Leaf on display in the Lincoln home. These gifts of well-wishers were all crafted in 1884-1898, according to the various trademarks. Left to right: Brush holder, chamber pot, and water pitcher by Alfred Meakin, 1881-1897. The silencer (center with vertical ribbing) R*ᵈ *date 1884, but no manufacturer's name. It has four holes in the bottom. Wash bowl is by Shaw, 1890-1898; the small nappy and the soap dish are by John Edwards in their Victory shape; also registered 1884.* (47)

MAD-3

shipped to the United States. I found one Shaw item in the Lincoln home; most were of much larger vintage such as this set by John Maddock and Sons.

In answer to my 1977 inquiry, Betty C. Monkman, Registrar in the Office of the Curator at the White House, replied that there were currently no pieces in the White House similar to the Tea Leaf photos I had enclosed.

Mrs. Lincoln had purchased two official services during her White House years and these were paid for by government funds. If Mrs. Lincoln had purchased any for her personal use the government archives would have no record of them.

This seems to put to rest the legend that Mrs. Lincoln had used Tea Leaf dishes in the White House.

Nevertheless, we can enjoy the photos and learn something of John Maddock and his sons. Maddock is also a good old American pottery name as we shall see. I will not be surprised to have Tea Leaf show up with an American Maddock trademark on it.

John Maddock was in Jervis' account of 1830 Staffordshire potters, and it is likely about the first time he and James Edwards were partners at the old Dale Hall Works on Newcastle Street in Burslem. (The date of the second time is elusive.) In 1839, Edwards left to go in business on his own and one Mr. Seddon took his place; the style was Maddock and Seddon until 1842, when he left also. Maddock was alone until his sons were taken in, in 1855. During this time he was busy with some new ideas for the industry and was granted patents for oven and kiln improvements. He had a fine reputation as a potter. The clay bodies he made were less apt to craze, as he used more expensive clays and fired at higher temperatures. The result was very little, if any, crazing, a common problem with any glazed earthenware. He was successful from the very first and seemed to be proof of the old axiom "Nothing succeeds like success." This carried through for his sons, also.

At the time John Maddock served his apprenticeship, six to eight years was the usual time required, and a working knowledge of the entire process of pottery making was absolutely essential, including engineering, designing, drafting, standards of production and foundry work, along with a knowledge of pattern making and machine shop work.

One had to be familiar with, and competent to operate, all types of tools used to work on wood, plaster, clays, metal, wax, or any other medium. An eye for color and a knowledge of chemistry (for mixing clays and paints) were essential. All these, plus the knack of finding time to cultivate friends/customers, to market wisely and to handle money well — were *some* of the essentials for a master potter. John Maddock *was* a master potter.

All of his sons seemed to have come to the United States at one time or another. Thomas came and stayed (more on him later); James and Henry came and went back soon to take an active part in their father's business. John Jr., stayed to establish a United States market, but he too later returned home and succeeded his father as president of the company, until his death about 1911. At that time, James, who was the only son left living in England, took the helm and admitted his nephew, John Francis, as a partner.

John Jr. had spent many years in this country cementing good business friendships and keeping the Maddock name in front of the buying public. However, his brothers, Henry and James, reaped the greatest benefits of his labors as they succeeded him.

Upon James' return to England after the Philadelphia Centennial Exposition in 1876, the home plant was expanded, and the number of workmen reached well over 600. This may all have been the direct result of James' trip to this country, as they had an exhibit at that exposition. That public showing exposed our crudity and opened our eyes to beauty we had temporarily forgotten; it created a wave of wants — new, finer dishes, ornate decorations — enriched table service in general. John Maddock and Sons responded with a degree unexcelled by most other potters.

Before 1876 they had made only white earthenware, superbly decorated by skilled engravers. Later they brought out their Cable shape (before 1879) and also began production of semi-porcelain using beautifully colored transfer prints. Their Cable design was of more extravagant interpretation than other competitors. More color and gilding were used. They also made decal transfers on less expensive wares, but they were very well done. This must have been about the time Tea Leaf was made part of their production. On the set in the Lincoln home, the body was nice and white with no crazing. The lustre was intact, and the whole assembly, when lifted, was heavy but had a comfortable feel. Their Tea Leaf design had only three lobes on each leaf instead of the usual five.

John Maddock's one aim from the first was that no competition should surpass him, and this idea was passed on to his sons. A little while later, their white ware was all completely vitrified, resulting in an even more superior product. In the 1890s, one of their successes was a fine reproduction of the old Blue Willow pattern in a rich dark blue, much like the earlier Spode reproduction.

"Royal" was included in each trademark, indicating a visit by a member of the royal family. I show only one trademark, but there were numerous others used as shown in Godden's *Encyclopedia of British Pottery and Porcelain Marks* — a book no collector of English ware can afford to be without.

James' tenure as head of the Maddock was evidently a happy time for everyone. He had a keen intellect and, as his father had done, made every effort to keep the Maddock name as a symbol of the best in housewares. He restricted his production to this, so the entire manufacturing process was under his close personal supervision. He was a congenial, liberal, progressive optimist — civic minded, especially interested in city government and, at one time, was mayor of Burslem.

During the British depression of 1887–1888, he kept a full force at work and the entire plant in operation. His employees appreciated this enough to later arrange a celebration and present to him two silver stands along with a large silver tray thus inscribed:

> We are proud of the high position the manufacturings of this firm have attained and still maintain on the market, and we highly appreciate the honorable, fair and kindly treatment your employees have always received at your hand, your uniform and thoughtful consideration for them in times of sickness, the efforts you have put forth — sometimes to your own disadvantage, to provide work for them when trade has been depressed, and your endeavors as chairman of the Board of Arbitration to secure and promote cordial relationship between capital and labor. As a testimonial of the honesty of these expressions of respect and esteem, we request your acceptance of the accompanying tray and two silver center stands.

There must have been a good bit of family business transacted while his brothers were all together for the Centennial Exposition in Philadelphia as John Jr. went home with James, and his former role of family sales representative here was transferred to Thomas, who continued in this capacity many years, all the while experimenting on the processes necessary to successfully produce our much needed American-made sanitary ware. It has been said that Josiah Wedgwood recorded 10,000 experiments that he made before success was final in his production of his famous Jasperware. I found no record of how many tests Thomas made, but his work, for a time, had to be some of the most discouraging in American pottery history. Before financial success was finally a reality, he carried his precious samples — wrapped in a sheet — lifted up on his shoulder, and walked the New York City streets seeking jobbers who would sell his new conveniences instead of those imported from England. "Time, toil, patience, and indomitable perseverence" finally paid off and we, today, can be grateful to Thomas Maddock* for our modern American-made bathroom facilities.

In 1896 "Ltd." was added to the John Maddock name; sometimes the trademark included the name of the town as well as *England*.

Made in England was added after 1935, and they are still in business.

Alfred Meakin (Ltd.)
1875 to present

Alfred Meakin made several body shapes, the most common of which I will designate, for lack of company name, as No. 1. Dishes in this photo are part of a 44 year collection. Only the tea pot lid is a replacement.
MEA-1   (87)

Sauce tureen, lid, ladle, and service tray, 6" x 8".   (91)
MEA-2

Alfred Meakin is a magic name among Tea Leaf collectors and is of course the mark which appeared on my grandma's Tea Leaf dishes. It seems, at least here in the Midwest, there is more Tea Leaf with the Meakin trademark than all the other marks combined. I doubt if there is a Tea Leaf collector who does not own at least one piece of Grandma's set, and we must include the avid hunter who has amassed a full elaborate dinner set with all accouterments. There are many collectors who refuse to buy pieces from another maker and yet find their search is quite rewarding because there is so much Alfred Meakin available.

The late Gladys Caruso recorded in *Spinning Wheel*, November, 1967:

> Alfred Meakin was one maker who sometimes used more than the minimum lustre decoration. Many collectors favor Meakin's work because of the beautiful color of his lustre, but other wares were so like his that a wise collector never turns down a fine specimen because of the mark.

Who *was* Alfred Meakin? Historians agree that he began potting on his own in 1875 at Tunstall when he took over the Victoria Works which had been built by John Tompkinson in 1858. It had been operated as Turner and Tompkinson until the latter's retirement; it was continued by Turner as G. W. Turner and Sons for a short time until the Meakin occupancy. About the same time, Meakin acquired the Royal Albert Works nearby from Turner and Goddard, as well as the Highgate Pottery from an unnamed company. His first trademark was a globe with the name Alfred Meakin emblazoned across the center; England was added in 1891; in 1897 Alfred Meakin became a limited liability company, and as same, is still in business.

Alfred Meakin began with a small, rather insignificant pot-bank and made it into one of the largest concerns in the Potteries, with sheer hard work, astute business judgment, and fair treatment of his fellow men. The hard work was evidenced in the vast amount of goods shipped to the United States for so many years, along with numerous expansion and renovation programs that brought dramatic changes to the physical plants.

---

* Thomas Maddock and Sons, *Pottery* (printed privately by this company, 1910).

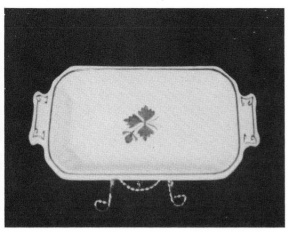

Relish tray, 4½" x 8¾". One of the most common pieces found today, other than plates and platters. (19)
MEA-3

Huge soup tureen, lid, and ladle — 9¼" diameter x 8½" high. Found in a shop in northern California by an advanced collector whose treasures came from there to Martha's Vineyard in Massachusetts and all points in between. (1)
MEA-4

Soap dish, lid, and drainer (30)
MEA-5

Meakin's business judgments were proven correct by his successful entry into the foreign markets, which had expanded rapidly after the close of our Civil War in 1865. The need for all sorts of ceramic products in the United States was a welcome challenge to him, and a lack of serious competition for a time also worked to his advantage.

The Philadelphia Centennial in 1876 caused an even greater demand for decorated dinnerware to replace the heavy, plain white ironstone which had reigned for so long on American dinner tables. Alfred Meakin joined J. and G. Meakin, and the Johnson Brothers (all relatives) to fill this void. Each in his own way provided beauty and quality for thousands of American tables with his ironstone, semi-porcelain, bone china, and other pottery products.

Meakin was a continuing promoter of the movement we now term the Industrial Revolution. Two of the greatest factors in his success were his early use of steam power and automatic machinery in his potteries. The steam-powered press, in 1856, had replaced the old sun-evaporation method used at the beginning of the clay preparation. The 1860s and 1870s brought steam-powered blungers and pug mills which did away with hand mixing and wedging, both laborious and time-consuming processes essential in preliminary clay preparation. Steam-powered plate jiggers and jolleys also improved the quality of goods and speed of production. Hollow ware presses for pitchers, large bowls, and the like, soon followed. The year 1880 brought bat-making machines which automatically measured the exact amount of clay necessary for a single plate or cup, thus bringing uniformity in size and thickness to the products. This same power was used on throwers' wheels and lathes, along with a device to control the speed of these machines. The manufacture of pottery machinery was big business by 1880–1885, and a certain Mr. Boulton was one of the innovators responsible for the establishment of that segment of the industry in Staffordshire.

Machines had been available since 1845 but workmen objected to their use, fearing the loss of jobs. Also, imperfections in the machinery delayed their adoption for general use. Alfred Meakin must have been a very special kind of potter to have been able to convince his employees of the advantages of these new-fangled methods. Help was available to him through publication of a new trade magazine, *The Pottery Examiner*, along with the formation of a new Pottery Board of Conciliation and Arbitration. Trade unions were reactivated and became a powerful voice for the workmen.

All this may surprise many Americans since we were almost a quarter of a century ahead of Staffordshire in our use of machinery. We did not have the opposition of entrenched "old timers," and some of those machines were American inventions.

In the advertisement of china houses which exporters opened in our country, I found no one who included Alfred Meakin among the polyglot of potters whose goods they handled; I therefore believe he immediately established his own methods of distribution. Much of his output was sold through mail-order catalogs of large American companies. There has been, for a long time, an exclusive representative here for Alfred Meakin; the present office is in the Chicago area.

Finally, a century of service by this public-spirited man and his company is an unsung anthem of the truth of the Golden Rule — to treat others as we wish to be treated. His one aim was to make the best possible product at the most reasonable price — an accomplished fact in his lifetime — and ours. The Staffordshire district is still the beneficiary of many public institutions — evidences of his generosity. His name, as a force for good, will long be remembered.

Chamber pot (no lid). Note the huge Tea Leaf. (78)
MEA-6

This sauce tureen with lid should have a ladle (which sold for 22¢ in a 1901 Montgomery Ward catalog) and a service tray. (74)
MEA-7

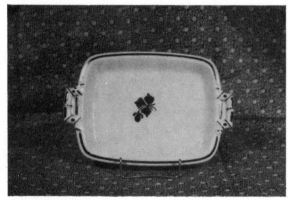

Service tray for sauce tureen (14)
MEA-7B

Donut stand. 8" square; straight sides. Mint! (69)
MEA-8

Early historians make so many references to potteries owned or operated by all the Meakins, it is difficult to determine who was where, and when. I make no real effort here to show family relationships as it seems all the Meakins were related. There are several Henrys and Georges for example, and it is often impossible, without further identification, to be accurate. We *do* know, however, the families of Meakin, Johnson, Ridgway, and Pearson were all related, and their activities in various potteries were intertwined.

In 1973 personal correspondence, I was advised by the Alfred Meakin Company that they were taken over in 1908 by members of the Johnson family and had been in their control ever since. The firm at that time was comprised of the Royal Albert and Newfield factories — two of the most modern in Stoke-on-Trent. They employed nearly 1000 in 1973.

In December, 1977, correspondence with A.G. Houldsworth, sales manager for Myatt-Meakin Ltd., informed me the Alfred Meakin (Tunstall) Ltd. Company had been taken over by the firm of Myatt Son & Co., who themselves were owned by Interpace Corporation of Parsippany, New Jersey. Later information from *Murphy's Industrial Manual* (February, 1974) indicated the price was $5,051,000.00. We cannot help but wonder if this was part of Alfred Meakin's wildest dreams one hundred and one years earlier! At least they are now part of an American company.

Mr. Houldsworth went on to relate that there was a thorough "housecleaning" of both patterns and shapes and many old records were destroyed — including those about our favorite pattern. He could not find even one old pattern book with the Tea Leaf design in it. Oh, if I had only written sooner!

He was also gracious enough to include some historical background on the Johnson family. There were seven boys, six of whom went into business. Two of them owned the Johnson-Richards Tiles Ltd., the largest in Britain. Two others originated the Johnson Bros. pottery which is now part of the Wedgwood Group, and the last two, Stuart and Frank, ran the Alfred Meakin (Tunstall) Ltd. (My early information indicated three brothers in the Johnson Bros. pottery.)

He also recollected that the three factories of Alfred Meakin were visited by King George V and Queen Mary in 1913. At that time they were presented a full dinner set in a specially commissioned decoration known as Bleu-de-Roi, which became one of their best-sellers for many years. In 1977 there were 2000 employees in four separate operations. In our correspondence, Mr. Houldsworth recalled that one of the last living granddaughters of the first Alfred Meakin had passed away in mid-1977. He also indicated there were no surviving old time employees.

According to the *Official Handbook of Stoke-on-Trent in 1978* (sent to me by Arnold Mountford of the City Museum – Hanley), Royal Albert Works was the largest producer of bone china in the world. They hold the Queen's Award for export achievement with 74 percent of their total production exported. They have never fallen below 60 percent since World War II. In the past ten years these works had doubled in capacity, and the main plant is one of the best planned and modernized factories in the area. Royal Albert is the only china with a ten year minimum available guarantee. The Newfield Potteries were acquired by Meakin in 1930 and renamed Alfred Meakin (Tunstall), Ltd.

One of the oldest works which came under the Meakin family control for awhile was the Abbey Pottery of Cobridge which was built in 1703. The name comes from occupancy by monks from the old Hulton

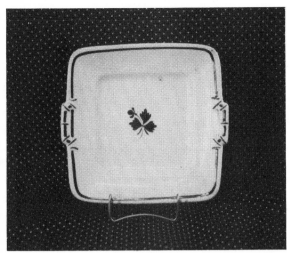

Square 8½" plate with solid handles. Could be used as a service tray for the square covered casserole but was probably a bread or cake plate from a large tea set. (69)
MEA-9

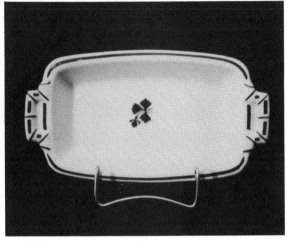

Relish tray — Bamboo shape (85)
MEA-10

Popular Bamboo style jugs came in graduated sizes from one pint to the large one for the bedroom wash set. This was the first piece of Tea Leaf owned by a newlywed collector in 1973. (38)
MEA-11

Abbey, which is less than two miles away. The first record I found of tenants was of one of the William Adams and his stepfather, Mr. Hales, who were potting there in 1787. The Adams sisters lived in the family home, Cobridge Hill, just across the road, so it seems logical the Adams operated the Abbey works a good many years. The next tenant mentioned was Edward Pearson, 1846–51, whose partner, Mr. Hancock, retired and left Pearson to carry on alone until his son, Edward Meakin Pearson (his mother was a Meakin), entered the business. About 1872 young Edward came to the United States and for twenty years was associated with several East Liverpool potteries, and later, the Wheeling Pottery of Wheeling, West Virginia. The elder Mr. Pearson had found an original timber in the roof structure of the Abbey Pottery which verified the 1703 construction date. He was also the originator of the Wheat or Ceres pattern, copied by so many potters in the 1860s.

After young Pearson left England the works were operated by Henry Meakin from 1872–1879, who made ironstone exclusively for the American market. I would not be surprised to hear of Tea Leaf with his name on it. When he relinquished control of the business it was taken over by Woods and Hawthorne (1879–1884).

The old pottery was honey-combed underground by coal mines and was finally pulled down sometime before 1902, according to Jervis.

Other Meakins connected with various potteries include:

1650	The old James Glass Pottery, Hanley, was later occupied by Samuel Keeling and Company; Meakin Brothers (1851–?); and later the Taylor Brothers. These old works were taken down before 1880, as Jewitt recorded.
1845	Meakin and Proctor — Lane End
1845–1855	J. Meakin — The New Town Pottery, Longton, later taken by J. and H. Proctor. This is likely the same works as the previous listing, and it may have belonged to James Meakin, father of J. and G. Meakin.
1865–1882	Meakin and Company, Elder Road Works, Cobridge. This company annually shipped 2,500 crates (about 300 pounds each) of white granite ware, which was shipped to the United States. I cannot help wondering if this is the old Abbey Pottery — renamed — as Elder Road is in Cobridge. Or is it the same Henry Meakin in a second pottery?
1870	Harry Meakin, Lichfield Street, Hanley
1873–1876	H. Meakin — no other information
1882	Henry Meakin — Grove Street, Cobridge
1883–1889	Charles Meakin, Eastwood Pottery, Hanley (formerly was at Burslem)
1883	Charles Meakin — established a pottery at Derby. No other information.

As can be seen, there were many potters by this family name, and possibly I missed some. There are numerous descendants of Alfred

Meakin in the United States. I have corresponded with or spoken by phone to several of them in all parts of the country, but none was able to recall specific interesting information about him. Perhaps someone now will come forward with pertinent reminiscences for all of us to enjoy.

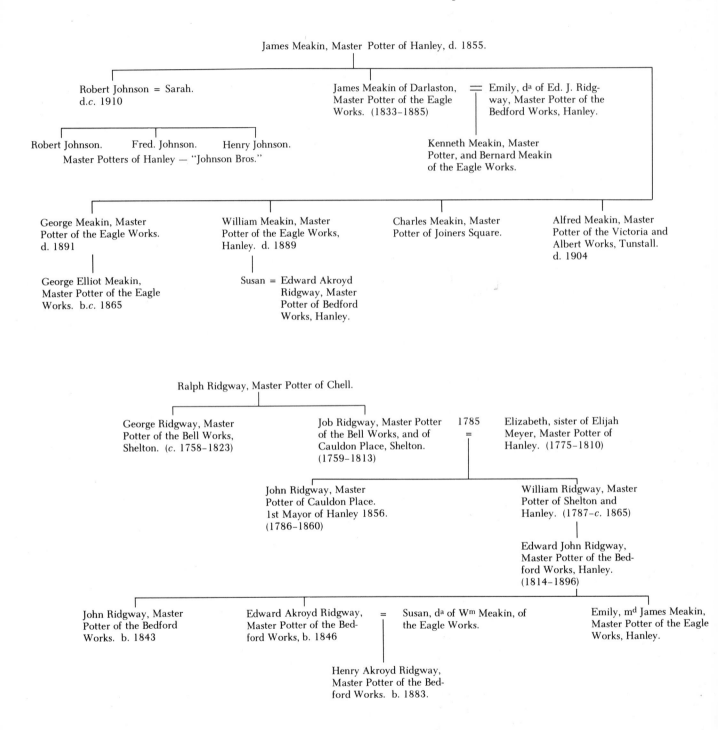

James Meakin, Master Potter of Hanley, d. 1855.

Robert Johnson = Sarah.
d.c. 1910

James Meakin of Darlaston, Master Potter of the Eagle Works. (1833–1885) = Emily, da of Ed. J. Ridgway, Master Potter of the Bedford Works, Hanley.

Robert Johnson.   Fred. Johnson.   Henry Johnson.
Master Potters of Hanley — "Johnson Bros."

Kenneth Meakin, Master Potter, and Bernard Meakin of the Eagle Works.

George Meakin, Master Potter of the Eagle Works. d. 1891

William Meakin, Master Potter of the Eagle Works, Hanley. d. 1889

Charles Meakin, Master Potter of Joiners Square.

Alfred Meakin, Master Potter of the Victoria and Albert Works, Tunstall. d. 1904

George Elliot Meakin, Master Potter of the Eagle Works. b.c. 1865

Susan = Edward Akroyd Ridgway, Master Potter of Bedford Works, Hanley.

Ralph Ridgway, Master Potter of Chell.

George Ridgway, Master Potter of the Bell Works, Shelton. (c. 1758–1823)

Job Ridgway, Master Potter of the Bell Works, and of Cauldon Place, Shelton. (1759–1813)

1785 =

Elizabeth, sister of Elijah Meyer, Master Potter of Hanley. (1775–1810)

John Ridgway, Master Potter of Cauldon Place. 1st Mayor of Hanley 1856. (1786–1860)

William Ridgway, Master Potter of Shelton and Hanley. (1787–c. 1865)

Edward John Ridgway, Master Potter of the Bedford Works, Hanley. (1814–1896)

John Ridgway, Master Potter of the Bedford Works. b. 1843

Edward Akroyd Ridgway, Master Potter of the Bedford Works, b. 1846

= Susan, da of Wm Meakin, of the Eagle Works.

Emily, md James Meakin, Master Potter of the Eagle Works, Hanley.

Henry Akroyd Ridgway, Master Potter of the Bedford Works. b. 1883.

From Staffordshire History by Josiah C. Wedgwood M.P. 1913

Common square butter dish with lid (drainer is missing). (30)
MEA-12

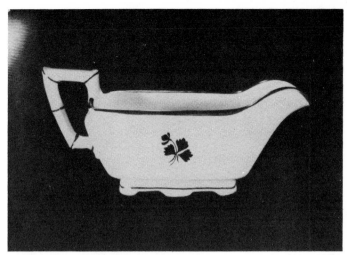

Gravy boat. The Bamboo handle seems too large for the rest of the piece, but it is still a desirable find. (59)
MEA-13

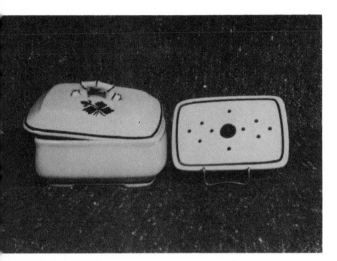

Soap dish, Bamboo style, 4½" x 6" (74)
MEA-14

Bamboo chamber pot and lid. Beautiful. (41)
MEA-15

Brush holder has been expertly repaired. No doubt this is the Bamboo style holder. (32)
MEA-16

Meakin's use of this square or rectangle shape in the commonly called Bamboo pattern and the fluted corner on another style I prefer to call #1 (because it is the most common body style) were only two of his presentations in Tea Leaf; both of these were also decorated with the Moss Rose pattern. A later body style—Chelsea—a name used in old Sears and Wards catalogs for plain white ironstone ware in this body style, similar to a thinner body by Johnson Brothers, was also very popular after the turn of the century. His earlier wares were often on the old Cable body style or other plain, heavy bodies. Much of his Tea Leaf was on hotel type ware, as many of those institutions were supplied with his dishes and toilet wares of this type.

Tea Leaf production ceased about 1910, not long after the acquisition by Johnsons.

Meakin used gold in decorating Tea Leaf at one time. One of my correspondents has twelve cups with gold trim rather than copper lustre. I have no date as to when the change to copper lustre decoration was made. Or was it used after the copper lustre fad waned?

There is so much in this saga. Who will complete the Alfred Meakin story?

Bamboo bowl and ewer set. Ewer is only 13" high. (58)
MEA-17

Trademark most common one, used 1891-97 at Royal Albert, Victoria, and Higate Potteries. (61)
MEA-18

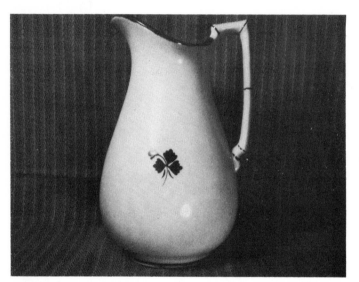

Trademark — Alfred Meakin LTD from 1897.
MEA-20

Ewer for wash set; 14½" high (78)
MEA-19

Showy covered dish in same style (21)
MEA-21

Squat teapot. This one-of-a-kind item heads the group of items in another Meakin body style; lighter weight with an embossed leafy floral design. 10" T-T (spout to handle) but only 7⅝" high. (54)
MEA-22

Yet another pretty plate (39)
MEA-23

Gravy boat — same style; 7" long
MEA-24

Round bowl, 9½" in diameter x 3¼" high. Tea Leaf is inside in bottom. (11)
MEA-25

The last body style I found a name for was "Chelsea" as shown in early day catalogs. This attractive three piece set is the most I saw in this style in any one collection. The vertical panels in four groups of four around each piece lend strength and beauty. Generous handles are quite nice and the Tea Leaves are larger than those on some other Meakin styles. (35)
MEA-26

Gravy boat. Hard to find but nice to hold, 8" long. (12)
MEA-27

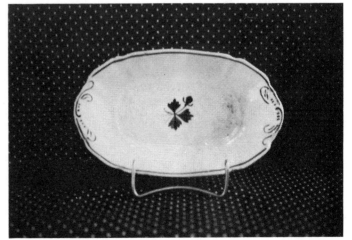

Service tray for gravy boat; 8¾" long (69)
MEA-28

Such a pretty covered vegetable bowl; 5½" x 11½". (12)
MEA-29

One of many open bakers made in graduated sizes. This one is 4" x 6". **MEA-30** (35)

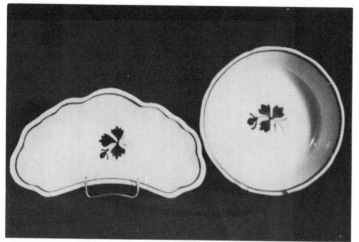

Bone dish and nappy. Bone dish 3½" x 6¾", scalloped and fluted. Nappy, 5"; no base rim. (30)
MEA-31

Ewer for a bedroom set, 14" high. No one can see the chunk which is gone from back side of the rim when it is filled with dried flowers and grasses.
MEA-32

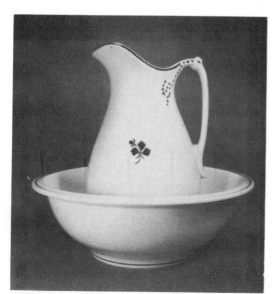

Bowl is deeper and the ewer fatter. Excellent cable detail on handle top.
MEA-33

Yet another unnamed body style is this covered casserole with unusual finials and handles. It, too, is quite heavy even for the 8" x 13" oval size. Superb for beef stew or chicken and dumplings. (11)
MEA-34

Waste jar (needs the lid); 12" high. Such a rare item is a conversa-tion piece even if it is poorly mended. (69)
MEA-35

Waste bowl — part of a tea set 6" diameter x 3¾" high **MEA-37** (64)

Waste bowl — also belonged in a tea set. 5½" wide x 3½" high. Note the hand painted Tea Leaf decal design where the lustre has worn off. The top is chipped in numerous places but the love and pride of a little girl, as she spent a whole nickel for this gift to her mother, makes this one piece more precious than all the rest of the owners collection. (8)
MEA-39

Deep compote with a rim foot. 9" in diameter x 6" high. This extremely heavy bowl may be part of the previous body style or it may be part of some other line as yet unidentified, as are the remainder of these Meakin pictures. Without catalogs or company information we can only be happy to have any of their wares to enjoy. **MEA-36** (12)

Round bowl, 9¼" x 3" deep with a thick piecrust rim which makes it easy to hold. Inside scallops and the deep base rim also help make this a most attractive bowl. (89)
MEA-38

Unusual 10" gravy boat in older heavy ware (89)
MEA-40

*This group of five small dishes were labeled children's dishes by the collector/dealer, but they are in fact, small sizes in hotel ware used as side dishes for vegetables, bread, fruit, or bacon. All are by Meakin except center oval one. It is by Mellor-Taylor. **None** of these is soap dishes. They are all about 4" x 6". The square one is 4½".* (91)
MEA-41

Jug, 3½" square at base x 5½" high. Note the design on the front under the lip, heavy lustre around the top, and unusual handle. (76)
MEA-42

Four bowls — center, very heavy rim foot, 6¼" oyster bowl; square nappies, one plain, one fluted corners (No. 1); 7" plate. Not pictured: a 12" flat soup plate! Why so large? (45)
MEA-43

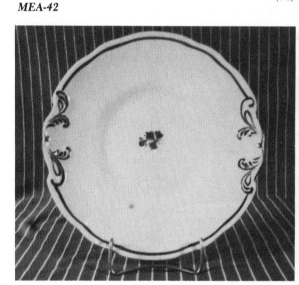

Another pretty Meakin plate, 9½", probably part of a tea set. This plate was shown in Aunt Polly's kitchen in the 1972 version of the movie "Tom Sawyer" made in Arrow Rock, Missouri. (11)
MEA-44

Similar to previous plate but larger (10¼")
MEA-45

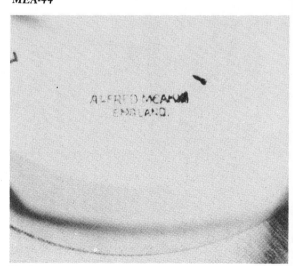

Trademark on left
MEA-46

Eighteen panel saucer — 6"; quite heavy and deep. It may have come with a handleless cup or been part of a "farmer's" cup and saucer set.
MEA-47

Service for eight, including cups in four styles. Serving pieces are included but not shown here. (34)
MEA-48

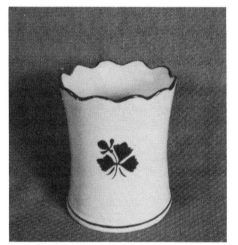

Brush holder (77)
MEA-49

Brush holder — 5¼"; pretty enough for a flower vase. Some even used it for a spooner, but it still a brush holder. No drain hole. (27)
MEA-50

Brush holder — 4¾" (84)
MEA-51

An exception — not the rule — in 100 piece dinnerware sets packed in a barrel which retailed for $7.00-$14.00. This 8" square baker, part of a 44 year collection of a western Illinois pioneer, is lasting proof of the workmen's variableness and the fact they had to sell everything they possibly could salvage. (87)
MEA-52

This Bamboo waste jar and lid was sold for over $400.00 in April, 1980 at a midwest antique show. (92)
MEA-53

J. & G. Meakin

1851 to present

The Meakins occupy a unique position in the Potteries . . . Their art . . . is for the multitude, not the millionaire.

W.P. Jervis: *The Pottery, Glass and Brass Salesman,* p. 13

Eight panel handleless cup with saucer (53)
MEA J&G-1

Trademark for above
MEA J&G-2

This Meakin firm was not only one of the largest exporters in Staffordshire, but was interested as well in the quality of life in the Potteries. This interest was not limited to producing the best dishes possible, but in making the community a better place to live.

James Meakin established a pottery at Longton in 1845 and moved to Hanley three years later. When he retired in 1852, his two sons, James Jr., and George, succeeded him as J. & G. Meakin. With attendant success in 1859, they built the Eagle Pottery at Joiners' Square which is about halfway between Hanley and Fenton. In ten years they were forced to enlarge those Eagle Works. They also had branches in Cobridge and Burslem. Before his retirement, their father had acquired the Eastwood Pottery in Hanley but, even with all these plants, they were not able to keep up with their orders all of the time and at least once commissioned George Jones, Stoke-on-Trent, to make some ironstone (or white granite) to help them catch up.

One of their experiments was an imitation of French china, but their prolonged production of children's gift mugs and plates, along with regular souvenir or gift plates, was definitely successful. Today these are very collectible items.

As stated in the Alfred Meakin chapter, the close of the American Civil War in 1865 opened new markets, and J. & G. Meakin were quick to grasp that golden opportunity. Their well-made, uniform, hard, white ironstone was serviceable, plain, and cheap — just what the pioneers needed as they settled the western part of our country. J. & G Meakin supplied not only the United States but Canada as well. One of their shipments in 1873 was sixty crates of white granite sent by sailing ship. Only a short time before, the entire annual output of another Meakin works was only 2500 crates. By the 1870s they had almost a monopoly on that facet of world trade.

One of their popular patterns had sheaves of wheat embossed on the white ware, very similar, if not identical, to some old wares of the very first embossed dinnerware. Pie crust trim was very popular on some of their bowls in the 1870s, but, by the '80s, flowers and fruit were much favored; peach flowers and fruit were found on some of their goods. Another style was Cable — often shown on hotel-weight ware. We see it today, so it was strong enough to last a century. Their Cable design was more pronounced than some, and really very attractive — even without other decoration.

In 1880, their stock was offered for sale, and they became a limited liability company. Not long afterward, George Elliott Meakin, son of George, who had recently entered the firm, was made chairman of the board.

In 1883, one of the Meakin girls married Fredrick Johnson who was president of the Johnson Brothers works.

James Jr., died in 1885 and his brother, George, in 1891, but the company kept growing and going forward; in 1911 someone noted they were still one of the largest exporters in Staffordshire. Someone else made note that the Eagle Works was carried on by Kenneth and Bernard, sons, and George M. of Cresswell Hall, a nephew.

In 1947 they issued a series of Romantic English scenes, and in 1958 the Eastwood Pottery was sold, while the Eagle Works was completely renovated and enlarged.

Today, 1981, they must still be doing lots of things right! In 1968 they merged with W.R. Midwinter Company. A complete modernization has taken place with an entirely new factory using the most up-to-date equipment. Midwinter was one of the first companies to use the new, modern shapes like Coupe — well known and·so popular. They have expanded even more since becoming a member of the prestigious Wedgwood Group in 1970. We can expect to see much more fine ware from this favorite old company.

Mellor, Taylor & Company
1880-1904

Large tureen and lid (no ladle or service plate). The vertical ribbing on this and following pictures is reminiscent of Burgess, Edwards, Grindley, and Enoch Wedgwood (Tunstall) Ltd. wares. The Mellor-Taylor pieces are scalloped around the outside edges of many pieces. (90)

MT-1

Gravy boat and tray, same body style (84)

MT-2

It is impossible to overrate pottery as a textbook — it was the reporter of antiquity whose records have remained.

William P. Jervis: *Encyclopedia of Ceramics*, 1902.

This is very true of Mellor, Taylor and Company of Burslem. Far too little is known of their history; but the great amount of wares (especially Tea Leaf) from their pottery which is now available speak to us of quality and durability.

In this company we again find both names go far back in Staffordshire annals, but without actual proof that each one named is a close family member of each line. Since Mellor is a rather unusual name, let us look at it first.

At some time it may have been Mueller or Miller. The first, William Mellor of Hanley, was mentioned several times, as he owned and worked the old Charles Street Works in 1758. This was the pot-bank which the Johnson Brothers took over in 1883 after more than a century of various operators. Jewitt noted that it still belonged to the Mellor family about 1880 as he completed his *Ceramic Art of Great Britain*. Mellor was one of the first half-dozen potters who made black basalt wares from the late 1750s through the end of the century. (He was a contemporary of Josiah Wedgwood and may have copied his work.) There was such a demand for coffee and tea wares in the United States and on the Continent that Mellor exported his entire output. It was fortunate that the toughness and durability made possible long trips, by pack-horse to ship-loading facilities, for overseas travel. Ordinary earthenware of the day had as much as one-third breakage loss while the loss in basalt ware was negligible. Boiling liquids had no effect on it, either.

The William *Miller* listed in Jewitt's list of potters was probably this same man — only the name was misspelled, as the 1802 list shows a widow, Mrs. Mellor, as carrying on. This was common practice, and often they enlarged and improved the works until a son was old enough to take over operation of the business.

Arnold Mountford listed one Benjamin Mellor as having made a harvest flask in 1775, inscribed with his name and date, which is now in a Staffordshire museum. It is decorated with scratch-blue, common in that day.

George Mellor, in 1784, was a painter at the Chelsea works in Derby, specializing in insects and flowers, while one William Taylor, at the same time and place, specialized in Oriental subjects and patterns. I wonder if this was where the family friendship began.

The Burslem pottery directory for 1818 listed John Mellor as a potter near the Market Place; he may be the partner in the 1834–1851 company of Mellor, Venables and Company at the Hale House in Burslem. They were on Ward's 1842 list as makers of china and earthenware blue, and other color printed American views, for the United States.

Creamer, 5" tall, and sugar with lid, 6¾" tall (35)
MT-3

Beautiful large ewer for bedroom set. Vertical ribbing at the base and full length panels on each side are interesting. Bowl (not shown) has outside ribbing also. (46)
MT-4

4¾" square nappy — also quite brown with no remaining lustre (35)
MT-5

In 1902 Jervis observed that Mr. Mellor was producing some extra fine crystalline glazes that needed no other decoration. This man was not further identified.

The other name in this partnership — Taylor — has been prominent since the 1650s when the Tofts, Simpsons, and others were busy turning out slip-ware.

A William Tallor (father or grandfather of the Derby painter?) was also plying this trade in Derbyshire at the same time. The name was also spelled Talor and Taylor. Another William Taylor was busy in Burslem making slip-ware two-handled jugs, small cribs, and the like, popular and profitable wedding gift items of the day. The Derby Talor made sure his plates were identified. He put his initials between the two central figures and spelled out, in full, his name around the feet of the two. The Burslem Taylor also left his wares well-marked and dated; both artistic wares are museum relics today. Jewitt* observes they were "most likely" of the same family.

Thomas Taylor was recorded in the 1710–1715 Burslem list of potters as having two places: one where he made moulds and another where he made "freckled" and stoneware. It seemed his mould works were right in the middle of Burslem, near the Wedgwood Brick House. This could well be near the Wedgwood Brick House, if not at the exact site, on which two Taylor Brothers — John and William — in 1750, each built their houses on opposite sides of the road. John named his place the Hill Top Works while William chose to be known as the Hill Pottery.

John was one who signed the price agreement in 1770, previously mentioned, and it was his daughter, Elizabeth, who was married to Thomas Wedgwood Jr., a relative of Josiah (probably a cousin). They were the parents of several children, including Ralph Wedgwood of Wedgwood and Company of Ferrybridge (not our Tea Leaf Company). Another son was John Taylor Wedgwood, an eminent engraver.

One Mr. Taylor (unnamed) was director of the Birmingham School of Art, who turned potter and created beautiful glazes different than had been used in England; he was a friend of Josiah Wedgwood.

John Taylor was still at the Hill Top Works in 1802, and William kept the Hill Pottery until after 1839 when it was taken by Samuel Alcock.

In 1786 George Taylor (1784–1811) and with George Jr. (to 1813), was a Hanley potter making slip-ware. One signed teapot of his is in The City Museum in Hanley. Later (1818) there was a T. and J. Taylor Company, and finally (1829) just T. Taylor. Later the works passed to William Ridgway who had several other pot-works. Jewitt records bare mention of the five other works in which a Taylor was involved from 1862–1898.

Jewitt's account also stated that in 1881 Mellor, Taylor and Company took the Waterloo Road Works and made the usual items in hard ironstone or granite, mostly for the American market, but was one of the few producers of cheaper white ware that sold part of their production at home. Thomas Hughes had been the previous proprietor, who moved to the Top Bridge Works in Longport, one of the old Davenport Works.

Other historians, including Godden and Jervis, say Mellor, Taylor and Company began in 1880; were at Top Bridge Works from 1882–1884; and for twenty years (1884–1904) operated at the Cleveland Works, Burslem. Where they were located does not matter as

* Jewitt, p. 435.

Waste bowl, 5" diameter **MT-6**   (53)

Open baker — oblong. This came in graduated sizes. **MT-7**   (59)

Oblong covered casserole with lid 7" x 9½" plus handles x 5½" high including lid. Have photographed two of these large pieces and they are one of the few items that lids do not fit. Evidently this large square was hard to work with. However, this body style with the lion head finials remains pristine white and retains the copper lustre. **MT-8**   (40)

much as the kind of goods they made. All I have seen have been good quality ironstone or semi-porcelain. They used underglaze scenes on their tableware; sometimes the name of the scene, imprinted on the reverse with the trademark, did not fit the scene, but the body shape was comfortable to hold; the glazes were excellent (no crazing), and the lids fit! A tiny lion's head is part of the finials on one shape decorated with Tea Leaf.

Another shape has small vertical ribbing around the base which I refer to as "melon-rib" because it reminds me of Mellor. The platters and some hollow ware pieces are ribbed around the border with bulging sides and curved ends.

Two of the partners, Henry Pratt and Thomas Taylor, were "graduates" of the Meakin Works, so the wares of the two companies are very similar. Excellent products, expanding markets, and repeat orders made it necessary to enlarge several times, so by 1902 this was one of the biggest and most modern plants in Burslem. No account was given as to final disposition of this manufactory; and no historian I found mentioned any history of the Mellor who was in the company. He may have been a silent partner.

Mention has been made that many old potteries did not mark their wares until 1891 when the McKinley Act required all imported ware be marked with country of origin. Many Staffordshire potters (especially Tea Leaf makers) marked their goods made for foreign markets long before they were required to — it simply was good business — good advertising! How much easier to reorder a favorite style or pattern if the original carried the name and address of the potter. We see very little Tea Leaf which is not well marked, with two exceptions: cups made anywhere, and Tea Leaf made in the United States. Even some of it is as well identified as the British ware, as the time of contempt for American goods was passing by the time our favorite design was so much in demand in the 1890s.

I have recalled many Mellors and Taylors, but most will agree the duplication of names in successive generations is too great to disallow some family ties. From all indications, all these men were good, or outstanding, artists who deserve to be remembered. There are some others we must also add to our list.

Of much more interest to most of us is that in 1829 a pair of Englishmen, James and William Taylor, went to work as throwers at the American Pottery Company of Jersey City, New Jersey, which was owned by David Henderson. Jenny Young, writing in 1878 in her *Ceramic Art*, acquaints us with salient points of this early American story. She says:

> It was here that the throwing and turning of earthenware upon English principle was first performed in America by William and James Taylor. This was also the first successful attempt to compete with England, and was made in connection with the manufacture of yellow-ware. Three years later, or in 1832, the same potters were making cream-colored ware chiefly from imported materials. To the decoration of a white ware the English process of printing was successfully brought . . . The firm made white granite and cream-colored ware until 1854. At that time the pressure of foreign competition was so great that they could not gain a foothold in the regular trade. Their wares were sold chiefly by peddlers and itinerant dealers, who were in the habit of going to the factory with wagons, when they knew that a kiln was to be drawn, and carting off the goods before they were trimmed.

In 1852 James Taylor, who had long since left Jersey City for East Liverpool, made the acquaintance of Speeler and William Bloor; went east again to Trenton. There they established the firm of Taylor and

Waste jar, 14" high with lid. Mint! (41)
MT-9

Two rectangle bakers in pleasant, practical shape. These and the platters, on page 103, are squarer than most pieces. Body shape name unknown. (40)
MT-10

Speeler, and began the successful manufacture of yellow and Rockingham ware but they were less fortunate in their production of porcelain and parian. By 1856 they were making white granite and were awarded a medal by the Franklin Institute of the State of Pennsylvania. It was inscribed "Reward of skill and industry to Taylor, Speeler, and Bloor, Trenton, New Jersey, for china, granite and earthenware, 1856." Mr. Bloor had joined the firm in 1854, upon his return from the gold rush (see chapter on William Brunt Jr.). Bloor returned later to East Liverpool, and applied his knowledge gained in the Jersey City pottery, to make the first commercial white ware in East Liverpool in 1862. John Goodwin (see chapter on Goodwin Brothers) joined Mr. Taylor in 1870 for a time. These men *may* have been friends in England, and I will not be surprised to learn some day this William Taylor was a close relative of the Mellor, Taylor firm who made so much of our fine Tea Leaf. To date I have seen no Tea Leaf marked with a New Jersey trademark but have no doubt it will show up before long.

Perhaps this thread of history, which ties Staffordshire with East Liverpool via New Jersey, will be strengthened by renewed interest in our pottery history of the past one-hundred fifty years which has not been studied in detail.

To the Taylors of Staffordshire, we in America owe an expression of gratitude for the white dishes on our tables; for the men who persevered to establish a thriving industry; and for the fine talent brought to our shores and shared with so many others in the pottery industry.

It is doubtful that all the men and/or companies listed in this chapter are all members of one of the two immediate families, but each did contribute something toward progress in the pottery world, for which I am grateful.

The Mellor name has not been prominent in our ceramic story, but anything new will be no surprise.

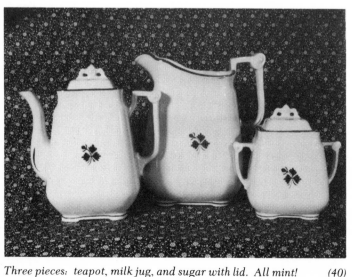

Three pieces: teapot, milk jug, and sugar with lid. All mint! (40)
MT-11

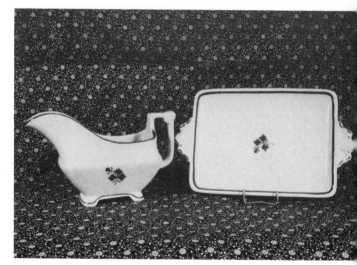

Gravy boat and tray which is 5½" x 9½" (40
MT-12

Two platters: 9¾" x 12¼" and 11½" x 14½" (40)
MT-13

Oval platter ? or service plate ? 8½" x 12¼". (35)
MT-14

Another oval platter or service plate, 9" x 12¼" (40)
MT-15

Brush holder, 3" x 4½" high. Light brown underglaze design seemed to be peculiar to much Mellor-Taylor ware. This holder had no drain hole. (74)
MT-16

MT-17

MT-18

MT-19

Trademarks on Mellor-Taylor ware

Powell and Bishop (and Stonier)

1876-1891

Group of items by Powell & Bishop: gravy boat and tray; sugar with lid, oblong covered casserole with lid, and square butter dish (no drainer). These are all on a very thin white ironstone body resembling semi-porcelain and decorated with gold overglaze which wears off easily. Three of the pieces bear an 1886 registration date. Powell & Bishop were in business 1865-78, then Stonier was added, but the original back stamp use was continued until Powell left and it became Bishop and Stonier 1891-1936. P&B-1   (3)

A wedding gift collection received in 1975 including one bone dish and one egg cup each worth enough to buy "every day" dishes and stainless steel flat ware for the newlywed couple. P&B-2   (3)

A ten piece bedroom set — all mint! P&B-3   (82)

Another class consists of firms who have come into existence in recent years, whose products are known in the market, and a few details concerning them may be of interest and possibly furnish data to some future historian.

W. P. Jervis: *A Pottery Primer,* 1911

I wonder if Mr. Jervis may have had Powell and Bishop in mind when he penned those words; there is so little information concerning this company, and so much Tea Leaf to be found with their back stamp, I began to fear I would find nothing to write about them. However, Mr. Jewitt devoted almost two pages to their story.

The first mention I found of either name was that Livesley and Powell, of Old Hall Lane and Miles Bank, made ironstone, cream-colored ware, and standard parian from 1851 until 1865. I have seen a twelve-sided white plate with a copper lustre band ¼" wide around the edge that bears their stamp. It dates from the 1850s; it is a beautiful bluish white craze-free piece. It was then I realized this was an old company whose workers may have forgotten more than some of the late-comers ever knew! An even greater treat was to photograph a handleless cup and a saucer (with sixteen panels). Both had the heavy lustre band, but the cup had a Coffeeberry motif like Clemenston's instead of the regular Tea Leaf. The owner had purchased them together but, since the saucer had no motif and was panelled (the cup was round — no panels), I feel the two did not belong together even though they were beautiful. If they *did* belong together, this would indicate a very early date for Tea Leaf which heretofore has not been verified. Mr. Livesley left the company in 1865, and the firm became Powell and Bishop (1865–1878). They took the old Stafford Street Works in Hanley after the departure of Furnivals from there. The company also occupied the Church Works where Ridgway had once operated, and the Waterloo Works. A different type goods was manufactured at each place.

At the Stafford Street shops, only earthenware was made but in numerous styles and decorations. They supplied home as well as foreign markets; they were one of the few Staffordshire potteries who catered to the Australian trade. All their lines were of excellent quality, whether the usual white or their Oriental Ivory which was their counterpart of Josiah Wedgwood's Queensware. Some services were very plain, others gilded and enamelled in elaborate ways, but all in good taste. They seem to have produced a greater variety than most companies. Their efforts were rewarded by medals they received at exhibitions in 1862, 1869, 1871, and 1875. They had a large exhibit at our Philadelphia Centennial in 1876, but I found no record of awards to them.

The Tea Leaf on our tables which bears their trademark probably was made in the old Church Works on High Street. Here they made only white granite (ironstone) for export to Canada and the United States. It, too, was of excellent quality, in various body styles and modes of decoration. Most of their Tea Leaf I have seen has been on a very lightweight body that resembles semi-porcelain but is really ironstone of fine quality. One square covered vegetable dish in my collection is cracked; nearby is a place where the glaze has flaked or peeled off, and the body is a very chalky white. There is some crazing around this break, but it is still a beautiful show piece.

When the company changed partners, they retained some of the trademarks; part of the very white Tea Leaf I have seen is marked Bishop and Stonier. The cups are especially pleasant to use as they are lighter weight than some of the older ones and they have very nice handles — easy to hold.

One autumn day several surprises were in store for me in Peoria, Illinois. The first I saw was a saucer with a variant design in black underglaze with the British Registry date May 22, 1867.

Enormous soup tureen, lid, and ladle (no service tray). Mint. **P&B-4** (60)

Trademark for Powell & Bishop **P&B-5**

Four pieces on a heavy, not-so-white ironstone with underglaze decoration in green. Some call this motif a rose, others a mum, yet another sees a clover. Whatever, it is attractive and a fine conversation piece. There is some lustre left on each piece but the green is also evident. The plate is embossed with a wheat design; the other pieces are plain. **P&B-6** (3)

There were three embossed designs around the inside of a rather wide band of lustre, and the center design resembled an old Clemenston variant with 11 dangling berries. This saucer — quite deep — was somewhat crazed and discolored but worth owning, and I was happy to be able to photograph it. Later the same day I repeated the process except my subject was another variant — this time a dark green underglaze. On my way home, a stop at a small shop was rewarded by finding the first piece of green underglaze Tea Leaf variant which was for sale. It was a heavy eight-inch plate with a design I hesitate to name — a clover? A rose? A mum? The glaze was fair and the plate very white and the price was right! All three variants were by Powell & Bishop.

A year later on a return trip from Arizona, I drove thirty miles out of my way to buy a green Tea Leaf cup and saucer for $15.00! When I reached home I found it matched my plate from Illinois. Such are the joys of a Tea Leaf collector.

My last Powell and Bishop cup and saucer are very heavy hotel-type ware with a very poorly done regular Tea Leaf on each piece. My only reason for purchase was that it was "different" from all this company's wares I had seen. It had nothing to recommend it.

This is the only English company I found who used a gold overglaze decoration. Of course, much of this gold has worn off. The decoration was not done in copper on the lighter weight bodies, but it had been applied on all the heavier types. The gold Tea Leaf of Powell and Bishop is so very different. I feel it must have been copied from the Gingko Tree leaf (see chapter on Tea Leaf Designs).

Powell and Bishop's third plant, the Waterloo Works, was built in the late 1860s or early 1870s to replace an old pot-bank of theirs torn down to make room for city improvements. The new location was near Nelson Place on the canal side across from a huge mill which they also operated. Here they made china, but all their decorating was sent to the Stafford Street Works to be done. Their products from here were also outstanding, much of it original with fresh ideas in body shapes and decorations. Lots of gold was used to imitate inlays, but all done in good taste. A departure from all white was a pale green body of china used in tea services, along with a very popular Victoria pattern.

I found no information as to what became of Mr. Powell, but a Mr. John Stonier was taken into the firm and, for a time, they were known as Powell, Bishop and Stonier, 1878–1891; from then until 1939 only Bishop and Stonier (Ltd.) names were on their back stamps. It is very possible there will be Tea Leaf with Powell, Bishop and Stonier, as well as just Powell and Bishop or Bishop and Stonier (Ltd.), which I have seen. Keep looking. As usual, I will show only the trademarks I have found on dishes I have photographed, even though this company also used several different ones.

Jervis noted that Mr. Stonier was a native of Staffordshire who had travelled extensively as a china merchant. He was in partnership with one Mr. Livingston in Liverpool when he left to join Powell and Bishop. Jervis recorded he was "of genial disposition and earned the respect of all who knew him." He died in 1897 while still in the firm of Bishop and Stonier. Godden indicated that Bishop operated alone, 1936–1939, as Bishop & Stonier with no further information available.

Powell & Bishop made this variant in underglaze with copper lustre on a medium weight style. The central decoration is quite unique. Three large and three small designs are embossed around the rim (10" plate). (3)
P&B-7

Several items with the later Bishop and Stonier mark   (35)
B&S-1

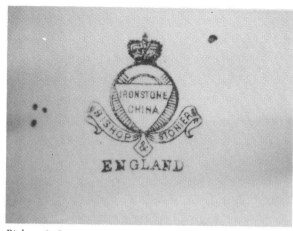

Bishop & Stonier trademark
B&S-2

Anthony Shaw

1850-1900

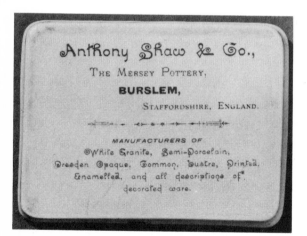

If I could collect Tea Leaf by only one potter, Anthony Shaw would be my first choice. The beautifully embossed pieces, in elegant glazes, make his ware outstanding on any shelf. He must have been a very interesting, distinguished gentleman to have expressed such lasting beauty in common potter's clay.

William Burton noted there were several families of Shaws in Burslem (1700–1750) but he did not specify relationships; and Geoffery Godden said there were twenty or more Shaw potters in Staffordshire. I feel there were many of these who were related, and perhaps some day a genealogist will confirm my thoughts, and verify the fact that Anthony Shaw's first-mentioned ancestors *may have been* Mary Shawe, heiress of Haracles, who was married to John Wedgwood of Blackwood in 1470; or Margaret Shaw, who became the wife of Thomas Wedgwood about 1750. They *may* also confirm that the Shaw who made clay pipes in Broseley in the 1630s was a relative; or they *may* find that Moses and Aaron Shaw, listed continuously from 1686 in the Burslem court rolls, were of the same family. These men had two of the five largest potbanks in Burslem. They had separate homes with their pot-works adjacent to their houses in the middle of town. They made dipped, stone, and "freckled" wares; and Aaron was still in business in 1750. Someone *may* even find that Robert Shaw, the 1692 slip-ware maker of Burslem, or Stephen Shaw, also a Burslem slip-ware artist in 1725, were related.

Ralph Shaw, an important Burslem potter of the early 1700s, is an excellent possibility, also. This man was noted for his black basalts, chocolate (or red) wares, slip-ware, salt-glazed stone ware, etc.; but when he was defeated in 1736 in court over a patent, he got mad, moved to Lillie, France, and established a pottery there — the first Englishman to take English potting secrets and methods to the Continent! But Staffordshire was home and some of his family returned in 1750. He invented a slip-ware kiln and, because of his curiosity and ingenuity, we have stilts and spurs used between dishes in the saggers to prevent them from sticking together during the long firing process.

Two other Shaws I definitely feel were ancestors were Alderman Thomas Shaw, a Liverpool delft-ware potter, 1716–1765, and his son, Samuel, who continued his father's business at Shaw's Brow. This area was named for these early men; it overlooked the Mersey River at what is now William Brown Road near the heart of Liverpool. Their early works began here and, in later years, the area was just a nest of potbanks owned by individuals. There were about 75 houses on either side

Sugar (no lid), 5" high; quite heavy body, dark lustre in wide bands; the first of several pieces in this five loop and panels of the Tulip style (as identified by Laura Ady). This piece has the earliest R⁴ mark I found: April 5, 1856. (12)

AS-1

Trademark
AS-2

A SHAW

Covered casserole 8" high x 10" long. A stunning piece with the nut finial (like a pine cone). Quite heavy, very white and has R⁴ April 7, 1856. Mrs. Ady also has a plate with same date stamped on it. Platters are oval. (1)

AS-3

This tureen, also a magnificent piece, is 15" long x 12" high with lid and ladle. Matches sugar bowl, above. (39)

AS-4

of the street with a population of almost 440, all employed in the potbanks. Richard Chaffers, father of William Chaffers, author of the magnificent *Marks and Monograms on Pottery and Porcelain*, was an early-day apprentice at the Shaw Delft-Ware Works under Alderman Shaw.

Other ancestoral possibilities were:

1777   Shaw was a partner at Caughley with Thomas Turner, but since he was a London china dealer he may have been of another family.

1798–1825   A. & J. Shaw, Lane End, part of a group of lesser known Lane End Potters. An ink stand inscribed in gold by James Shaw from this area has been preserved.

1802   Charles Shaw, Tunstall, china dealer and packer

1828–1853   Ralph Shaw, Longton, built the Victoria Works which was held for many years by members of the Shaw family. He may have been a son or grandson of the first-mentioned Ralph Shawe of Burslem.

1828   Simeon Shaw, historian, published his *History of the Staffordshire Potteries* and may be part of the Shaw family puzzle.

1864   The Church Gresley Potteries, Swadlincote, established in 1790, were occupied sometime between 1790 and 1864 by Shaw and Harrison.

Anthony Shaw is first mentioned as having been at the Child Works in Tunstall, an old pottery built in 1763 which had a series of tenants. He went there in 1841 when the previous owner, Joseph Heath and Company, left; but no date was given for his removal. It may have been 1850 when he took the Mersey Pottery in Burslem. He possibly was associated with other potteries for short periods during the early part of the 1800s, but historians are silent on these years for Shaw.

It was the ironstone, stone china, or white granite which brought great wealth to the Staffordshire potters. We fail to appreciate the technical skill and the excellence of the fine white bodies which, in some cases, were almost like parian. It was strictly an English product which we copied and still enjoy so much. As a rule, foreign merchants shipped only their best to the United States; in this way our potters were constantly challenged to better and greater production and, even today we are the beneficiaries.

All of this must have been true for Anthony Shaw, as he completely rebuilt his Mersey works in 1866, and his success continued until his death when the responsibility fell on his son, Edward.

The year of 1882 was when the son was taken into the business, and the style changed to Anthony Shaw & Son. But it was the old Mr. Shaw, himself, who, long before, put the name of the town he lived in on his back stamp, so there was no doubt where his waves of white ware came from as they rolled onto foreign shores.

If only our American potters had become so proud and so bold — sooner than they did.

First of several pieces in Lily-of-the-Valley embossed body style. This pot is 9½" high, dazzling white, with bell shaped finial like a true lily-of-the-valley. Extravagant lustre tastefully used. (11)
AS-5

Sugar with lid, 6½" high, also comes in smaller size. The creamer is done in a very light brown . . . unusual. (60)
AS-6

Small milk jug, 7½" high (82)
AS-7

The son was not the potter his father had been — the works deteriorated and, after Edward's death in 1900, the works were closed for a couple of years or so until they were re-opened by Arthur J. Wilkinson.

Anthony Shaw is credited with being the first to use decalcomania transfer printing on his ironstone and cream-colored wares, his specialties for the United States market.

At the Paris Exhibition of 1856, he was given a medal for excellence of the wares he displayed there.

It is common knowledge that Anthony Shaw is credited with being the first to make our Tea Leaf pattern, which he called Lustre Band and Spray.

The late Thelma Shull reported the British Registry date of 1856 on an oval covered tureen with Tea Leaf decoration, but it could have been some time before it was actually made and sold, as that registry date is for the patent on the body style. When it was made is not so important as that it is still beautiful and useful.

This was about the same time screen wire was invented here in the United States, first made on hand looms in St. Louis, Missouri. Before that time, cloth was hung at the doors or the shutters lowered to keep out the pesky flies. In 1857 power looms were in use, but screen wire was not available commercially until 1895 and came into general use during the next decade. These dates coincide almost identically with Anthony Shaw's history. How much nicer our dinners, served on Anthony Shaw's Tea Leaf, have been with the use of screen wire.

One of Shaw's best-remembered creations was the Cable body style from the late 1860s which was popular the next ten years or more. It was widely copied by numerous potters, but none made prettier Cable services than the creator, himself.

Another popular body style was the Fuchsia, a beautifully embossed style that was stunning in plain white, but took on added elegance when highlighted with copper lustre.

One of his best-loved body shapes was Lily-of-the-Valley. It was produced with decorations other than Tea Leaf, and some of it was sold plain white. The Tea Leaf is outstanding.

Even the plain square, rectangular, or hexagon shapes, so popular in the 1880s, were truly elegant and made beautiful table settings, with their glimmer of copper lustre decorations.

Mention was made of gilt decoration by Shaw (not copper lustre), but I have not seen it as yet; however, it may turn up tomorrow. Neither did I find his dinner services shown in our mail-order catalogs, so his distribution must have been in his own china house or personal representative.

If you wonder why so many old tureens and sugar bowls are discolored while the lids are white, consider Mrs. M. W. Kamm's suggestion that herbs, spices, and lumps of raw dark sugar were stored in them for long periods by some women, and the acids affected the glaze. Of course, grease from the warming oven storage and lye soap used in the dish pan did their share, too.

Oh, for the "good old days" of 1948 when an Anthony Shaw Lily-of-the-Valley teapot and sugar bowl were advertised in *Spinning Wheel* for $20.00.

Anthony Shaw used ever so many trademarks, but only those I have found on Tea Leaf are shown here.

Oval covered vegetable dish; one of the loveliest pieces made; 7½" x 12½" x 7½" high. (64)
AS-8

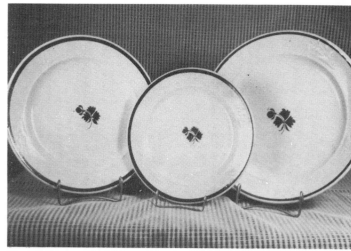

Here is the so-called "Green Tea Leaf." These three plates all in same body shape, have varying amounts of lustre remaining on them but each definitely has the underglaze decoration done in a bright dark green, which is a pleasant diversion. No one I have contacted knows why but someone may give an answer now. (49)
AS-9

The first in a large group of Cable body style items. Notice the "rope" around each side of the finial and at the top of the handle. The shape is bulbous, plain, and quite heavy. Much of it is crazed and discolored. This teapot is 8½" high. (15)
AS-10

This complete bedroom set is a good prize for anyone to cherish. Bowl and ewer are Lily-of-the-Valley style while the remainder of the pieces are on the Fuchsia body shape. All are complete and mint. The brush box is 8" long x 4" high and has two inside ridges for brushes to rest on. (1)
AS-11

Cable style sugar; no lid. Very brown stained around lower part; 5" high. (93)
AS-12

Cable style creamer; this may be a creamer for a child's mush and milk set. It is smaller than most. (60)
AS-13

*A double treat: sauce tureen, lid, and ladle; 6½" long, dated 1884. Covered
vegetable casserole and lid; 9" long. Mint.* (1)
AS-14

*This round tureen may be a variation of the Fuchsia
body style. While it is very striking, the lid and ladle
add much to the beauty.* (82)
AS-15

Gravy boat and mug 3¼" high in same cable style (17)
AS-16

*Relish dish; 9¼" long. Doubtless this is the same cable style
by the simplicity and the two groups of three dots at each end* (11
AS-17

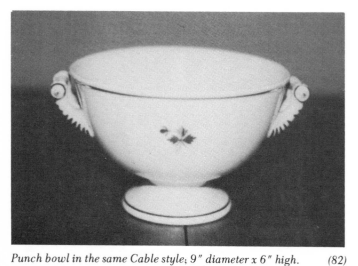

Punch bowl in the same Cable style; 9" diameter x 6" high. (82)
AS-18

*"Gozunda" because it "goes unda the bed." Cable pot but wrong
lid. It now hangs full of English ivy in my bedroom window.*
AS-19

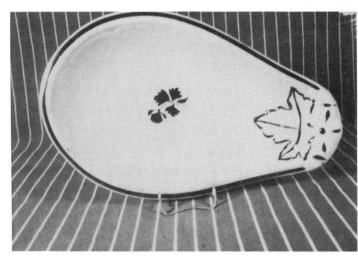

Bowl and ewer. Excellent view of Cable design on handle of ewer (13" high); bowl is 15" in diameter. (67)
AS-20

"Dripping Spoon," or relish tray; 9" long. (11)
AS-21

Such a set as this would add much to the breakfast table to get us off to a good day. (1)
AS-22

*Tea pot; 10½" high, blue-white, no crazing. A copy of this was featured in **Woman's Day** magazine in 1972 as part of a display in the Essex Institute at Salem, Massachusetts and bears the trademark shown below.*
AS-23

Service tray for an oval tureen such as the one pictured on 110. I have two alike except one was made 1860–1882 and the other by the son who carried on 1882–1898. It is much lighter weight.
AS-24

Trademark on much of older Shaw ware made 1860-1882
AS-25

Newer mark, probably one of the last ones used
AS-26

Creamer in a square style popular beginning in the 1880s   (69)
AS-27

Sugar with lid in same body style. This pair is like the set shown in **Staffordshire Pottery** *by Josiah C. Wedgwood, M. P. and Thomas H. Ormsbee, on page 152. Both these pieces bear the Registration No. 2965 which means the body style was registered in 1884; however, it had to have been manufactured after 1891 as the company began using this particular back stamp 1891-1898 when the son was taken into the business. This information by personal correspondence from Arnold Mountford, F.M.A., Director, City Museum & Art Gallery, Stoke-on-Trent. See end of Enoch Wedgwood (Tunstall) Ltd. chapter for complete story.*
AS-28

This must have been a very popular Shaw style. This sauce tureen, 5" x 8", has a coveted ladle.   (69)
AS-29

The only piece in this body style which as been crazed or brown; 8" tall; super lustre. R^d No. 2965 (1884).   (84)
AS-30

No one made more or prettier tureens and covered pieces than Shaw. This complete sauce tureen is only 4" x 11" including handles, and the tray is 6" x 10". The ladle is 7½" long. This hexagon shape sported short, stubby feet on some pieces but not all. (35)
AS-31

A complete soup tureen, 9" x 11", lid, ladle, and service tray along with a small relish tray — would be show pieces anywhere. (54)
AS-32

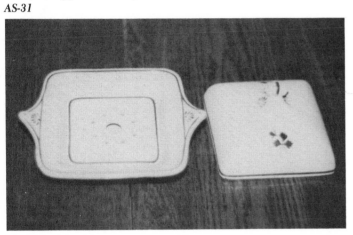

*This **may** be a butter dish but is likely a soap dish because of all the holes in the inset. 6½" square x 5" high.* (82)
AS-33

If one squared style was good, two must have been better. This covered vegetable casserole (7" x 12" x 6" tall) certainly is a beauty and the only piece I found with this finial. It was in mint condition.
AS-34 (59)

"Square" hexagon open piece, 8½". It may have had a lid at one time. Two pieces were found the same day, 35 miles apart. Never saw any more. (35)
AS-35

Hexagon relish tray, 4" x 6" plus handles
AS-36

4½" nappy
AS-37

Hexagon creamer, 6" tall   *(12)*
AS-38

Matching sugar. The owner calls it a "cracker jar" and it may well be. The twelve-panelled heavy bowl, 10" in diameter, was found by the present owner out by the drain spout to catch rainwater for shampooing the hair of the elderly lady who had owned it many years. The 5½" tall creamer is much lighter weight ware in semi-porcelain made after 1898, according to the backstamp. It is on the order of the Meakin Chelsea shape of the same period. **AS-40** *(1)*

Matching chamber pot; probably had a lid.   *(40)*
AS-39

The cup and saucer are unusual, as most Shaw cups have the Tea Leaf inside in the bottom. These may be a "marriage" as no cups were marked, but the saucer is Shaw. Teapot is Meakin.   *(54)*
AS-41

*These two gravy boats are: (left) Lily-of-the-Valley **without** excess lustre; the one motif is outside under the spout. (Right) possibly of one of the earlier shown panelled styles.*
AS-42

Oval baker in hotel ware with wide rim, 7½" x 10"
AS-43

Even these footed compotes came in graduated sizes. This one is 9" diameter. (89)
AS-44

Some compotes came with a shorter foot and more or varied scallops such as this one; 9" with one large, then two smaller alternating scallops. This style is older according to the trademark. (11)
AS-45

This magnificent piece is easily the most outstanding item in this entire book! Nowhere else have I seen an open-work piece of such beauty and detailed decoration! It is all the more precious to the owner because a friend purchased it for $10.00 and it was so dirty they could not see the pattern. (26)
AS-46

One of a group of graduated sized bowls with registration date of Dec. 7, 1878. Each company made numerous styles in these varied sizes. (41)
AS-47

4½" square nappies with fine scalloped edge. See butter pats in same style. (85)
AS-48

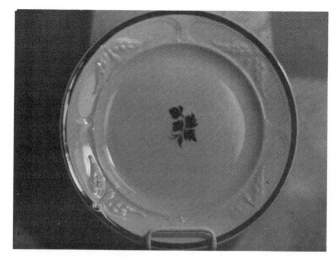

Unusual 10" plate, heavy lustre band, and four panels with four unusual sprays of grain. (1)
AS-49

Relish dish or gravy boat tray with unique basket weave design around inside. No lustre; quite stained. (49)
AS-50

Service tray for sauce tureen; 6" x 9¼" (84)
AS-51

Brush holders (left): Shaw, 5¼" high, bulbous shape. (Right) Furnival, 5" high x 2½" diameter. (41)
AS-52

Chamber pot and lid. One of the prettiest. (67)
AS-53

Soap dish, drainer, no lid; about 4" x 6"
AS-54   (78)

Two impressed marks used frequently with another mark, 1860-1882. Mersey Pottery, Burslem. **AS-55**

Shaw trademarks with Buslem 1860-1882; Mersey Pottery, Newport Lane, Burslem.
AS-56

Two backstamps used by Anthony Shaw, 1891-98. Only slight variation. Used at Mersey Pottery, Burslem.
AS-57

Most common mark used 1882-1898. With or without R^d No. or other impressed marks.
AS-58

Mark often seen 1891-1900. Notice SONS.
AS-59

Only time I saw this globe mark for Anthony Shaw & Co. 1898-1900, when the works were closed and later sold. The R^d No. is a 1889 date.   (61)
AS-60

Edward Walley
1845-1856

Genius and invention have seldom been more usefully employed than in the improved production of pottery.

Simeon Shaw: *History of Staffordshire Potteries*, 1829

Walley was not exactly the most common name in the Potteries, so it was relatively easy to trace Edward Walley for the short time he was active. Little says Elijah Jones was at the Phoenix Works in Shelton for a short time around 1830–1832 when these works were taken by Joseph Clementson in a partnership with a Mr. Read. Jones moved to the Villa Pottery at Cobridge and a decade later took in Edward Walley as a partner. They operated as Jones and Walley for several years, then Walley was alone and his style was simply "Edward Walley" until 1856. Some indicate Walley was active until 1865. Cobridge is the only location we hear of Walley operating a pottery. Possibly this was his ancestral home. As for other Walleys in the Potteries:

1795–1865   One John Walley who was a potter at Cobridge; made the usual Rockingham tea pots, small novelties, jet black figures, and ironstone for the American market. No mention of relationships was found, but he could easily have been the father, brother, uncle, or cousin of Edward.

Godden mentioned several other Walleys.

1850–1867   John Walley, High Street, Burslem.

1813   John Walley, Market Street, Tunstall.

1853–1854   John Walley, Hope Street, Hanley.

1825–1855   John Walley was a Staffordshire potter in a partnership with William Smith of Stockton-on-Tees. (Chaffers and Jewitt recorded this association)

1802   A list of trades in connection with potters included Peter Walley as a dealer in earthenware at Hanover Square, Burslem.

This is not a very large family list, nor are they widely scattered, so they could well have all been of the same family. The spelling variation with or without the *h* was rather common.

There was no further mention of Edward Walley after 1856; it will be a challenge to learn more of this potter.

Elizabeth Collard explained in great detail that with the advent of ironstone in England, French exports were affected, especially after Staffordshire potters cornered the American market. The French countered with offerings of cheap white porcelain (really no match for genuine ironstone). Since Canada had strong French connections, it was easy to see why the Canadians would buy French imports. However, the British are, if anything, tenacious; so they came right back with ironstone made by slightly different formulas and glaze colors — AND new names like: Limoges P.G. (Parisian Granite), used by Bridgwood; Parisian Porcelain; Opaque Porcelain or Porcelain Opaque; Demi-Porcelain; or Edward Walley's Paris White. Every Staffordshire exporter had his own pet solution to this competitive problem of selling ordinary ironstone to unseen buyers. After all, there was no reason to stand idly by and let France monopolize this lucrative market.

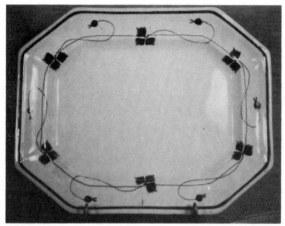

This octagon shape is about the same size as platter on page 120. It bears, in upper right hand corner, the shadow of a decal which had been moved.
WE-1

This 10" octagon plate was the first piece I had seen in this old variant but it was easy to identify by Kamm's Old China Book. (25)
WE-2

The Pre-Tea Leaf pitcher, 5½" tall, that was in a 25¢ basket of junk. (24)
WE-3

WALLEY trademark, 1845-56
WE-4

WALLEY trademark on oval platter
WE-5

Before that time, very little ironstone or cream-colored ware was sold in Canada (most of it went to the United States), but Edward Walley seemed to have a special inside track with the Canadian government, so he was able to elicit special orders from the government, as well as several large institutions, and numerous orders for domestic use. As I read Simeon Shaw's 1829 report of Cobridge, I could better understand a possible tie and offer a logical explanation: The Church. Shaw recounted that Cobridge contained a number of houses and was in both Burslem and Stoke parishes. There was a Free School, built seventy years before, used occasionally to benefit the "poorer classes." There was, in addition, a neat chapel with a Sunday School room operated by the Methodist New Connection. Then . . .

> . . . a very large Roman Catholic Chapel and also a convenient school room for educationg youth by a method which embraces the usefulness of the systems of Bell and Lancaster yet differs from both. At the Grange, new this place, formerly a very secluded spot, are the remains of an old Catholic Chapel, a mere thatched shed; probably the place of resort to that body of Christians, at the time when bigotry was rampant.

Since Canada was settled by many members of the Roman Catholic faith it seems reasonable to me that Edward Walley possibly would seek and enjoy doing business with people who had common interests and possibly other ties with him. Francis Clementson did the same thing—only he was a Methodist!

The maple leaf and the beaver are national symbols in Canada, and Walley worked these designs in many of his productions. Indian Stone was the name he chose for his fine white ironstone; he also made Flow Blue and Gaudy Dutch, as well as uncolored wares. Many of his dinner-service cups were made without handles, as this was the style in demand in his hey-day. The Niagara shape, registered in 1856, was one of his outstanding successes used for dinner, dessert, and tea sets, along with toilet sets. I have seen mention of a Lustre-berry variation by Walley, but have not seen it yet.

One of his most eye-catching patterns was one with his many-sided plates, on the order of those made by Livesley and Powell, which had only a single wide band of copper lustre at the edge. Walley added a scroll to each panel below the band which certainly added just the right touch of distinction.

It is inevitable that some dishes which came from the ovens were defective in some way, quite often so crooked that it was impossible for a bowl or plate to sit flat on the table (such as my special square baker by Alfred Meakin). However, anything that would hold food or beverage was considered salable, according to Arelene and Paul Greaser in *Homespun Ceramics.* These rejects were often sold to schools established to train young or beginner decorating students; or else they were used right in the home pottery for the same purpose. After the apprentices had decorated them with spattered, sponged, or simple primitive drawings, the dishes were sold. In Scotland and Britain it was known as sponge-ware while here in the United States it was called spatter-ware because of the colors appeared to have been applied by flipping a charge of paint from a brush rather than stippling with a piece of cut sponge, root, or a brush. This style was especially popular in Pennsylvania Dutch communities and today is becoming rather scarce at antique shows and flea markets.

Since in the 1850s much of the dish production was unmarked, it was a surprise to me to learn from Ms. Collard* that Edward Walley's

---

* Collard, p. 147.

name was added to the list of potters already identified by the Greasers as having made the original dishes to which this type of decoration was applied—either on white ironstone or cream-colored earthenware, with or without his trademark.

Each of the few Edward Walley pieces I have seen have been in the Pre-Tea Leaf design. They were all on very superior body of blue-white color that I doubt would ever chip. The very first piece I saw was a plate belonging to my friend, Betty Grissom of Peoria, Illinois. It was featured later in an article she wrote for *Spinning Wheel*. The second item was a little creamer which belonged to a friend near Columbus, Ohio; she had gotten it in a whole basket of junk at an auction for a quarter. Oh, the luck of some people! But I had my day . . . on the way home on that trip, I found my oblong platter in a musty old Missouri river town shop that probably had not made a sale that day (or week?). In the same shop I also found my handleless black Coffeeberry cup and saucer! The platter, which has no foot-rim, is quite heavy. The leaves around the edge of the well are held together with a continuous squiggly line of pea-green which looks out of place; however, the leaves are a very beautiful, dark, rich copper lustre. The platter carries a remnant of a mistake—the decorator put a leaf motif in the wrong place—but moved it to the correct position; yet, the shadow of the original placing will always be an underglaze reminder of human frailty.

After that good fortune, I drove the last 250 miles home nonstop, as I could think of nothing which would be more appropriate to end a happy day.

We should all keep looking for any Pre-Tea Leaf or variants by Edward Walley, to complete this elementary identification of his work.

Walley's variant is on extremely heavy blue-white body in the Niagara shape (according to back stamp). This oval platter is 11¼" x 14¼". The underglaze designs are in green with rich dark copper lustre. Each leaf and bud are connected by a fine squiggly green line. (1)
WE-6

Enoch Wedgwood (Tunstall) Ltd.
1860 to present

Several items in two basic Enoch Wedgwood (Tunstall) Ltd. body styles: We see the vertical ribbing and scalloped edges on one and stark simplicity on the other one. Both are pleasant to use and beautiful to behold. The square open baker comes in usual graduated sizes as does the rectangle platter; the far square plate is a service tray for a tureen; the small sauce tureen is minus the ladle; butter pats and butter dish are intact, and the large covered vegetable is a show piece. (17)
WW-1

There is magic in the name Wedgwood in the pottery world and our Tea Leaf story is no exception, but there is a difference . . .

Let me state first that the Tea Leaf we use today was **not**, and I repeat **not**, made by the great Josiah Wedgwood at his Etruria Works, or by his descendants, regardless of what anyone may tell us who has Tea Leaf to sell or show.

To begin, Josiah Wedgwood was born 1730 and died 1796, so it would have been totally impossible for him to have ever made any Tea Leaf. His successors made a "stone china" which resembled French Porcelain, for about ten years, ending in 1825, but not in any great amount and examples are very rare. "Pearl china" was made by the same group from 1820-1868 and "Pearl" or "P" was incorporated in the printed marks along with their trademark which is the one word **WEDGWOOD**, in capital letters. There was **never** an *"and company"* added. This applies to all types of ware made by the company started by Josiah himself and continues to the present day by his sons or members of their immediate families, operating now as Josiah Wedgwood and Sons, Ltd., Barleston Stoke-on-Trent.

The Wedgwood & Company in which we are all interested was at the Unicorn Pottery and Pinnox Works in Tunstall where Mr. Edward Challinor was in business at an earlier date, and who was succeeded in 1835 by Podmore, Walker and Company. Enoch Wedgwood was the "and Company" of that firm. Podmore and Walker left and, in 1860, Enoch Wedgwood with his younger brother, Jabez Charles Wedgwood, founded (Enoch) Wedgwood and Company. Enoch was born in 1813, a son of Isaac and Charlotte Wedgwood. In 1855-56 he was Chief Bailiff of the County of Stafford.

Square covered dish 8½" x 6" high; simply plain. (69)
WW-2

Service tray for above or a nice cookie plate (69)
WW-3

Rectangle 7" x 10" x 5" high. Quite heavy. (84)
WW-4

When Jewitt was writing in 1878, Enoch's eldest son, Edmund, was in charge of the extensive works situated on about an acre of ground and which gave employment to almost 700 people. It was one of the best arranged and substantially built works in the area; to continue this image, they produced the higher types and quality goods in all the usual table services and miscellaneous items. They served Continental, Colonial, and American as well as home markets. In fact, they were one of the largest pottery exporters, and their "Imperial" ironstone china was an excellent staple line made in a wide variety of bodies, shapes, colors, and decorations.

The company philosophy seemed to be two-fold: first, to produce the best quality; the most beautiful ware possible, adapted to ordinary use, so that everyone who bought their products could be surrounded by beauty and quality.

They were one of the major suppliers of china for use on ships, in hotels, restuarants, and other commercial institutions. In 1870 this was big business. They did not go into production of ornamental pottery, but they did issue some historical pieces and blue-printed wares along with good quality Blue Willow ware.

The second part of their philosophy was their policy of not trading on the well-known name of Josiah Wedgwood, but building their reputation on their own production merits.

This was called to my attention in reading Jervis' summation in his *Pottery Primer* (1902) and further emphasized in extensive personal correspondence with the present personnel. I had written to ask if there was a family tie between the Josiah Wedgwood family line and the Enoch Wedgwood line, as well as any other history.

In this correspondence they re-affirmed that there was **no** family tie between the two companies and to be very sure there was no confusion they sent a form letter which is mailed to all prospective clients, outlining the proper procedure for addressing the company: The full name is to be used: ENOCH WEDGWOOD (TUNSTALL) LTD., all in the same size letters so the Wedgwood was in no way emphasized. Further, it was to be written all on one line if possible and never on more than two lines. The following descriptive terms were not to be used in connection with their name: "Genuine," "Famous," "Original," "Expensive," or "Fine." It seems to me they have gone to great lengths to be sure they do not trade on the Wedgwood name as some earlier businesses had done.

Their products are fine earthenware known here in the United States as "ironstone." (Josiah Wedgwood & Sons Ltd. makes china and earthenware, according to these letters of correspondence.)

Due to a fire many years ago no old records and/or history is available, except that they operate two potteries. One, in Tunstall on Brownhills Road, is a late nineteenth century replacement for the old Pinnox & Unicorn Works. Naturally, it is much larger and better equipped. In 1977 there were about 950 employees producing some 50,000 dozen pieces per week—90% of which is exported. An average of 50% or more comes regularly to the United States but in 1976 that percentage raised to 70% because of their award-winning line of "Liberty Blue" made especially for our Bicentennial year. This was their third such award in less than ten years.

Their other plant was acquired in 1974 from A. G. Richardson. It is in Cobridge — The Britannia Works — and they continue use of the brand name Crown Ducal Ltd. There were about 240 employees in 1977.

Gravy boat, 3½" x 7" x 3½" high. Mint.   (71)
WW-5

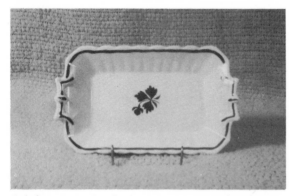

Relish tray, 4½" x 7½"; some crazing and staining.
WW-6

Versatile open baker 5½" x 7¾" with vertical ribbing inside. **WW-7**   (58)

Two 4½" nappies, front and back view
WW-8

Since so much of their ware is sent to our country we can still enjoy the quality and beauty of the wares by this venerable old company.

Because so many references have been made concerning the photo on page 152 of *Staffordshire Pottery* by Josiah C. Wedgwood M.P. and Thomas H. Ormsbee, this needs clarification also. Many readers have concluded this was proof that Tea Leaf was made by the original Wedgwood company. It was a surprise to me to find the examples chosen for that book by Wedgwood & Ormsbee were made by Anthony Shaw and Son.

I show several photos in the Anthony Shaw chapter of identical pieces as shown in the Wedgwood book, which are trademarked Anthony Shaw. Some have the British Registry Number which dates them 1884, and the earliest date on any Tea Leaf I have seen is 1856.

This photo was part of an attempt by the late Mr. Ormsbee to include all the popular *types* of English earthenware in his resumé. This learned gentleman may never have been introduced properly to our lovely, simple pattern, as his interests were on more expensive and ornamental wares.

Such a pretty creamer. Enoch Wedgwood (Tunstall) Ltd. body style was the model for the Red Cliff china copied by Hall China Company during the 1950s. See pages 175-181 to compare.   (82)
WW-9

Matching sugar; no lid. Both are 5½" high.   (78)
WW-10

Soup tureen 8" x 11" x 7" high, lid, ladle (not original), and service tray 9¾" x 12¾", which may be a platter as it has no handles. All quite brown and crazed, but still hold a lot of stew or chili for a crowd.
WW-11

Mark used after 1862.
WW-12

*This graceful bowl and ewer set was pictured in the **Antique Reporter** in an article written by Mrs. Clarence Peterson of Galva, Illinois.* (9)
WW-13

Brush holder from a bedroom set, 5" high (89)
WW-14

Butter dish base, 6¾" square plus handles. Unidentified body style. (60)
WW-15

Trademark used from 1891-1900. LTD. added after 1900.
WW-16

James F. Wileman
1864-1892

Only pieces by this owner which I have seen. Creamer is 8½" high. (90)
WM-1

Trademark for above.
WM-2

Wileman was the last English potter to come to my attention when, in 1978, I found a handleless cup with saucer in the booth of a Wisconsin dealer at an antique show in Kansas City. The ware is a beautiful blue-white color and later four-petaled flowers with no crazing. The design is a variant with a stylized four petal flower and several viney leaves. It was a pleasure to put together the history of this fine old company as I sipped coffee from this lovely old cup.

The Foley Pottery of Fenton, home of the James F. Wileman Company, has a long, illustrious history. It was named for the Foley family who was an earlier large land owner in the area. The pottery was built by John Smith in the early 1820s and first tenants were Elkin, Knight and Bridgwood who were famous for their Willow ware and Broseley patterns, as well as other blue-printed wares. Simeon Shaw commented in 1829 that the Foley Potteries was a "new and very complete establishment." Ward praised them also, in 1843; then silence until Jewitt recorded in 1878 so much pertinent information about them. Lesser companies were in and out of business with little or no mention ever made of their existence.

When Samuel Bridgwood retired from that first company of occupants of the Foley Pottery the style changed to Knight & Elkin; later to John King Knight alone, until 1853. Henry Wileman entered the picture then as a partner. He was a former London wholesale china dealer which probably was a tremendous asset to their successful operation as Knight and Wileman. Upon Knight's death, Wileman carried on alone until 1864 when his two sons, James F. and Charles W., succeeded him. During this time, Henry built the nearby Foley China Works.

As so often happens, brothers/partners soon part company; in 1866 they did just that. James took the Foley Potteries where earthenware was the important product. Charles chose the Foley China Works which specialized in china making. James' style was *James F. Wileman*, using the name or initials in the back stamp. He produced all the usual goods: black basalts, printed wares, cream-colored wares, white granite; and he was especially noted for fine lustre wares. His output was made specifically for export to Australia, Ceylon, India, Java, and South Africa, as well as the United States.

Charles retired in 1870 and his brother became head of both firms; soon he took in as partners, J. B. and Percy Shelley, operating then as Wileman & Company. An even finer quality of china was then put into production under Shelley's management. At J. F. Wileman's death and the retirement of J. B. Shelley, the business passed to Percy Shelley. He in turn retained the services of Fredric A. Rhead and something else new was added — art pottery. Later, *another* Fredrick Hurten Rhead, probably his son, migrated to the United States and was instrumental in raising our standards of excellence in the art pottery field through association with various potteries in Ohio, Missouri, New York, and California.

As we look at Henry Wileman's predecessors, we may find an answer to where his peculiar variant design originated. Partners from 1827-40 were Elkin, Knight and Bridgwood. This Samuel Bridgwood produced a variant design commonly known as Bridgwood's Clover Leaf. These are very similar except that Bridgwood's was done in gold overglaze on porcelain, while Wileman's was an underglaze design on ironstone with a rich, dark copper lustre overglaze color. In these two we can see the constant process of evolution in design that keeps a little nostalgia of the old combined with a new touch for tomorrow.

Chances are excellent that much of James F. Wileman's ware came into the United States through the wholesale house of Burgess & Goddard with offices in New York City. They were also distributors for John Edwards, Wedgwood & Co., Samuel Bridgwood & Son, along with several other Staffordshire potters.

Anyone can expect to find another item made by J. F. Wileman; it should be given a choice place in one's collection.

Arthur J. Wilkinson and Ltd.
1879 to present

Wilkinson was another Cable body style producer; this could well have been his first line. **WI-1** *(13)*

Lid and back stamp Royal Staffordshire Pottery, Burslem; 1891-1896; Ltd. added 1896. **WI-2**

Perhaps because his name was not well known in the Potteries, Arthur J. Wilkinson operated partially under another name for awhile. It happened this way:

In 1879 he bought the old Central Pottery in Burslem from Richard Alcock; he chose for his style "Arthur J. Wilkinson, late R. Alcock, Burslem," until he was better known in business. The name change — dropping the "R. Alcock" style — was not made until 1881. There were a couple of patterns in earthenware shown in 1879 (Queen and Empress patterns) which carried the trademark of Richard Alcock, but the same ones shown in 1883 were labeled Arthur J. Wilkinson. He *could* have been a young man just beginning his business career.

According to Jewitt, the old Central Pottery had formerly been worked by Hopkins and Vernon; Hulme and Booth; Thomas Hulme; Burgess and Leigh; and finally Richard Alcock who greatly enlarged, remodeled, and rebuilt the entire works. At Alcock's death in 1881 it passed to Wilkinson who continued the same lines of production as previous owners: white granite for export to the United States. Mr. Wilkinson also introduced the use of gold lustre on granite, but I suspect this soon evolved into our copper-lustre Tea Leaf.

Whether he sold the old Central Pottery when he moved in 1885 to the Royal Staffordshire Works in Burslem, or if he simply added to his holdings, is not clear; it matters little except that his coverage of the export market may have been greater. These old works had been established in 1865 with numerous intervening owners. His style there in the new location to begin with was Wilkinson and Hulme, but soon was changed to Arthur J. Wilkinson. Ironstone and cream-colored ware were again the principal productions as these were the most sought-after items. "Ltd." was added in 1896 and they were still in business in 1964, according to Godden.

The years 1945-1952 were the times of most dramatic change when much thought was given to all the British potteries under government control to modernize them, but the cost was astronomical and the plan impractical; it was finally left to the individual potters to solve their own problems. The result? Few family businesses are completely independent today. Just as here in the United States, various mergers, consolidations, trusts, and cooperatives have provided more efficient production and sales; so, many smaller groups working together have affected the most worthwhile changes with the least loss of family pride and honor. Some of these potteries kept right on operating while rebuilding, enlarging, and modernizing in a big way — no small feat. I found no specific references as to which group the Wilkinsons are in but Geoffrey Godden, the foremost English pottery historian today, brings us up to date with a report on Wilkinson's part in the Art Deco segment of our twentieth century history. The term "Art Deco" evolved out of the 1925 Paris Exposition. In general, the designs are chunky and angular in contrast to the flowing lines of the Art Nouveau concept, but both are loosely applied to most novel offerings of that time, 1920-1935.

These footed compotes were a long-time favorite and were made in graduated sizes. This one is 11" wide and 5" high.
WI-3

Gravy boat, very narrow, (2½" x 8½" long). (35)
WI-4

Round butter dish, lid, drainer; 6½" wide. Mint. (35)
WI-5

One Clarice Cliff kept excellent records of her work at the Royal Staffordshire Works and the adjoining Newport Pottery which Wilkinson had also acquired. Her challenge was most fascinating: a warehouse chock-full of jugs, vases, candlesticks, bowls, etc., from an earlier day — all undecorated. With a skeleton crew of two girls, she was allowed to experiment with designs. Eventually their offerings were put on sale and, to the astonishment of everyone, they sold like hot cakes. Her fresh, simple designs of circles, diamonds, squares, and bands, all in bright colors, relieved occasionally with simple landscapes, were like a breath of spring. Soon buyers were clamoring for more, and the staff increased to 300 decorators. Art Deco was launched and the scope has widened to a variety of artistic designs and trends.

Clarice Cliff was in Kansas City, Missouri in December, 1979, doing a one woman show.

Wilkinson certainly was not a new, unfamiliar name in the pottery trade; there were others before him.

1745-1777 — Andrew & Thomas Wilkinson, Holland Manor, Wicksworth House

1803-1882 — R. J. Wilkinson – Wear Pottery, Sunderland

1862 — Wilkinson & Rickuss – Kensington Works, Hanley

1864-1866 — W. Wilkinson & Wardle, Denaby Yorkshire

1882 — J. Wilkinson, Don Pottery, Swenton, Yorkshire, D.B.A. Samuel Barker & Sons

Relatives? Does someone know? Presently, we only know these Wilkinsons were all potters in a very small area.

Jervis recorded that Arthur J. Wilkinson made semi-porcelain of good quality and his shapes and designs were distinguished by originality. Much of his Tea Leaf was made on lighter weight bodies as the old "Thrashers" china was losing popularity — women were tired of the heavy old stuff by 1891. There was only bare mention of his acquisition of the Mersey Pottery in 1904 from Anthony Shaw's son, so I doubt if our favorite design was applied to goods shipped from there.

In all this, Arthur J. Wilkinson, Ltd., was truly a leader. We could call them part of the New Breed.

Showpiece soup tureen; complete. (22)
WI-6

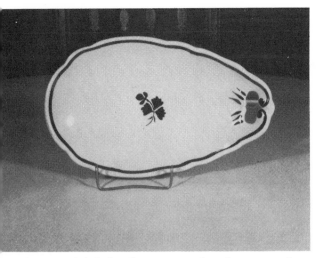

Relish tray with hole/handle; or, it may have been meant for a dripping spoon to use on the stove a lay a messy spoon in. (39)
WI-7

Another style; same possiblities (75)
WI-8

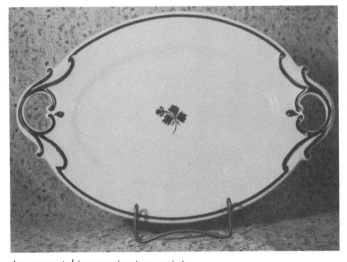

Brush holder with drain. Quite plain; all these pieces had the same trademark as the one shown on page 125. (1)
WI-9

An eye catching service tray; mint.
WI-10

Square covered vegetable on left is marked simply WILKINSON & HULME, BURSLEM, ENGLAND.
WI-12

Ornate teapot, 10" high (53)
WI-11

Fancy milk jug, 7" tall (11)
WI-13

Matching sugar bowl with lid (58)
WI-14

Sauce tureen and lid but no ladle; 6" x 8½". "Wohl Bouillion" printed on side; probably a gift or premium from that store. This was a wedding gift to the owner — 1975. (83)
WI-15

Covered vegetable casserole, 7" x 11" (including handles) x 6" tall. A real beauty! (78)
WI-16

Gravy boat; mint; huge Tea Leaf; 8" long.
WI-17

Soap dish, lid, and drainer (3)
WI-18

auce tureen, lid, and ladle in a more ornate but heavier body style;
" x 8" x 4½" high. (35)
VI-19

Matching creamer for sugar bowl below.
WI-20

Yet another body style; square sugar bowl with lid; 4½" x 6½" tall.
Interesting decoration by handle; otherwise, very plain and heavy.
WI-21 (85)

Vaste bowl; straight sides. (16)
WI-22

Waste bowl; rounded base; both 5½" in diameter. (74)
WI-23

Good use for an odd or damaged piece that is too good to throw away!
WI-24   (12)

Teapot, 8½″ tall; mint, and still another body style.   (1)
WI-25

Distinctive ewer for bedroom set. Excellent lustre, huge Tea Leaf, ornate handle. **WI-26**   (29)

Simple brush holder but pretty!   (64)
WI-27

A.J. Wilkinson trademark
WI-28

American Pottery Background

According to John Spargo's writing in the *Early American Pottery and China* there had been very little, if any, accurate information compiled about potteries in the United States before 1684. He observed that the establishment of a pottery was not an event worth recording such as were saw-mills, grist mills, or even distilleries. However, in 1950, Lura Woodside Watkins' book, *Early New England Potters and Their Wares*, was published, wherein she had assembled more complete accounts of that area.

The first records from Massachusetts probate inventories in 1644 included: "glasses – trayes & earth weare & other lumber" in one list, while "Earthen potts," "milk pans," "Potts-with-honey" were mentioned in various inventories in 1646, 1657, and 1652, respectively.

Ms. Watkins indicated these allusions were not *proof* of local potters, but since earthenware valued at four or five shillings (five to six dollars) was found in nearly every home, it was undoubtedly native red-ware. Because stoneware from Germany and delft-ware from Holland were often itemized in those inventories, she was further convinced earthenware was of local make and went on to identify some of the local artisans.

It was natural for the first potteries to be on or near the sea; therefore, we are not surprised to find numerous kilns in the 1600s in Massachusetts coastal areas along with documented evidence of pottery making at New Haven, Connecticut about the same time.

Brick-making kilns often precede or accompany pottery making kilns; therefore, we were not surprised to find proof of this near Salem, Massachusetts when the Rev. Francis Higginson, in 1629, told of having good clay there to make bricks, tiles, and earthenware as they needed. At that time they were getting a kiln ready to make bricks and tiles with which to build their houses. That bed of clay mentioned was seventy feet deep and provided clay for a long, long time to one of the greatest pottery-making centers in New England.

There is evidence of pottery making in Virginia also in the 1600s; while in New York, in 1657, a New Amsterdam (New York City) list of residents includes one "Dirck Claeson – Pot-baker." Forty years later in those New York City rolls we find mention of one "John DeWilde Pott-maker," "Dirck Bensen – Pott-baker," and "John Euwaste – Pott-maker." We do not know where they worked, for how long they continued, or what they made, but each is mentioned by numerous early historians.

There were remains of a kiln below South Amboy, New Jersey which possibly was built by Dutch settlers, while one of the first and best recorded histories was of a pottery established at Burlington, New Jersey in 1684 by Daniel Coxe of London for the making of "white and Chiney-ware."* This was probably a salt-glazed white delft-ware which was also known in New England, and that England herself had not surpassed at this time. There is also a possibility it was a fine-textured, salt-glazed stoneware. It was *not* what we think of as white ware or china today.

It was more than fifty years later that experimental grades of porcelain were made in this country, but by then many on both sides of the Atlantic were trying to reproduce the quality ware of the old Chinese porcelain.

About 1738 samples of China-ware from the Orient were sent to a master potter in Savannah, Georgia, one Andrew Duché, who used them as models. He is noted as one of three American porcelain makers before the Revolutionary War. Born in Philadelphia in 1710, son of a stoneware potter, he had migrated south, worked in Charleston, South Carolina, New Windsor, and finally Savannah, where he received help to establish a pottery from General Oglethorpe, founder of the Georgia Colony, and the Earl of Egmont, one of the trustees of the colony.

Before 1743 he had ferreted out the secret of good Chinese quality porcelain, because several years before (1738) he had discovered kaolin (china-clay) from which he had made very fine ware. A year or so afterward he found a small mountain of petuntse (feldspar) near Ebenezer, Georgia. A combination of the two was used by him then, and it is still the basis for making true porcelain today.

In 1740 fortune favored him a third time when he located a five acre tract of land with "ironstone" clay with which he made much useful common ware, while he experimented with making porcelain.

Duché received through General Oglethorpe and the Earl of Egmont about everything he asked for in the way of men and supplies. One of these requests included: "two pot painters (decorators); pig-lead; blue smalt; block tin; and an iron mortar and pestle† . . ." everything with which to decorate porcelain in the manner of the Chinese. But even all this was not enough to satisfy this man, or to quell the political and personal squabbles attendant to the pottery. Finally, in 1743, Duché left Savannah, but turned up later in the year at the Bow Pottery in Chelsea, Middlesex, England.

In his later years he returned to the United States as a merchant and landowner. He died in Philadelphia in 1778.

A letter dated 1745 from William Cookworthy, a British chemist, indicated he had talked to Duché and had seen samples of this kaolin recently found by Duché in America; and he had ordered some for himself‡. Mr. Cookworthy was granted the first Royal patent for true English hard paste porcelain in 1768. That same year he discovered the kaolin and feldspar beds of clay at Cornwall, which is in the very tip of England only 200-300 miles southwest of Staffordshire. These were very satisfactory for his purpose; they were superior to the kaolin of the "Chirakae nation." From then on hard paste porcelain was a reality in England. The Cornwall clays are still being used.

---

* Helen Comstock, edition, Concise Encyclopedia of American Antiques (New York: Hawthorn Books, Inc., 1968, 1st edition, 2nd printing, 1967) p. 869.

† Comstock, p. 872.

‡ Barber, *Pottery and Porcelain*, pp. 59-61.

In 1744 Thomas Frye and Edward Heylin of Bow in Chelsea obtained a patent for producing a ware "made of the same material as china."§ They were using a formula told to them by Andrew Duché, while the three of them were together at Bow and using the clay from America called "china-clay" or kaolin. According to Mr. Barber this first chinaware made by Heylin and Frye was made "from an earth—the product of the Chirakee nation in America and called by the natives 'unaker'." This evidently was a soft-paste type for which Bow is still famous.

Mr. William Goss commented in *The Pottery and Glass Trades Review** of England for 1878-79 "The specifications of this patent is of startling interest. Who would have thought the first English China we have any record of was made from American china clay?"

This raises a question in my mind! Was the English porcelain for which William Cookworthy was granted the patent in 1768 — also made entirely from American clays? These patents along with Mason's ironstone patent are still the basis for most of our dinner ware today.

In her *Life of Josiah Wedgwood*, Miss Elza Meteyard records that Mr. Wedgwood was much afraid of losing the American pottery market after he saw the quality of the clays shipped to England from the colonies. He was also alarmed at the great number of potters who were recruited to work in the pot-works in all parts of this New World; and he was perturbed because they were paid higher wages than had been paid in England — even though he was more liberal in payment than most other British potters. He bought, for his own use, large quantities of clay from the Carolinas, as well as a superior grade from Florida. In no time kaolin and petuntse were part of most cargos on ships returning to England from the colonies as other potters copied Wedgwood. Much kaolin used later in Trenton, New Jersey and East Liverpool, Ohio came from extensive beds in Jackson County, North Carolina.

Mr. Spargo in retrospect recorded,

> "How ill-founded and vain the fears of the great English potters were, we know. We smile at the vast gulf that yawns between scared fancy and sober fact. The South Carolina potteries were small and their owners eked out a precarious existence for a few years, when they disappeared altogether. One result they had which Wedgwood was not farsighted enough to foresee: the migration of the potters to the New World brought to the Old World new supplies of kaolin. For several years Wedgwood used considerable quantities of South Carolina clay. Subsequently he used clay from the Pensacola district of Florida instead, finding it of superior quality. It is interesting to know that the oldest specimens of old Bow china, the earliest in England, were made from American clay, and that American clay also went into making of Wedgwood's finest wares.**

The following vignette conveys the hope and heartache, desperation, and finally defeat which dogged so many early potters.

Another porcelain pot-works of importance was the China Works in fashionable Philadelphia, begun about 1770, operated by Gouse Bonnin, previously at the Bow Pottery in England, and George Anthony Morris. They did a great deal of advertising during the two years they were in business. They first wrote of their porcelain being equal to that of

§ John Spargo, *Early American Pottery and China* (New York: Garden City Publishing Company, Inc., 1926), pp. 20-21, 61-62.

* William Goss, in E.A. Barber, *Pottery and Porcelain*, p. 60.
** Spargo, pp. 65-66

England, then advertised for workmen skilled in all branches of potting. Barber reprinted the appeal that followed to those parents:

> as are inclined to bind their children's apprentices to either of these branches, must be early in their application, as only a few of the first offering will be accepted without a premium; none will be received under twelve years of age or upwards of fifteen.

Apprentice time was usually seven years and was a common practice carried to the New World by migrating potters.

A short time later they were advertising for bones, paying twenty shillings (£1, or about $2.50) per thousand pounds and down, delivered to the China Works at Southwark.

Not long afterward they applied to the Philadelphia assembly for financial aid but there is no evidence it was given. They also advertised for zaffer, for making "blue ware," twice more for children apprentices, fifty wagons of white flintstone, and finally a public appeal for charity for foreign workmen without further means of support.

The factory was closed in 1774 (Morris had already retired); the real estate was sold, and Mr. Bonnin went back to England, a very disillusioned man.

According to his son, Mr. Mease, the gentleman who had financed their venture received, for his £500 investment, a blue-printed dinner service! A broken fruit basket is the only specimen that remains of this set of dinner ware. It is on display at a Pennsylvania museum. It is white earthenware of good quality, similar to Bow pottery of the period, but it is not bone china.

It is known their clay came from White Clay Creek near Wilmington, Delaware, and from Charleston, South Carolina. There is proof they experimented with making bone china (the bones were used for this), but most of their two year production was an assortment of general china, both useful and ornamental. A century later the "useful" ware (whiteware) and the bone china "experiments" were profitable realities in numerous potteries throughout Pennsylvania, Ohio, and New Jersey.

Our Tea Leaf evolved from these American pioneer potters who were spurred by Staffordshire competition. We are all the richer for it.

There are many more exciting stories of potteries and people that could be told here, but for our story, mention is made of those that had a more direct influence on the Tea Leaf saga. Long before James Bennett established his pottery in East Liverpool, Ohio (population 500 in 1840), others had been using the plentiful clays found in a twelve mile strip along the Ohio River. They were making necessary pots and jugs and firing these in crude home kilns. The Indians who inhabited this part of Ohio showed rudimentary knowledge of pottery making long before the white men came.

Early nineteenth century pioneers there were John Kountz who operated a pot-bank between East Liverpool and Wellsville in 1817; Joseph Wells, for whom Wellsville was named, began potting in 1820 making red-ware and stoneware, continuing until 1856. In the meantime Philip Brown, Oliver Griffith, and Samuel Watson as well as others were busy potting at Lisbon, ten miles to the north of Fawcettstown, as East Liverpool was then known. There were also various potteries at Salem, Ohio from 1806. All these workmen helped prove the clay to be good and profitable to work.

No wonder then that as James Bennett traveled, he heard of the clay of Columbiana County, Ohio. In England he had been a packer in a yellow-ware pottery in Wooden Box, Derbyshire, just east of the Staffordshire district. Upon his arrival in the United States in 1834, he

First pottery in East Liverpool Ohio. Built and operated in 1839.

worked for a time in New Jersey, but later walked all the way to Troy, Indiana to work in a pottery owned by James Clews of the earlier English Blue Staffordshire fame. Bennett was a skilled and ambitious potter from a family of potters. Consequently, when malaria forced him to leave Indiana he traveled back east toward New Jersey, stopped to work for a short time in Cincinnati, then migrated further east by riverboat. On this predestined trip he met two men from East Liverpool: William G. Smith, a riverboat trader, and James Pratt,** who operated a machine shop. They convinced him to stop there and look at the area. "Eureka! The mind, the place, and the raw material had met."††

In essence this story of Bennett and East Liverpool **is** the story of American-made Tea Leaf as most of the American Tea Leaf we see today was crafted in this picturesque "Staffordshire District of America."

The clay was very much like that used to produce good yellow-ware in Bennett's native Derbyshire. He was without funds but Benjamin Harker and Anthony Kearns, East Liverpool residents, helped with money as well as labor, and the pottery was finished in the spring of 1840. Mr. George Smith and Mr. Josiah Thompson also helped Bennett by giving him credit at their store in East Liverpool. (The Thompson family later became one of our Tea Leaf potters. See that chapter.)

The one-kiln pottery was located at the southeast corner of Second and Jefferson, between the Ohio River and the newly laid Cleveland and Pittsburgh railroad track. The main building was two stories high and about twenty feet wide and forty feet long, made of hand-hewn timbers, covered with clapboard, with a roof of shaved oak shingles. The kiln stood alone surrounded by a wide shed. A "slip" kiln and clay grinding apparatus, operated by one horse, occupied part of the area, and the balance of the plot was used to "weather" the clay, by exposure to the elements. Whether Bennett used clay that belonged to Harker from along the river, or if it came from clay beds above town, leased from George D. McKinnon, the first white child born in Columbiana County, may never be known.

The contents of the first kiln, burned in 1840, were mostly earthenware "mugs, jugs, pans, and other domestic wares of fairly good quality" according to Barth in his *History of Columbiana County*. He went on to assert:

> a great crowd assembled to witness the process and view the results of the departure!

The Bennetts stayed on in East Liverpool until 1846, then moved to Pittsburgh and later to Baltimore. The last vestige of that Bennett pottery disappeared in the flood of 1852.

Two crates of the ware were purchased by Isaac W. Knowles, then barely twenty-one years old, who took his purchase down the Ohio River in a trading boat, peddling it to the settlers as he stopped. Bennett himself took the remainder out through the country and peddled it also; the total profit for both men was about $250.00. (See the Knowles, Taylor, Knowles chapter.)

Two other men inextricably tied in history with James Bennett were Benjamin Harker and John Goodwin, of whom I shall write more later. (See chapters elsewhere in this book on each.)

Along about the time the Bennetts were getting started in East Liverpool, many other English potters joined the earlier mentioned

---

** This is the same who built the gas works in St. Louis and Kansas City. Harold B. Barth, *History of Columbiania County*, 1924.

†† Quote of Harold Barth, Ibid.

immigration societies in Britain and migrated to this city. Some were aided financially by relatives such as the other Bennett brothers, Edwin, Daniel, and William, and a dishmaker by the name of Edward Tunnicliff. They, along with numerous others, all came to the East Liverpool area, and it was soon known as the "Staffordshire District of America."

Because these people often brought familiar potting family names to this side of the Atlantic, it sometimes is hard to tell whether a given pottery is English or American. They often used famous British company names as part of their own American company titles — like Benjamin Harker and Sons, the second pottery established in the city — who adapted the name "Wedgewood" Pottery (notice the extra "e"), or "Herculaneum" used by Jabez Vodrey.

Mr. McCord§§ recorded that there are few stories of hardship and privation in the early history of the middle-west that equal the experiences through which East Liverpools residents passed in the 1850s.

Laborers were not usually paid in money, but quite often by orders at the stores in town. The pottery wares were peddled throughout the country and exchanged for anything that could be obtained: poultry, flour, cornmeal, cheese, eggs, wool, etc. These were brought back into town and given to the workers in lieu of cash. Those men who had invested all they had in their little potteries looked to their workmen for support, and those workmen did not fail them even though the pay was poor, and at times irregular.

McCord went on to tell how, after a crop failure in 1854, during that winter, one firm paid one dollar in cash in three months time on their payroll; the rest was in store orders. Also that winter flour was very scarce and could only be obtained by special order. Many men who were considered prosperous a short time before worked on streets for one dollar a day and took their wages in cornmeal. Others begged or borrowed from a wealthy friend — a dollar or two with which to pay taxes on their property. That year corn sold for ten cents a bushel in Indiana, but there was no transportation between that crop and East Liverpool, so cornmeal sold there for eighty cents. Cows sold for three dollars — if anyone had three dollars.

Yet through it all, these hardy people had a vision, and by 1860 the tide had turned and better times for most were on the horizon.

One of the brightest stars on that horizon was the discovery of natural gas and oil in 1860 and by 1866 gas fired potteries were in common use. William B. McCord, in his *History of Columbiana County*, wrote:

> The pioneer pottery manufacturers of East Liverpool were the first in the world to relegate to oblivion, as a commercial factor, the "potters" wheel, famed in story and song, as the implement of the worker in all ages. This was because of the introduction of machinery and labor saving devices in East Liverpool potteries, a decade before the English potters learned its worth and adapted it."

Wooden machinery was used at first; some of it was made by Isaac Knowles who was a carpenter turned potter, while some of it was introduced by John Goodwin after a trip to the north woods of Minnesota.

In only sixty-five years East Liverpool attained production of forty-five percent of all pottery made in the United States.

---

§§ William B. McCord, History of Columbiana County (Chicago: Biographical Publishing Company).

The following is a complete list of potteries in East Liverpool. It was compiled by Wilbur Stout of the Ohio Geological Survey (1923) and revised by the late William H. Vodrey, Jr. in 1945. It was printed in the *Bulletin of the American Ceramic Society* in August, 1945.

Record of Pottery Industry in East Liverpool District
Revised by William H. Vodrey, Jr., East Liverpool, Ohio *
East Liverpool, Ohio

Year estab-lished	Dates of changes	Names of original companies and their successors	Location	Kind of ware
1830?	1852?	Longs Run or Sprucevale Pottery	Northwest corner Section 15, St. Clair Township	Rockingham and yellow
1840		James Bennett	Southeast corner 2d and Jefferson Sts.	"
	1841	Bennett & Bros.	"	"
	1844	Thomas Croxall & Bros.	"	"
	1852	Plant destroyed by flood		
1840		Benjamin Harker, Sr.	River Road east of Homer Laughlin Pottery	"
		Benjamin & George S. Harker–Etruria Pottery	"	"
	1846	Harker, Taylor & Co.	"	"
	1851	Harker, Thompson & Co.	"	"
	1854	George S. Harker & Co.	"	"
	1879	"	"	White granite
	1890	Harker Pottery Co.	"	Semiporcelain
	1931	Moved to Chester, W. Va.		
1842		Salt, Mear, Ogden & Hancock—Salt & Mear—Mansion House	Northeast corner 2d and Washington Sts.	Rockingham and yellow
	1850	(William G. Smith & Benjamin Harker, Sr.)		
		Harker & Smith (also James Foster & D. & J. S.)	"	"
	1857	James Foster & William Garner	"	"
	1863	Croxall & Cartwright	"	"
	1888	G. W. Croxall & Sons	"	"
	1898	Croxall Pottery Co.	"	"
	1912	Suspended		
1844		John Goodwin	Southeast corner 2d and Market Sts.	"
	1845	"	"	Rockingham, yellow, and knobs
	1853	S. & W. Baggott — Eagle Pottery	"	Rockingham and yellow
	189–	Plant closed		
	1902	Mountford & Co.	"	Stilts, pins, and spurs
	1939	In operation		
1845		Ball & Morris — Union Pottery	Southeast 2d St. and Cherry Alley	Rockingham and yellow
	1855	McGilvary & Orr	"	"
	1857	Croxall & Cartwright	"	"
	1898	Croxall Pottery Co.	"	"
	1914	American Porcelain Co.	"	"
	1932	Suspended		
1847		William Brunt, Sr.	West side Market St. at 1st St.	Rockingham, yellow, and knobs
	1852	William Brunt & William Bloor	"	"
	1853	William Brunt, Sr.	"	"
	1881	Henry Brunt & Son — Riverside Knob Works	"	Clay and porcelain knobs
	1895	William H. Brunt	"	"
	1911	Riverside Knob Co.	"	"
	1917	General Porcelain Co.	"	"
	1930	Riverside Knob Co. (John C. Miller)	"	"
	1891	Henry Brunt & Son — Riverside Knob Works	"	Electrical porcelain
	1895	George F. Brunt & C. F. Thompson	"	"
	1907	G. F. Brunt Porcelain Co.	"	"
	1911	General Porcelain Co.	"	"
	1930	Riverside Knob Co. (John C. Miller)	"	Knobs
1847		Woodward & Vodrey — Herculaneum Pottery	South side East 4th St. from Walnut St. to Elm St.	Rockingham and yellow
	1848	Woodward, Vodrey & Booth	"	"
	1849	Woodward, Blakely & Co.	"	Rockingham, yellow, and terra cotta
	1857	Discontinued business		

* For original listing, see *Ohio Geol. Survey Bull.* [4th Series], No. 26, pp. 74–81 (1923).

Record of Pottery Industry in East Liverpool District

Year estab-lished	Dates of changes	Names of original companies and their successors	Location	Kind of Ware
1853		Knowles & Harvey—Plant No. 1, Old End, East Liverpool Pottery Works	Northeast corner 6th and Walnut Sts.	Rockingham and yellow
	1867	Isaac W. Knowles	"	"
	1870	Knowles, Taylor & Knowles—Plant No. 1, Old End	"	"
	1872	Knowles, Taylor & Knowles	"	White granite
	1890	"	"	Semiporcelain
	1929	American Chinaware Corp., Plant E	"	"
	1931	Suspended		
1880		Knowles, Taylor & Knowles—Plant No. 2, New End	West side Walnut St. North Potters Alley	White granite
	1890	"	"	Semiporcelain
	1929	American Chinaware Corp., Plant E	"	"
	1931	Suspended		
1879		Surles & Gamble	Northeast corner Buckeye Alley and Bradshaw Ave.	Rockingham and yellow
	1882	Flentke, Harrison & Co.	"	"
	1885	Knowles, Taylor & Knowles —Plant No. 3, Buckeye	"	White granite
	1890	"	"	Semiporcelain
	1929	American Chinaware Corp., Plant E	"	"
	1931	Suspended		
1888		Knowles, Taylor & Knowles—Plant No. 4, China Works	North side Bradshaw Ave. east of Plant No. 3	Porcelain and lotus
	1898	"	"	Semiporcelain
	1929	American Chinaware Corp., Plant E	"	"
	1931	Closed		
1857		Vodrey & Bros.—Palissy Works	Southeast corner 4th and College Sts.	Rockingham and yellow
	1879	Vodrey & Bros.	"	"
	1896	Vodrey Pottery Co.	"	Semiporcelain
	1928	Suspended		
1847		John Henderson—Salamander Pottery Works	South corner Broadway and St. Clair Ave.	Rockingham and yellow
	1857	Morley, Godwin & Flentke	"	"
	1870	"	East side Broadway, 5th to 6th Sts.	"
	1874	"	"	White granite
	1878	Godwin & Flentke	"	"
	1882	William Flentke	"	"
	1886	Standard Co-Operative Co.	"	"
	1890	" No. 1	"	Semiporcelain
	1926	Suspended (moved to New Cumberland, W. Va., as Cronin China Co.)		
187–		Flentke, Worcester & Co.—Buckeye Pottery Works	South corner St. Clair and Broadway	Rockingham and yellow
	1877	Flentke, Harrison & Co.	"	"
1859		William Bloor—East Liverpool Porcelain Works U.S. Pottery Works	Northeast corner Walnut and Third Sts.	Porcelain and novelties
	1862	William, Brunt, Jr., & Co.—Phoenix Pottery Works	"	Rockingham and yellow
	1878?	William Brunt, Son & Co.	"	White granite
	1894	William Brunt Pottery Co.	"	Semiporcelain
	1926	Hall China Co.	"	"
	1930	Moved to Klondyke Plant		
1859		William Brunt, Jr., & Co.—Phoenix Pottery	Southeast corner Walnut and 4th Sts.	Rockingham and yellow
	1865	Thompson, Jobling, Taylor & Hardwick—Lincoln Pottery Works	"	"
	1867	West, Hardwick & Co.	"	
	1879	"	"	Cream-colored
	1882	"	"	White granite
	1884	George Morley & Son—Lincoln Pottery	"	White granite and majolica
	1890	Discontinued business		
	1894	East Liverpool Pottery Co.	"	White granite
	1896	"	"	Semiporcelain
	1903	East Liverpool Potteries Co.	"	"
	1905	Hall China Co.	"	"

(1945)

Bulletin of the American Ceramic Society—Vodrey

Year estab-lished	Dates of changes	Names of original companies and their successors	Location	Kind of ware
	1913	Hall China Co.	Southeast corner Walnut and 4th Sts.	Porcelain
	1930	Moved to Klondyke Plant		
1930		Hall China Co.	Northeast corner Elizabeth and Harvey Ave.	"
1859		Elijah Webster—A. Webster & Co.	East side Jackson St. at 1st St.	Stoneware
	1864	Manley & Cartwright—Industrial Pottery	"	Rockingham and yellow
	1872	Manley, Cartwright & Co.	"	"
	1880	Cartwright Bros. Co.	"	"
	1887	"	"	Yellow and cream-colored
	1890	"	"	White granite
	1891	"	"	Semiporcelain
	1924	Suspended		
1863		John Goodwin Novelty Pottery Co.	Southeast corner Broadway and 6th St.	Yellow ware and novelties
	1865	Marks, Farmer, Manley & Riley—A. J. Marks & Co.	"	Rockingham and yellow
	1869	McNicol, Burton & Co.	"	Rockingham, yellow, and white granite
	1892	D.E. McNicol Pottery Co.	"	Yellow, cream-colored, and white granite
	1930	Moved to Clarksburg, W. Va.		
1903		East Liverpool Electrical Porcelain Co.	West Side Boyce St. between Mapletree Mapletree and Elmtree	Electrical porcelain
	1912	General Porcelain Co.	"	"
	1916	Bisque Novelty Work (George S. Thompson)	"	Novelties, doll heads, etc.
	1919	D.E. McNicol Pottery Co.	"	"
	1931	Trymore Clay Products Co.	"	"
	1933	Bellmar Pottery Co.	"	"
	1935-1937	Goodwin Pottery Co.	"	"
1895		Edward O'Connor	East side Starkey St.	Rockingham and yellow
	1902	D.E. McNicol Pottery Co.	"	"
	1921	In operation		
	1927	Hall China Co.	"	Porcelain
	1930	Moved to Klondyke		
1904		Anderson Porcelain Co.	South side Harvey Ave. between Myrtle and Putnam	Electrical porcelain
	1911	General Porcelain Co.	"	"
	1916	Louthan Manufacturing Co.	"	Electrical porcelain and gas porcelain
1866		Starkey & Simms—Star Stoneware	Southeast corner Dresden and 8th St.	Stoneware
	1868	Laughlin & Simms	"	"
		Ferguson & Simms	"	"
		N. M. Simms & Co.	"	"
	1875	Brunt, Bloor, Martin & Co.—Dresden Pottery	"	White granite
	1882	Potters' Co-Operative Co.	"	"
	1890	"	"	Semiporcelain
	1925	Dresden Pottery Co.	"	"
	1927	Discontinued business		
1867		Hill, Brunt & Co.	Southwest corner 5th and Walnut Sts.	Rockingham and yellow
	1874	John Wyllie & Son—Great Western Pottery Works	"	White granite
	1891	Union Pottery Co.	"	"
	1896	"	"	Semiporcelain
	1904	Discontinued business		
1868		McDevitt, Cochran & Co.—California Pottery	California Hollow	Rockingham and yellow
	1871	McDevitt & Moore	"	Majolica and jet ware
	1900?	Discontinued business		
1868		Thompson & Herbert	River Road, east of Sugar Alley	Rockingham and yellow
	1870	C.C. Thompson & Co.	"	"
	1884	"	"	Yellow and cream-colored
	1890	"	"	Cream-colored and white granite
	1918	"	"	Semiporcelain
	1938	Suspended		

Record of Pottery Industry in East Liverpool District

Year established	Dates of changes	Names of original companies and their successors	Location	Kind of ware
1867		Burgess, Webster & Viney Webster, Viney & Co.	South side West 8th St.	Stoneware
	1871	Starkey & Ourly—Star Pottery	"	Rockingham and yellow
	1872	Samuel Worcester & Son	"	"
	187–	Bulger & Worcester	"	"
	1886	Discontinued business		
1863		Agner & Foutts—American Pottery Works	Northeast corner 2d and Market Sts.	"
	188–	Agner & Gaston	"	"
	1887	Sebring Pottery Co.	"	"
	1900	Sevres China Co.	"	White granite
	1908	Warner-Keffer China Co.	"	Semiporcelain
	1910	Suspended operation		"
1857		Joseph Foster & George Garner	Northeast corner Broadway and 6th St.	Rockingham and yellow
	1860	Joseph Foster & James Rowley	"	"
	1865	Foster & Rigby	"	"
	186–	T. Rigby & Co.—Broadway Pottery	"	"
	1872	John Goodwin	"	White granite
	1876	Goodwin Brothers	"	"
	1893	Goodwin Pottery Co.	"	Semiporcelain
	1913	Davidson & Stevenson, lessees	"	Electrical porcelain
	1919	Hall China Co.	"	Semiporcelain
	1930	Moved to Klondyke Plant		
1872		R. Thomas & Sons Co.	North side West 7th St.	Clay knobs
	1884	"	"	Clay knobs and porcelain wiring knobs
		—American Knob Works		
	1885	R. Thomas & Sons Co.	"	Low-voltage porcelain
	1897	"	"	High-voltage porcelain
	1927	Moved to Lisbon Plant		
1873		Laughlin Bros. Pottery—Ohio Valley Pottery	River Road, east of Thompson Pottery	White granite
	1879	Homer Laughlin Pottery	"	Porcelain
	1897	"	"	Semiporcelain
	1903	National China Co.	"	"
	1911	Harker Pottery Co., Plant 2	"	"
	1931	Moved to Chester, W. Va.		
1858?		Booth Brothers		Novelties and heating stoves
	1865	Discontinued business		
1868		Jackson Brothers	Northeast corner 7th and Jefferson Sts.	China and parian
	1870	Discontinued business		
1865?		William Colclough	Northwest corner 6th and Sugar Sts.	Porcelain, clay pipes, and novelties
	1895	Discontinued business		
1867?		Jacob Morton		Clay pipes
	1870?	Discontinued business		
1848?		Wyllie Brothers		Rockingham and yellow
	1854?	Discontinued business		
1877		Benjamin Harker & Sons—Wedgewood Pottery	River Road, east of Harker Pottery	Cream-colored
	1881	Wallace & Chetwynd—Colonial Pottery	"	White granite
	1896	"	"	Semiporcelain
	1903	East Liverpool Potteries Co.	"	"
	1905	Colonial Co.	"	"
	1929	Suspended operations		
1879		Burford Brothers	Northwest corner Green Lane and East 7th St.	Floor and wall tile
	1881	"	"	Cream-colored and white granite
	1896	"	"	Semiporcelain
	1905	Standard Pottery Co. No. 2	"	"
	1920	Potters' Co-Operative Co.	"	"
	1925	Dresden Pottery Co. No. 2	"	"
	1927	Discontinued business		

(1945)

Year estab-lished	Dates of changes	Names of original companies and their successors	Location	Kind of Ware
1881		Frederick, Shenkel, Allen & Co.— Globe Pottery	River Road, east of Colonial Pottery	Rockingham and yellow
	1888	Globe Pottery Co.	"	Semiporcelain
	1903	East Liverpool Potteries Co.	"	"
	1905	Globe Pottery Co.	"	"
	1913	T.A. McNicol Pottery Co.	"	"
	1926	Suspended		
1874		Golding Sons Co.	Southside West 4th St.	Flint and feldspar
	1937	Suspended		
1887		Potters Mining & Milling Co.	North side Railroad St. east of Boyce St. and east of Trenle Pottery	"
	1939	In operation		
1903		Ohio Silica Co.		Flint
	1924	Suspended		
1920		General Pulverizing Co.	Southeast corner Minerva and Walnut Sts.	Feldspar
	1920	Plant burned		
1890		Burgess & Co.—American China Co.	South side West 8th St.	Bone china
	1893	West End Pottery Co.	"	Semiporcelain
	1938	Suspended		
1894		East End Pottery Co.	North side Railroad St. east of Boyce St.	White granite
	1903	East Liverpool Potteries Co.	"	Semiporcelain
	1905	East End Liverpool Co.	"	"
	1910	East End China Co.	"	"
	1915	Trenle China Co.	"	"
	1917	Trenle Porcelain Co.	"	Electrical porcelain and porcelain
	1937	Moved to Ravenswood, W. Va.		
1895		French China Co.	West side Pearl St. at Michigan and Elizabeth Sts.	Semiporcelain
	1901	Smith-Phillips China Co.	"	"
	1929	American Chinaware Corp., Plant F	"	"
	1931	Johnson China Co.	"	Semiporcelain and and porcelain
	1937	Specialty Porcelain Works (Boch)	"	Electrical porcelain
1899		National China Co.	North side Railroad St. between Virginia and Boyce	Semiporcelain
	1903	Homer Laughlin China Co., Plants 1, 2, and 3	"	"
	1929	Moved to Newell, W. Va.		
1890		Corns Knob Works	Laura Ave.	Door and furniture knobs
	1900?	Benty Brothers	"	Artware
	1906	Craven	"	
	1910?	Suspended operations		
1907		Adamant Porcelain Co.	North side West 6th St.	Electrical porcelain
	1912	"	"	Sanitary ware
	1915	T.V. Milligan Porcelain Co.	"	Electrical ware
	1929	Peach Porcelain Co.	"	"
	1932	Ceramic Specialties Co.	"	"
1883?		Burgess & Co.—American Stilt Works	Southwest corner—4th and Cherry Alley	Stilts, pins, and spurs
	1894	Plant dismantled		
1893		Burton & Garner	South side Ravine St. between Blakely and Bradshaw	Pins, stilts, spurs and knobs
	1898	Corns & Williams	"	Specialties
	1903	Suspended		
1880?		Robertson & Co.—Diamond Stilt Works	Northwest corner Union and 1st Sts.	Stilts, pins, and spurs
	1882	Rowe & Mountford	"	
	1891	"	"	Potters' supplies and white granite
	1894	George C. Murphy & Co.	"	White granite
	1896	"	"	Semiporcelain
	1903	East Liverpool Potteries Co.	"	"
	1904	Discontinued business		
1890		Potters Supply Co.	West side Washington St. at 1st St.	Stilts, pins, spurs, etc.
	1940	In operation		

Record of Pottery Industry in East Liverpool District

Year estab-lished	Dates of changes	Names of original companies and their successors	Location	Kind of ware
1902		Louthan Supply Co.	Southwest corner Jefferson and West 8th Sts.	Heating porcelain for electricity and gas
	1916	Louthan Manufacturing Co.	"	"
	1922	Moved to Klondyke		
1868		Fowler & O'Connor—Phoenix Terra Cotta Works	North side Bradshaw Ave. opposite Ravine St.	Terra cotta
	1873	Suspended		
1874		Thomas Haden	West 7th St. near Market St.	Decorating shop
	1879?	Suspended operation		
1874		Joseph Dennis	Northeast corner Washington and Pink Alley	"
	1886	Suspended business		
1877		George F. Humrickhouse	Southwest corner Broadway and Potters Alley	"
		James H. Baum	"	"
	1884	Thomas Haden	"	"
	1888	Suspended business		
1879		John F. Steel	Grove Alley between 4th and 5th Sts.	"
	1891	Discontinued business		
1885		George Buxton	Rural Lane near Jackson St.	"
	1891	Discontinued business		

WELLSVILLE, OHIO

Year estab-lished	Dates of changes	Names of original companies and their successors	Location	Kind of ware
1826		Joseph Wells		Stoneware
	1856	Discontinued business		
1878		Morley & Co.—Pioneer Pottery	Southwest corner Commerce and 9th Sts.	White granite and majolica
	1890	Pioneer Pottery Co.	"	White granite and semi-porcelain
	1896	"	"	
	1900	Wellsville China Co.	"	"
	1933	"	"	Porcelain
1882		John Patterson & Sons Pottery Co.	North side 12th St. at Anderson Ave.	Rockingham and yellow
	1900	Patterson Brothers Co.	"	"
	1917	Sterling China Co.	"	Vitrified hotel china
	1939	In operation		
1886		Webster, Campbell & Co. School House Pottery	Northwest corner 6th and Washington Sts.	White granite
	1888	James H. Baum	"	Cream-colored, sanitary ware, and white granite
	1904	McNicol-Smith Co.	"	"
	1906	"	"	Semiporcelain
	1907	McNicol-Corns Co.	"	"
	1928	Corns China Co.	"	"
	1932	Plant burned		
1894		Burgess & Co.	Southwest corner Lisbon and 3rd Sts.	Stilts, pins, and spurs
	1935	Suspended		
1845		George & John Garner, Enoch Bullock	"	Rockingham and yellow
	1847	Suspended		
1867		Leonard Jones	Southwest corner Lisbon and 3rd Sts.	Terra cotta
	1870	George Jones	"	"
	1880	Suspended		
1852		John Lyth & Sons Co.	South side Wellsville at Corporation Line	"
		Ohio Terra Cotta Works	"	"
	1905	Suspended		
1898		United States Pottery Co.	Southwest corner Main and 20th Sts.	Semiporcelain
	1903	East Liverpool Potteries Co.	"	"
	1936	Purinton Pottery Co.	"	"

(1945)

Bulletin of The American Ceramic Society—Vodrey
SALINEVILLE, OHIO

Year estab- lished	Dates of changes	Names of original companies and their successors	Location	Kind of ware
1902	1904	Dresden China Co.	North side Main St. at first bridge	Semipocelain
	1910	National China Co.	"	"
	1929	American Chinaware Corp., Plant G	"	"
	1931	John Winterich	"	"
	1937	Plant burned		

LISBON, OHIO

1900		Thomas China Co.	South side Washington St. at crossing, Lisbon	"
	1905	R. Thomas & Sons Co.	"	Electrical porcelain
	1939	In operation		

CHESTER, WEST VIRGINIA

1900		Taylor, Smith & Taylor Co.	River front	Semiporcelain
	1939	In operation		
1900		Edwin M. Knowles China Co.	East end Phoenix Ave.	"
	1931	Harker Pottery Co.	"	"
1913		Davidson-Stevenson Porcelain Co.	North side Newell Rd. at Corporation Line	Electrical porcelain and novelties
1921		Davidson Porcelain Co.	"	
	1936	Suspended		

NEWELL, WEST VIRGINIA

1848		Larkins Brothers—Virginia Pottery	East end Grant St.	Rockingham and yellow
	1857	William Thompson		
	1861	Suspended		
1907		John Boch	Northeast end 6th St.	Electrical porcelain
	1937	Moved to Klondyke		
1910		Novelty Clay Forming Co.	Northwest corner 3d and Harrison St.	Clay novelties
	1919	Boch-Metsch Porcelain Co.	"	Electrical and heating porcelain
	1922	Metsch Refractories Co.	"	"
1913		Edwin M. Knowles China Co.	North side Harrison St. at 5th St.	Porcelain
	1939	In operation		
1907		Homer Laughlin China Co., Plants 4 to 8, inclusive	North side Harrison St. between 5th and 10th Sts.	"
	1939	In operation		

OTHER POTTERIES IN EAST LIVERPOOL DISTRICT

1842		George McCullough	Liverpool Township	Terra cotta and brick
	1846	Philip F. Geisse	"	"
	1852	N.U. Walker & Co.—Cliff Mine Terra Cotta Works	"	"
	1900	Suspended		
1876		Herman Feustel	Northwest corner State and Chestnut Sts., Leetonia, Ohio	
		Bradshaw Pottery Co.	Rogers, Ohio	
		Ohio China Co.	East Palestine, Ohio	

Vol. 24, No. 8

East Liverpool, Ohio

In the East Liverpool Museum of Ceramics there is a large collection of original paintings that were executed by Ronald Schweinburg in 1941, along with a group of portraits by David G. Blythe, painted sometime before his death in 1865.

Since Schweinburg was not a potter, he had little conception of the various phases of that art; to achieve the realism desired, old time pottery men who had actually performed the tasks were used as models to depict pottery making from approximately 1840–1895.

David Blythe had painted the portraits of founders of that industry from personal sittings by the individuals while he lived among them . . . they were all part of those "early days."

He had a combination of great wit, talent, charm, and a temper to match his red beard. As a youth he drew sketches with burnt wood on a shed door. Then someone arranged for him to serve an apprenticeship under Joseph Woodwell, a fine wood carver, in Pittsburgh. Later, back in East Liverpool, he eeked out a livelihood as an itinerant portrait painter and many of those paintings hang in the Ceramics Museum today.

About 1846, Blythe married Julia Keffer of East Liverpool, but within a year she died of typhoid fever. During this time he had also painted a 300 foot panorama with the idea of making a good profit, but the death of his wife and failure to sell the panorama drastically changed his life and painting styles. For years he wandered restlessly with "old demon rum" as a close companion. From portrait painting he turned to caricatures.

Except for Western Pennsylvania and Eastern Ohio, Blythe was unknown until the Carnegie Institute of Pittsburgh, Pennsylvania had a showing of his paintings in 1932. Today the paintings of David Blythe are esteemed for the human emotions they evoke. His characters manifest the roughness and economic struggles, along with great strength of character, refined with a definite sense of social awareness, in that frontier community.

Mr. James Bennett (1812–1863) by David G. Blythe. First potter in East Liverpool, Ohio in 1840–1852.

Mr. Isaac W. Knowles (1819–1902) by David G. Blythe. Bought two crates of Bennett's ware from first kiln drawn and sold it from his boat on a trip down the river. Later, he established "Knowles, Taylor, Knowles China Co."

Bennett Pottery (1840) by Ronald Sweinburg. First pottery established at Second Street and Jefferson.

What delightful caricatures his talent and wit might have drawn from the showing of his paintings in their present surroundings! Oh! The ironic amusement that would have guided his brushes to know that just one of those paintings now is worth much more than he earned in his entire lifetime. To see his paintings is not only an insight to David Blythe the painter, but it is a rare opportunity for us to get better acquainted with these intrepid men of yesteryear.

These pictures show only part of the people mentioned throughout our story. Doubtless, someone else will, in time, add to this fascinating history on paper or canvas.

Jabez Vodrey (1795–1861) by David G. Blythe. Another early day potter whose descendents are still active in ELO business. He also arrived in town during the 1840s.

*Benjamin Harker Sr. (1793–1858) by David G. Blythe. Aided Mr. Bennett in first pottery and established the second pottery in E.L.O. which was the oldest in operation in the United States by one family. The Harker Pottery was sold in 1972 to the Jeanette Glass Co. They **may** have made Tea Leaf.*

William Bloor (1821–1877) Partner/friend, brother-in-law of Wm. Brunt, Jr. Made the first commercial white ware in East Liverpool, Ohio.

John Goodwin (1816–1875) by David G. Blyte. Another early day potter who came to East Liverpool in the 1840s from Staffordshire.

Grinding Clay To A Fine Powder by Ronald Schweinburg. This crude machine was probably powered by one horse. Notice the size of the wheel behind the workman. This required very hard physical labor for very low wages.

Slip Kiln by R. Schweinburg. After the clay was reduced to a powder it was mixed with water in the manner shown here.

*Wedging the Clay by Ronald Schweinburg. The next process in producing pottery was working the clay much as bread is kneaded . . . by pulling, rolling, shaping, and cutting with wire as shown by the man on the right. This helped remove air and to feel the impurities in the clay as it was handled. This was a **man's** work as evidenced by the muscles on these two men! These are actual workers who modelled for these paintings.*

These photos were taken in 1973 while the pictures were still hanging in the east wing of the museum, when it was housed on the second floor of the Carnegie Public Library building. There were certain problems of lighting and perspective which are apparent but the beauty, detail, and craftsmanship of the paintings are still very much in evidence. My own visit to some remaining landmarks are included for added human interest.

All of the Schweinburg and Blythe photos were taken by courtesy of the East Liverpool Historical Pottery Museum.

The Throwers by Ronald Schweinburg. Each piece of pottery ware was formed individually by highly skilled men. Many people today can throw a vase or built it up in one of various ways. But the art of throwing a plate or platter is all but lost.

The Jiggerman by R. Schweinburg. In the early days, each piece was formed by use of a simple machine called the "jigger." As the wheel turned, the clay was flattened and pressed into the desired shape by the artist jiggerman.

The Wheel and Jigger by the Author. This wheel and jigger was used many years in the old Croxall "Mansion House Pottery Co." It stood in the west wing of the old museum, mute testimony to years of labor. If the artist was available these tools stood ready for use at the turn of the wheel. The jigger was connected to the huge wheel by a pulley made of leather or rope. The wheel was turned by hand by a young boy. It was usually one of the first jobs available to a boy when he started to work in a pottery.

Copper Engraving by R. Schweinburg. A method of decorating the ware that was desirable but complicated. It required a steady hand, perfect vision, and unlimited patience. Long ago it was replaced by faster, easier methods: decalcominia and stenciling or photography.

Kiln Placing by R. Schweinburg. That box on the head of the workman is a segger (or sagger). Loaded, it weighs 30–50 pounds. A sagger-man carried one on his head and another in his hand as he went inside the kiln. He often had to climb the ladder to reach the top of the kiln, which was possibly fifty feet high, to load it with wares to be fired. A sagger-man could always be recognized on the streets, as he invariably carried groceries, etc. on his head. His cap was padded, but 50 pounds is still a heavy load.

The Decorator by R. Schweinburg. These artists seemed to have more prestige than the jiggermen or the throwers. But the decorators would have had no work without help of the previous workmen. Notice the better clothes and more pleasant surroundings. The man is even wearing a tie!

The Presser by R. Schweinburg. This work-man's job was also highly skilled. There is quite a trick to pressing a hollow piece into a mold, so it comes out perfectly formed, and then to get it out in perfect condition. Try it!

Kiln Firing by R. Schweinburg. After the kiln was loaded, the doors were closed and sealed with clay. The firing began and everyone had to wait for the temperature to reach the proper level, then to be lowered very gradually until the wares could be touched with bare hands. This usually required seven to nine days the first time, but less in the decorator (muffle) kiln as the temperature was not raised as high.

Drawing Kiln by R. Schweinburg. The big day! Everyone gathered 'round to see how the firing went, and to pass judgment on the quality of the kiln. A good draw . . . rejoicing! A bad draw . . . disappointment . . . even total loss of the business if working capital was inadequate.

Shipping By Water by R. Schweinburg. This looked easy, but actually was very deceiving. Imagine a boat such as this one floating and churning in rough water. No wonder lots of pottery is found in riverbeds! It was the cheapest transportation available, but always risky. A river boatman had to be an adventurer at heart.

Carnegie Public Library East Liverpool, Ohio. The entire second floor at this beautiful old building was occupied by the Pottery Museum in 1973. At a later date it was moved to a new home across the street and reopened in 1980.

Packing Ware by R. Schweinburg. This was a very important step in production. No one could afford the breakage that would surely result from poor packing. Packers were often sent along with big orders to see that proper handling methods were used. The barrels were quite heavy and very clumsy to handle. Each barrel held approximately one hundred pieces. Straw was a common packing material.

The Early Pottery Salesman by R. Schweinburg. More commonly known as the peddlar. Oh, happy day! When he came in his wagon or his cart with all the shiny new dishes, along with many other necessities. Farm produce was often accepted instead of money. Many a potter accepted cornmeal, chickens, apples, potatoes, or whatever was available, in lieu of cash payment, for a week's salary.

New Home of The East Liverpool Ceramic Museum. The former post office building, erected in 1908, just across the street.

KT Knowles, Taylor & Knowles Co. An original plant picture.

Restored Potter kiln Second and Broadway, constructed in 1974. Site of the first Bennett pottery.

Thompson Hotel. One of the outstanding landmarks of another era is now gone. This old hotel at Third and Broadway offered the very best in accomodations for travelers. The unique building feature was the floor of the lobby. Names of seventeen potters in the tile floor begin at the door and continue to the far side, a distance some forty feet. There is still hope the floor can be placed in the Ceramics Museum. This hotel was demolished to make way for the new freeway. The light area on the right side of the front corner is a scar covering the original grand entrance.

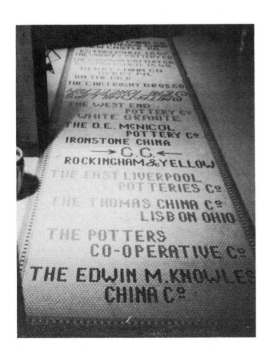

Thompson Hotel Tile Floor
  The Edwin M. Knowles China Co.
  The Potters Co-Operative Co.
  The Thomas China Co., Lisbon, Ohio
  The East Liverpool Potteries Co.
  The D.E. McNicol Pottery Co.—Ironstone China C.C.
    Rockingham & Yellow
  The West End Pottery Co.
  Smith-Phillips Semi-Porcelain
  The Cartwright Bros. Co.
  Derby China Co., Derby, PA on the P.R.R.
  The Goodwin Pottery—Established 1844
  The Vodrey Pottery Co.—Established 1857
  New Castle China Co., PA—Semi-vitreous china
  The Dresden China Co., Salineville, Ohio
  The C.C. Thompson Pottery Co., C.C. Rockingham
    & Yellow Ware
  The William Brunt Pottery Co.
  The National China Co.
  J.T. Croxall Potters Colors & Materials Mfg. Chemist

William Brunt Jr. & Company (W.B. JR. & CO)
1859-1903

Saucer, 5½" diameter; very ordinary but proof of manufacturing.
BR-1

Trademark of above.
BR-2

Another early-day East Liverpool potter was William Brunt Jr., who left the Staffordshire district of his native England with his father, and brother, Henry. They migrated first to Illinois as farmers but in the early 1840s they moved to East Liverpool where the father opened a tavern south of the town hall on Market Street. He hired Isaac Knowles to build a home for them on the riverbank at the western edge of the city, a site later occupied by the Cartwright Company quarters. The Vodreys and the Brunts arrived in town about the same time to begin their separate businesses there.

In 1847, Mr. Brunt Sr. began the manufacture of yellow ware in a small plant, The Riverside Knob Works, at First Street and Peach Alley facing Market Street. Here he pioneered in making yellow ware door knobs. That, before long, was a profitable operation which in years to come supplied nearly all that type knobs for the entire United States.

It was in this plant in the early days that William Brunt Jr. learned the pottery trade as he helped his father and brother at several intervals. Since he was a restless adventurer, when the gold rush craze was at its height young Brunt and his brother-in-law, William Bloor, went to California to seek their fortunes. Bloor returned in 1854 and Brunt a year later, each with about $5,000 to show for his efforts.

Brunt again assisted his father and brother upon his return, but the annual Ohio River floods which brought disaster for the potteries along the riverbank were the direct cause of him leaving the family business at the foot of Market Street. The son, during a very severe rainstorm, is said to have remarked to his father that they should "swim ashore and build a pottery on dry land."* The elder Brunt was infuriated and suggested the ambitious "young'un" find a high and dry site that suited him and go in business for himself. Young Brunt accepted the challenge and, with the nest egg he had brought home from California, purchased part of a big pottery at a sheriff's sale. His associate in the venture was again his brother-in-law and friend — William Bloor of Trenton, New Jersey, who had been attracted to East Liverpool by the sale. They were the only bidders on what Jabez Vodrey had not taken over in the huge, defunct Woodward, Blakely and Company plant. Vodrey had taken part of the plant with one kiln.

In 1859, William Brunt Jr., bought at that sheriff's sale the north half of the original works, which had the remaining two kilns, located at the corner of Walnut and Third Streets. He named it the Phoenix Pottery and, for several years, made yellow ware, which was so popular at that time. Bloor took the remaining south part on Walnut near Third. His part previously had been used for storage; therefore, his first project was to build one kiln and a clay shop; then he began to make a dream come true — to make the first white ware in East Liverpool.

By the following spring Bloor's success was heralded by favorable comment from a rival newspaper in Wellsville. This was almost unheard of as the East Liverpool and Wellsville editors spent much time writing disparaging items about the other city. However, even public acceptance of his heavy, yet attractive, white ware could not forestall the Civil War, with the end result that by 1862 he was forced to give up the venture.

Young Brunt bought his friend's pot-works, which gave him three kilns and much more space. This was not the blessing it could have been as most young men were gone to war. He enlisted also, leaving his plant in the charge of one John Thompson, his chief packer. Upon his return

---

* Much of this story is recorded by McCord, *History of Columbiana County*.

in 1864 he found his pottery abandoned, as Thompson had left town to avoid the draft. Finally, at the end of the war, Thompson returned and eventually was one of the buyers of the north (upper) end, along with William Joblin, James Taylor, and John Hardwick, etc., who operated a pottery as West, Hardwick and Company.

During the Civil War the stores of the town were left to old men, women, and boys to keep open; there was no pretense of running factories. Grass and jimson-weed flourished at Second and Broadway — the two busiest thoroughfares, while women and babies actually suffered for the bare necessities of life.

In due time it all ended; the "Boys in Blue" came home and put new life into the potting industry. In the next six years, 10 more new manufactories opened for business. Odd makeshift buildings were passé — new substantial ones and, for that day, modern ones — were in demand. Money came easier, peddling days were gone, steam was the motive power of the new factories, and transportation facilities were improved tremendously with new railroads into the city.

Our friend, Brunt, went back into the old Bloor plant to produce yellow and Rockingham ware with great success. He later added to the company his son, William III, and his son-in-law, Brad Louthan. The plant was converted to the manufacture of ironstone and decorated ware under the name of William Brunt, Sons and Company and incorporated in 1894 as William Brunt Pottery Company. It was some time before this incorporation that the Tea Life pattern was made there.

Shortly Mr. Brunt retired. Louthan went into business for himself, the concern declined, and finally ceased operation. It eventually became part of the Hall China Company in 1926.

In 1867 William Brunt Jr. rebuilt part of his old plant; and, in partnership with his brother, Henry, and Colonel Harrington R. Hill, a well known local attorney, built the Great Western Pottery at Fifth Street and Walnut. It was frame construction — 40 by 109 feet and two stories high, with an extension north along Apple Alley for plant machinery, two kilns, and clay houses.

The new pottery was built with an eye to economy and efficiency of operation by shop and kiln arrangements, to make use of assembly-line production methods introduced as part of the Industrial Revolution. It was by far the most pretentious plant in town, and many held great expectations for the future of this new venture. To match the spirit of the day, William Brunt Jr. brought from the old Woodward-Blakely plant a huge yellow ware pitcher about five feet tall (really a potting marvel at that time) and placed it on the roof of the new works where it remained for years. This new plant was located at the rear of his new residence on Broadway (later the site of the East Liverpool government building).

The opening of a new factory had become an outstanding social event, celebrated by receptions and the like, attended by "invitation only" with young soldiers as heroes, and a new social spirit, the likes of which had never been seen or heard before in East Liverpool. Both Mr. Brunt and Colonel Hill were charter members of the Odd Fellow Lodge, and that organization hosted the huge reception when the new Great Western Pottery opened.

The production included brown and jet ware door knobs, Rockingham novelties, and yellow ware. After Colonel Hill retired, the Brunts sold the works in 1874 to John Wyllie, Sr., and his son, John Wyllie, Jr. from England (via Pittsburgh in the 1860s).

Seemingly, William Brunt had a "nose" for defunct potteries and sheriff's sales. In 1875, just after he sold the Great Western Pottery to the Wyllies, he attended a sale and bid on the old Dresden plant which had been established in 1865 on the southeast corner of Eighth Street (West Market) on the city's far north side. Nathaniel Sims and Tom Starkey had taken what formerly was a grist mill and converted it to a two-kiln stoneware works. Brunt was not serious in his bidding and was quite surprised when the auctioneer "knocked" it down to him! For the third time, he took a floundering pot-works and turned it into a successful operation — for a time. He developed a bad case of "white ware fever" and was soon anxious to get into that new field of production which seemingly offered such great opportunities. (Knowles, Taylor and Knowles; John Wyllie; Homer Laughlin; and Harkers were already successful in white ware manufacture.)

Brunt again included his brother, Henry, and his good ally, William Bloor, who had returned to East Liverpool after 10 years in Trenton. George Martin and Samuel Emery were also partners in the new firm known as Brunt, Bloor, Martin and Company. Within a few weeks after the purchase, plans were drawn up for a new white ware plant and executed with dispatch. An excellent grade of white goods was produced from the very beginning, and the shops — new and modern for that day — attracted first-class workmen.

There are those who feel the Tea Leaf may possibly have been made here; but, according to the trademark — "W.B. Jr. & Co.," this was used only in the earlier days at the old pot-works on Third to Fourth Streets, Walnut to High Alley. At the Great Western plant and this Dresden pottery, the titles included the names of the other partners. According to a *Record of Pottery Industry in East Liverpool District* compiled by William H. Vodrey Jr. in 1945, the signature of William Brunt Jr. and Company was used in both "upper" and "lower" works; but, since we know this ware was popular towards the end of the century, it is logical it was made in the remodeled lower works which had been held formerly by William Bloor.

Several years before, Bloor had sold many of his formulas for white ware and glazes to his brother-in-law and Colonel Hill while they were operating the Great Western Works. It is no wonder there were high hopes for success in this venture. They did, in fact, exhibit at the Philadelphia Centennial in 1876, with less than a year's experience, and received medals of merit for some of their wares, along with award winners — Homer Laughlin and Knowles, Taylor and Knowles — quite an honor for such a small, new company; but it was recognition due William Bloor's pioneer work in producing white ware. This was an especially effective endorsement in view of the fact the competition was dominated by Trenton, New Jersey potters. Because of Mr. Bloor's generosity in sharing information on white ware manufacture with competitors in Trenton and East Liverpool, he hastened the day Americans were eating from white ware made in our own country by our own workmen. He, in fact, started the white dinner-ware manufacture in these two cities, which today is part of a thriving ceramics industry.

Things went fine until 1882 when a strike was called following organization of the Knights of Labor which was resented by the "boss potters." After 39 weeks the strike ended; the Brunt, Bloor, Martin and Company was sold to a stock company of workmen directed by H.A. McNicol, a businessman, who operated in various capacities until his death, when it passed to his sons and heirs as directors until 1927, then it was finally closed. It was renamed the Dresden Pottery after this sale. McNicol was a successful operator from the start in spite of two fires and numerous other problems.

Isaac Knowles was the second one to make white ware after Bloor's initial venture; the Harkers and Homer Laughlin were also successful in their introductions of whiteware; but Brunt, Bloor, Martin and Company failed to reap their just share of benefits because of insufficient capital at critical times.

In 1874 William Bloor brought in the first man to decorate exclusively white ware in an East Liverpool pottery: a German artist named Ludwick. They also supplied independent decorators with plain ware to be decorated and sold independently of the pottery. There were four such shops in town: John F. Steele on College Street north of the Vodrey Pottery; James Dennis on lower Market Street who, at one time, employed twenty to thirty decorators. William Higginson was on upper Walnut Street just south of Knowles, Taylor and Knowles until 1890; and Thomas Hayden, on Seventh Street, was in successful operation until a much later date.

These men stayed busy, as most small pot-works did not have facilities to decorate, or to fire after the decoration was applied in order to make it permanent.

Liquid gold was an important factor in decoration; the secret of converting pure gold to a liquid which could be fired and become a durable decoration was a well-kept trade secret of two large chemical companies, Hanovia and DuPont, who made a fortune from sales of their product. Many East Liverpool decorators thought they had perfected the process, only to find their experiments had consumed all their holdings and yet failed to be successful. In 1905 the New York firms still held fast to their secrets.

This has to be the explanation why much of the American Tea Leaf designs did not last; and, since there was no underglaze decoration (for some unexplained reason), there was nothing of lasting beauty.

Perhaps neither the decorators nor the potters dreamed that we — a century later — would wonder where the golden Tea Leaf went. How could they know their newly tried decorating methods would not stand a century of use and still be in mint condition? After all, much of the lustre of English ware *is* gone; but we are not so acutely aware of it because the underglaze decoration is still there.

The great revolution of the 1870s in the plants, wares, and methods brought all sorts of changes and gave East Liverpool a permanent place in the industrial history of the nation. Change meant heart-breaking struggle, as most of the capital with which experiments were conducted and failures borne, was the indomitable "staying power" and perseverance of pioneers in the movement. There was no patronage.

England, France, and Germany had supplied the American markets with white ware for all purposes; they had a vast wealth of great pottery families to back them, as well as paternal governments which provided laboratories and chemists and paid the bills for experiments to improve ceramic quality, thereby putting a premium on skill and industry.

Americans had not known first-class dinner ware except imported products, for at first, American-made wares were laughed at and held in derision. But — the 1870s was the decade that brought drastic changes. By 1879 this was the list of East Liverpool potteries and their size by the number of kilns:

> The total valuation of the product of the district at that time was placed at about $1,500,000 per annum.
> A list of the firms engaged in manufacturing pottery in 1879, the number of kilns each operated, and the character of product follows:

Firm	prod.	kilns
Wm. Brunt, Jr., & Co.	stone china	5
Homer Laughlin	stone china	5
Knowles, Taylor & Knowles	stone china	5

Brunt, Bloor & Martin	stone china	4
George S. Harker	stone china	4
Godwin & Flentke	stone china	2
John Wyllie & Son	stone china	2
Vodrey Bros.	stone china	2
Benj. Harker & Sons	"C. C."	2
West, Hardwick & Co.	"C. C."	3
Goodwin Bros.	"C. C."	3
Burford Bros.	"C. C."	1
C. C. Thompson & Co.	R. & Y.	5
Croxall & Cartwright (two plants)	R. & Y.	4
Agner, Foutts & Co.	R. & Y.	4
S. & W. Baggott	R. & Y.	3
Manley & Cartwright	R. & Y.	3
McNicol, Burton & Co.	R. & Y.	2
Flentke, Harrison & Co.	R. & Y.	1
Bulger & Wooster	R. & Y.	2
McDevitt & Moore	R. & Y.	2
H. Brunt & Son	Knobs	2
Richard Thomas & Son	Knobs	1

In 1925 Mr. Barth recorded a total of 285 kilns with ware capacity unsurpassed in a single community in the world. There were over 7,000 men and women employed in about 30 active potteries; there were also 10 electrical porcelain plants; five companies making potters' supplies; and several large cooperage plants.

> As the years have passed the importance of East Liverpool as a pottery center has grown, until today its activity is not equaled in any similar territory in the world.†

THE BUFFALO POTTERY COMPANY
1901 to present

Platter, 11″ × 15″. Rounded ends and 13 one-inch idented lines on each side. Really poor quality, stained, crazed, design in copper lustre overglaze almost gone; little lustre on rim.

BUF-1

The element of surprise has been one thing that has kept interest in "Grandma's Tea Leaf" at such a high level; we never know which source will have just the very item we have hunted for ages. So it was, when a letter from the Buffalo China Company came on a bleak November day and I found the answer to the "Vassar mystery." Thereby hangs this tale:

My daughter, Helen, had found a big rectangle Tea Leaf platter in a northeast Missouri "antiques and junk" shop, for 75 cents! I could hardly wait to see it when she said it was "different" with only the word "Vassar" stamped on the back; secretly, I felt sure it was American-made and certainly one I had not seen. It was very brown, scuzzy, crazed; the lustre almost gone; even most of the Tea Leaf design had disappeared. Frankly, it was not very pretty, and the thought flitted through my mind that it was worth only 75 cents!

But, on the other hand, *someone* had made it, and that meant another company to research. As I carried my "prize" into the house, I dropped it; but it broke in several large pieces which were easy to glue together. Even with its usefulness ended, it was on display as a background on a top shelf just to haunt me — WHO made it? WHO? WHO?

For almost two years, the question went unanswered until a photo came from Lois Lehner with a Buffalo Pottery trademark and the word *Vassar* on it. (But, the body-shape and decoration were totally different from my platter.)

I had previously written to the Buffalo people inquiring if they had ever made Tea Leaf and had received a pleasant reply to the negative. My second letter had included the photo and pictures of my platter, front and back. Their answer was the sunshine of that dismal November day — Yes, it was their work!

†M.K. Zimmerman: *Crockery and Glass Journal*, Dec. 18, 1924.

Back stamp. Acknowledged as that of Buffalo Pottery.
BUF-2

Next to the Tea Leaf story, the twentieth century Buffalo Pottery saga is more American than any fiction ever dreamed by an inventive writer. It is the story of a genie who turned a bar of yellow laundry soap into a world-renowned pottery, and changed the marketing and merchandising habits of the entire United States. Of course, John Durant Larkin had some excellent helpers, but it was his imagination and ingenuity which found expression in the John D. Larkin Company, and later in the Buffalo Pottery Company.

With permission of the publishers of *The Buffalo Pottery Book* by Violet and Seymour Altman, I will review some of that story as it relates to our Tea Leaf chronicle.

Larkin was born in Buffalo, New York, in 1845. His parents were English immigrants, and when John was seven, he and his six brothers and sisters were left fatherless. He stayed in school for five more years but then, of necessity, went to work as a messenger for Western Union; later he worked for a millinery concern; and by the time he was 16 he took a job with Justus Weller, a local soap-maker. Within ten years of his initial employment by Weller, he became a partner. In 1874 he married Hannah Frances Hubbard, an older sister of Elbert Hubbard, the famous author and artist, whose parents had also originally lived in Buffalo. Elbert was John D. Larkin's best helper and friend.

Larkin was anxious to go in to business for himself, and 199 Chicago Street, Buffalo, New York, was the site for his first soap-making manufactory — a small, two-story building. His one item — Sweet Home Soap — was sold by peddlers who used-hand carts to traverse the city streets.

In a short time he was joined by D. J. and W. H. Coss who handled production; and his brother-in-law, Elbert Hubbard, whose advertising and sales promotion facilitated the rapid growth of the young company. In a year or so they had outgrown their first two-story building and moved into a new plant which had three floors.

New products were constantly added, and the practice of including premiums with the order was also an innovation. Elbert Hubbard initiated the first mail-order business with merchants; but later Larkin products were sold directly to consumers, much to the chagrin of the merchants. The money saved by selling directly to the users was given back to them in the form of premiums equal to the amount of their purchases.

Within ten years, two shifts of workers, daily, were required to keep up with the orders until a third new plant was opened in 1885. This one had five stories and cost $12,000.

Hubbard's next brainstorm was a Combination Box containing 100 bars of the yellow laundry soap plus almost twenty bars of assorted toilet soaps and eleven pieces of silver-plated tableware — all for $6.00 to be paid for in thirty days. To handle the avalanche of bookkeeping problems, a new system using index cards rather than bound ledgers was instituted; thus the J. D. Larkin Company is credited with being the first to use this card system. An added benefit to the company was a huge, ready-made mailing list already compiled by use of this new card system.

There seemed to be no end to growth. New offerings in merchandise and premiums called for increased production at all levels.

From the small, two-story building in 1875 to a plant with 64 acres of floor space in 1914, plus seven branch offices with warehouse facilities, there was good reason for the Buffalo Chamber of Commerce to state that the local company was the largest manufacturer of soap and related items in the world.

The Larkin Company was mentioned in the Encyclopedia Brittanica because Frank Lloyd Wright designed its office building in 1912. It was his first attempt at commercial building design and was considered to be years ahead of its time because of ventilation and lighting systems and planned efficiency for use by the 1,800 clerks and typists, plus the executives and their secretaries. These employees were in addition to the 2,500 or more involved in production.

To keep up with the demand, Larkin began to manufacture or fabricate many of its premiums; the natural result of this trend was the establishment in 1901 of the Buffalo Pottery Company to provide first-class dishes and the like for premiums as well as general sales. These were shown in catalogs issued twice a year, for a time.

The pottery was chartered in 1901 but it was two years before it was in actual production. The first general manager was Louis Brown, a former salesman, who had called on Larkin while employed by the Crescent China Company of Trenton, New Jersey. He brought along several fine craftsmen including William J. Rea, who began at the age of 14 as an apprentice at the Mayer China Company in Beaver Falls, Pennsylvania. He had also worked in Ohio and had been in charge of a pottery in New Jersey for ten years. The Buffalo plant was his dream come true in concrete, bricks, and glass, as it was built according to his design and specifications. As we could expect, he had learned his trade very well at Mayer; one of his first successes was the underglaze process used to produce the first American Blue Willow ware. We recall Mayer was a leader in under-glaze decoration from their inception in 1881.

Another star in Rea's crown was the successful recruiting of skilled artisans whom he persuaded to come to work for him on a piece-work basis, which meant an excellent salary for excellent workers. They soon had a staff of 250.

The original buildings formed the largest fireproof pottery in the world when built. There was 80,000 square feet of floor space with 400 windows in the eight buildings. It was operated completely by electricity — another first. It was a beautifully clean, light, airy place to work.

Good construction planning eliminated wasted motion in the production lines from the time the clay was loaded at the point of origin until it was shipped out as finished ware. A minimum of handling was always the goal. Every device known in mechanical production to insure uniform high quality was used. Without thermostats (which had not yet been introduced), dedicated, experienced men used specially made ceramic cones to indicate proper heat in the kilns. Even here in the beginning of the twentieth century, men carried the loaded saggers, unsupported, on top of their heads as they climbed the ladders to reach the topmost rows of the kilns.

Their system for decorating, glazing, and firing at high temperatures produced high-quality semi-vitreous ware, guaranteed not to craze. Most of the merchandise was made for the parent Larkin Company, but by 1911 much of it was distributed throughout twenty-seven countries of the world.

Until the advent of the Buffalo Pottery Company, ceramic premiums given by Larkin were often seconds from American potteries, but after 1904 they publicized the first line-quality products of the new plant. Their earlier imported wares had been first quality goods from England, France, and Germany.

In the year 1915 vitrified china was introduced, and the company name changed from Buffalo Pottery Company to Buffalo China Company. A new addition to the plant was made which almost doubled the work area and added several new kilns.

As the letter from Buffalo noted, our platter was made before this time. Perhaps some of our readers will have other pieces of Tea Leaf by Buffalo Pottery Company, received as premiums from the Larkin Company, or purchased in a home town store, which will be in much better condition than the one shown in the lone photo in this chapter.

During World War I the plant provided enormous amounts of ware for all the military service branches as well as hospitals and merchant ships. Semi-vitreous ware was discontinued entirely in favor of the better quality vitrified goods.

After the armistice, some much finer dinnerware was made for Larkin as well as the general public than had previously been available.

Our 1977 Thanksgiving dinner in a fine Kansas City restaurant was served on Buffalo china and, as we ate, it was pleasant to recount the interesting story of this fine company, about which I had just completed the original manuscript that very morning.

When William Rea retired in 1938, he was replaced by Robert E. Gould who had started his ceramic career in the East Liverpool area, first at R. Thomas & Sons Company of nearby Lisbon, then later at Taylor, Smith and Taylor just across the Ohio River in Chester, West Virginia. He was a graduate of Ohio State University in ceramic engineering, and intervening years had been divided between a large European firm and the Tennessee Valley Authority at Norris, Tennessee, as their chief ceramic engineer. Under his guidance, another modernization program was undertaken to bring in the very latest in kilns, newer methods, and equipment. The end result was a most efficient, automated pottery.

In 1925, under William Rea, copies of the beautiful Barberini-Portland vase, made famous by Josiah Wedgwood, had been reissued. Wedgwood had given one of the first seven copies to his good friend, Joshua Mayer. It had been passed down to his grandson, Ernest Mayer, of Beaver Falls, who had been Rea's mentor at the start of his potting career. After years of experimentation and research at the Buffalo Pottery a matchless copy was cast under Rea's direction and six vases were issued. In "The Antique Trader" for July 23, 1980 one of these six vases was offered for sale. It was from the estate of Ruth Larkin Robb, granddaughter of John D. Larkin. It was in mint condition and the asking price was around $2,000, but at press time it had not been sold.

However, it was the production of the commercial and institutional type wares which placed Buffalo Pottery third largest in that category in the United States.

Practically all Buffalo Pottery is plainly marked and dated with a variety of back stamps. My platter seems the exception (perhaps they were not so very proud of it). Nonetheless, if they produced Tea Leaf in any amount, someone may have specimens which are easier to identify. We shall see.

Today, Mr. Harold Estey, grandson of John D. Larkin, with over thirty years of service with the company, is the president. Another grandson, John D. Larkin Jr. has been associated with the company in various capacities.

Cartwright Bros.
1864-1924

One of the most elusive examples in this Tea Leaf saga was ware made by the Cartwright Bros., who joined the growing list of potters producing this simple design in 1881. The only specimen of Tea Leaf in the East Liverpool Historical Society Museum in 1973 was a soap dish, but since it was behind glass I was unable to photograph the trademark; however the legend beside it identified this dish as Cartwright Bros. ware. It is the only Cartwright piece I have found in all my travels, so if anyone has other specimens they have rarities indeed!

This photo was taken in the East Liverpool, Ohio Historical Society Museum in 1973 when it was housed in the second floor of the Carnegie Public Library. All the items shown were by Cartwright as indicated by the legend in front of the top, right vase.
CA-1

The first mention of the Cartwright name in the Potteries comes from Simeon Shaw* who, in 1828, noted that two butter-pots, made in the 1640s, had been unearthed in Burslem, center of the butter-pot industry from the earliest days. These pots were well made of common clay, without glaze, and were marked in "rude letters" *Cartwright* on a relief two inches in diameter. This was the warranty that the pots were of the proper size.

At that time shysters (as now) tried to hoodwink the butter-buying public by various means: false bottoms, or too heavy or too light weight wares to insure proper weights of butter to the ultimate consumers. Finally, in 1670 Parliament passed a law that these utensils had to weigh not more than six pounds, had to hold fourteen pounds of butter, and were to be of hard quality to prevent them from absorbing water from the butter. To insure and/or enforce the law, surveyors (inspectors) were hired to spot-check the contents; so rather than depend on weight alone they used an auger-type "butter boare" which was inserted obliquely to the bottom, removed, and checked/tested to assure that the butter was the same all the way through. This was, after a fashion, an early day pure food act.

Now, back to the Cartwrights. This first man could not have been classed with so many other "poor butter-pot makers" because there is recorded proof that at his death, in 1658, he directed that "£20 yearly be given to the poor of Burslem forever." Probably not all Burslem butter-potters were equally affluent, but we can believe that not all Burslem potters were poor men.

W.P. Jervis and Chaffers identified one Richard Cartwright and Sons as making butter-pots in Burslem from 1640–1675. In those days the potter and his family usually constituted the whole working staff. Later Josiah C. Wedgwood listed in the Burslem rolls one Thomas Cartwright as making butter-pots "at the west end of town" from 1710–1715. There was silence in history until 1837 when Jewitt noted that Moses Cartwright had established the Swadlincote Mills; then in 1869 at the Longton Borough Pottery, Cartwright and Edwards built an extensive, model factory. The ovens were on a downdraft system with smoke conveyed to large chimneys into which all kilns worked; all the clay preparation was done by machinery; the water was taken out of the clay by pressure instead of by a slow process of evaporation as in earlier days; the throwing wheels and jiggers were turned by steam power, and the workshops had drying stoves so no open fire was used in drying the wares. Yet they were noted as producers of "ordinary earthenware."

According to *The Crockery and Glass Journal*, December 18, 1924, this is part of the Cartwright family history:

William Cartwright was born in Staffordshire in 1834. His father was also William Cartwright, a native of Shropshire, who, when yet a young man, located in Staffordshire and took employment in the potteries.

Thomas Cartwright, a son and brother, came to the United States in 1844 and located in East Liverpool. A year later the family arrived. In 1846 William Sr., upon becoming dissatisfied with local conditions, returned to England, but again returned to East Liverpool in 1853, where he continued in the pottery business until his death in 1876.

From 1846 until the disastrous flood of 1853 that destroyed the original Bennett plant, four Croxall boys had operated that kiln — but with their pot-works washed away a new firm was organized: John and Thomas Croxall, Joseph Cartwright, and Jonathan Kinsey. They pur-

---

*Simeon Shaw quoted in *History of Straffordshire Potteries*.

chased the two-kiln Union Pottery at Second and Cherry Alley which had been built by Mr. Thomas Ball and Mr. William B. Morris in 1848. Mr. Morris was an uncle of Andrew Carnegie, the steel magnate who spent many boyhood summers there at his uncle's home.

At one time this small plant had been burned down by a female employee who was disgruntled "because she had to work in the pottery." It was immediately rebuilt and continued in operation.

In 1863 the Croxall-Cartwright combo purchased the Mansion House Pottery; as a result they had two potteries with two kilns and continued in business for many years with the necessary expansion of facilities.

Their partnership was changed with the passing of Mr. Kinsey and the retirement of Mr. Cartwright; the style was changed to John Croxall and Sons. John Croxall was considered the dean of potters and was still in good health at eighty-one in 1905.

After almost sixty-five years of operation, the old Mansion House Pottery was torn down in 1912 so the lot could be used for a six-weeks evangelistic campaign by William "Billy" Sunday. Later it was purchased by the city and converted to a playground.

At the start of the Civil War, four Cartwright sons had entered the military service. At the close of their service duty the boys all returned to East Liverpool and resumed work in the potteries, which led to the formation of the partnership between William Cartwright and Holland Manley; they bought, in 1864, the stoneware plant built by Elijah Webster on the riverfront, as well as the old William Brunt house next door, and shortly began the remodeling and building of substantial structures. Upon this site they were successful producers of yellow ware and Rockingham from 1864–1880. They had one kiln, with a story and a half main building, eighteen by thirty feet. Samuel Cartwright, William's brother, entered the firm in 1872. Manley retired in 1880 and the name was changed to Cartwright Bros.

In 1881 they began making their version of our Tea Leaf design and other potteries in the Ohio Valley quickly followed suit. Their Tea Leaf design was known as Lustre Spray and/or Edge Line and Sprig. This was also the year the telephone was put into use in East Liverpool. In addition, Cartwrights produced the Willow pattern and supplied the American version of the Indian Tree pattern as well as several other standard old English designs for the United States Market.

In 1887 sons of the founder were taken into the firm and the name became Cartwright Bros. Company, and it was still in business in 1905.

E.A. Barber,† in 1893, noted that "at their Industrial Pottery works they manufactured: c.c. goods, plain and decorated, and specialties in ivory decorated ware." They made white granite after 1887.

In 1902 W.P. Jervis recorded that "Cartwright Bros. of East Liverpool, Ohio had six kilns and were producing cream-colored ware, and decorated staples. William Cartwright was president and treasurer; S.R. Cartwright was general manager, while John T. Cartwright was secretary."

Their home was next to St. Stephens Episcopal Church but has since been torn down.

During the time I was in East Liverpool in 1973, Miss Ruth Cartwright, 72, passed away on October 3. She was the last direct descendant of the family still living in East Liverpool. Her father was Fredrick Cartwright; she also had spent her entire life there, and served many years as assistant librarian of the Carnegie Public Library.

---

† E.A. Barber, *Pottery and Porcelain.*

The following excerpt is from the *Sixth Annual Tri-State Pottery Festival Handbook*, 1973.

One of the first notable events in East Liverpool was a Fourth of July celebration. A barbecue was held on the site of the future Cartwright Pottery. The attendance was a large one approximately four thousand people. William Larwell, one of the first lawyers in the area, read the Declaration of Independence. The area of Second Street was the scene of a parade including a company of militiamen commanded by John Wilcox. During the drill following the parade Captain Wilcox accidentally shot off one side of his whiskers. So the highlight of merriment for the day became, not the historic date, location, or crowd, but that of a "two-faced captain."

Cumbow China Decorating Co.
1932-1980

Pitcher, 4" high; purchased at flea market ($4.00). Note hammered effect.
CU-1

Cumbow was one of the first American companies to come to my attention in 1973. They are decorators only — not manufacturers — currently producing Tea Leaf. A delightful correspondence ensued with Mrs. Mabel Cumbow Ruskin, widow of the founder, in which she recounted that Mr. Jacob Zacariah Ruskin was born in Zurich, Switzerland where his people had been in the pottery business for about five hundred years. He established the Cumbow China Decorating Company in Abingdon, Virginia in 1932, and named it after his father-in-law, Anderson Hendricks Cumbow. The city of Abingdon was named after a town in England which was founded in 632 A.D. As an artist-designer it was natural that one of his very first patterns was named Abingdon. Since Tea Leaf was also of English origin, it was also natural that he used this motif in decorating.

In 1961 they began decorating a plain English ironstone with this design that harmonized so well with the Early American furnishings which were so popular at that time. Since then, they have used various plain wares from both England and America to fill the demand for Tea Leaf decorated china. One of their prettiest items is a squatty teapot. Several years ago I had an opportunity to buy a small collection of it, but, through ignorance I passed it up.

Some time ago, a small mystery was solved when Mrs. Ruskin identified as theirs, a small pitcher I had purchased at a flea market for four dollars. It was off-white with an orange peel finish ("hammered" she called it). The shape and "feel" were nice; the lustre was excellent, and it was "Oh! So pretty!" when filled with a small bouquet of spring violets or buttercups. To me it was meant for flowers — not cream — but Mrs. Ruskin advised that it was part of a three piece set — a creamer, sugar, and tea pot.

My first assumption was that it was a reproduction made in Japan or Germany which had been mentioned in various collectors' publications. The tiny three-leaf sprig on the bottom of that little treasure was not much to go on.

Late in 1977, I was able to order a cup and saucer from Cumbow and was pleasantly surprised to find my favorite motif on ware made by Simpsons, Ltd., in England, an affiliate of the Pfaltzgraf Company of York, Pennsylvania. It also was clearly marked as having been decorated by Cumbow. The panelled tall cup with the comfortable handle and the matching saucer are a joy to use. Cumbow decorates a full line of dinner ware, so a matching service is available.

In addition to china decorating, they also do restoration of fine ceramics, and as I learned when I sent some pieces to be mended, they were honest to tell me which pieces were not worth the cost of repair.

Cup and saucer ordered from Cumbow, 1978. Off-white. Earthenware (not ironstone); 12 panellel cup, flaring out at rim; 3½″ wide × 3¼″ high; comfortable, large handle. Saucer, 6″ in diameter, quite deep, also 12 panelled, convex at rim. Both on Simpson Ltd. blanks. Beautiful dark overglaze copper lustre.
CU-2

Crumbow trademark
CU-3

Three cups and saucers in squat style with deep rounded saucers. Purchased 1980. On Johnson Bros. blanks.   (90)
CU-4

Back stamp on all pieces at left. Notice patent number 187996.
CU-5

Note: Mrs. Ruskin passed away in March, 1980. The Company was closed and an October auction was the means of final dispersal. There is no more Cumbow China Decorating Company.

East End Pottery

1894-1909

This two-kiln works was established in East Liverpool in 1894 on the north side of the Cleveland and Pittsburgh Railroad on Railroad Street just east of Boyce. This is in the city's far east end just off Pennsylvania Avenue, the main highway from East Liverpool, northeast to Midland, Pennsylvania and points beyond.

The partners were Sampson Turnbull, Joseph Daekin, Edward J. Owens, and Gus Trenle, all practical potters. They made white ironstone (see the trademark) and semi-porcelain in decorated wares. W.P. Jervis remarked in his 1902 *Pottery Primer* that the Philadelphia Exhibition of 1876 had called attention to the lack of our use of decorated dinnerware (people had been using plain white, possibly with embossed designs). The foreign exhibitors brought their very finest and latest

Very attractive creamer, 6" high with same beading. One of their best pieces. (10)
EEP-1

Only mark I found on East End Pottery ware
EEP-2

creations to this show. Naturally, competitors took advantage an copied to their hearts' content. If all these partners were "practica potters," it is almost certain they changed their decorating style, thu their line did *not* read " 'plain' and decorated wares" as so many bio graphies of various potters had before.

Turnball and Daekin had retired before 1900, when they joined fiv other potteries in a cooperative venture under the name of East Liver pool Potteries Company, but that lasted only until 1903. This combin was formed to compete with Homer Laughlin; Knowles, Taylor & Knowles; W.S. George Potteries; Taylor, Smith and Taylor, and th Edwin M. Knowles Pottery, known in that area as the "Big Five." Members of this group were: East End Pottery; East Liverpool Potter Co.; The United States Pottery; Globe Pottery; Wallace and Chetwyn Pottery; and George C. Murphy Pottery.

After their unsuccessful merger, it reverted to the East End Potter for five years until 1909; then East End China Company, and finall reorganized to Trenle China Company — all the time since 1903 wit Gus Trenle at the head. Following a fire in 1912, they rebuilt wit added space and equipment. Gus Trenle was an old timer in Eas Liverpool and the father of Janice Brookman, an assistant librarian, wh was so much help to me in gathering all this material.

By 1917 the operation was changed to the manufacture of electrica porcelain and the name again changed, this time to Trenle Porcelai Company.

H.B. Barth reported in 1925 they had "constantly increasin success" and William Vodrey accounted for them in his pottery recor in 1945 that, in 1937, the company had moved to Ravenswood, Wes Virginia.

The photos shown here of the East End ware are of superior whit granite — ironstone — bodies, the tea pot and large wash bowl show n crazing and are very white, just as is the creamer. However, the platte is somewhat crazed and stained, while the square covered dish shows small amount of discoloration. Probably these last two items were use in the ovens, or at least in the warming ovens of Grandmas' stoves.

The company used several marks, but the one shown here is the onl mark I have seen on the Tea Leaf pieces. (The pitcher is unmarked.)

Group of items all made at East End Pottery: covered vegetable, 8" square, has fine beading on finial and handle matching right; the round ewer is 13½" high; one of several cups 3¼" high (no saucer); oval soap dish, no drainer, with overhanging lid, 5" × 6" with beading also; oval tea pot (no lid), 7½" high. All white, good quality ironstone with dark gold overglaze decoration.
EEP-3

Platter, very crazed and stained; most of Tea Leaf worn off bu good lustre on edge band. Same covered dish as in photo at left
EEP-4 (78

Goodwin Brothers Pottery Co.
1843-1911

Another of the early day potters who worked with James Bennett was John Goodwin, who went in business for himself in 1844. This tea pot made by Goodwin Bros. was the cause of all the research and the trail that led me to East Liverpool. The following account comes from the pen of Lucille T. Cox, who for many years was a resident of East Liverpool. My attempts to locate her were unsuccessful. According to my best information she left that city about 1953–4, and her whereabouts are unknown. Her eloquent use of words tells the John Goodwin story far better than I can. This was printed in the *Bulletin of the American Ceramic Society*, Vol, 21, No. 11, November 15, 1942, and sent to me by Mrs. Virginia Voedisch, librarian of this organization, whose help in so many, many ways was most welcome.

THE BULLETIN

OF

THE AMERICAN CERAMIC SOCIETY

4055 N. High St. Columbus, Ohio 43214

Volume 21	November 15, 1942	Number 11

THE STORY OF JOHN GOODWIN, PIONEER POTTER

By Lucille T. Cox

John Goodwin, one of the pioneer potters in America, was born in Burslem, England, in 1816. He worked in the James Edward Pottery in Dale Hall, Burslem, until 1842, when a strange event took place in his life.

During the opening years of the nineteenth century, England was faced with the problem of too many people. Her industrial towns were crowded centers of a teeming population living in filthy disease-ridden quarters. Compulsory emigration became the order of the day.

The *potters* in Burslem were *each given a number*. At stated times, drawings were made, and the men possessing the called numbers were required to leave England in a fortnight or face life imprisonment. They could go to one of the English colonies or, by special permission, to America. John Goodwin's number was selected in January, 1842. He had no choice but to sell his belongings, poor and meager as they were, send his wife and young daughter to his wife's parents, and leave England. He had no assurance that he would ever see his family again.

America or the colonies? John Goodwin chose America and embarked for New Orleans on a sailing vessel. He was sixty-one days on a mid-winter ocean in a coffin ship carrying a passenger list many times too large for its accommodations.

From New Orleans, the emigrant worked his way up the Mississippi as a roustabout on river steamers, stopping at St. Louis and finally Cincinnati.

The History of the Upper Ohio Valley, a volume published in 1891, tells of the next and final deciding step in his selection of a future home: "His next stopping place was Cincinnati, whither he went for the purpose of securing employment, but finding a scarcity of work, he started to Pittsburgh. While en route to the latter place, he learned there was a small pottery at East Liverpool, Ohio, so he concluded to make this town his objective point." He arrived in this river hamlet May 25, 1842.

Mr. Goodwin secured his first job in the factory of James Bennett,

The lone piece of Goodwin's pottery to come my way. This is the piece that led me to East Liverpool, Ohio, and opened up the world of American-made Tea Leaf to me. 9" high; no finial on lid; very brown and crazed; poor lustre. Oh, what tales it could tell! But so important to the book!
GB-1

Trademark on above
GB-2

the man who built the initial pottery in the town.[1] Later that same summer, he formed a partnership with Thomas Croxall and Edward Tunnecliff to make their own pottery. They had less than one hundred dollars and no equipment.

Benjamin Harker[2], who two years before had started a pottery on the Ohio River road east of the village, leased them his shop on equal shares. The plant consisted of a one-room cabin, a sliphouse, and an outside kiln. The blunger used in mixing the slip had been made by Isaac Knowles, the town carpenter[3]. All of the equipment was extremely primitive, and the ware produced was of inferior quality.

After several months of trying to make creditable ware, John Goodwin became impatient. He was certain that something was wrong with either the body or the firing and determined to investigate the cause. Finally, the Englishman decided that the ware was not being fired at the proper temperature.

Accordingly, one morning, he appeared in the kiln shed and announced to his partners that he was going to fire that particular kiln of ware.

Thomas Croxall, who had charge of the firing, was astonished almost beyond expression. "Ye 'ave na call to say I canna fire th' oven," he protested angrily. "Man an' lad I've fired ovens in th' ould countree for many a year."

Mr. Goodwin reiterated doggedly that he was going to fire the oven. His partner's indignation did not alter his determination. The potter was certain the ware was not being fired properly and he intended to correct this fault.

The first step was to tear out the fire pots and make them larger. Then he set about prewarming the kiln before loading it. When it had reached what he considered the proper temperature, he carried the filled saggers unassisted to the kiln, placed them, closed the opening with brick, and set about firing the kiln. The wood was piled in until the pots were crammed. The heat began to roll and the black smoke poured from the stack, but Mr. Goodwin did not relinquish his vigilance.

Mr. Croxall watched the proceeding with anxious eyes. Finally, he could no longer control his alarm. "John," he made one last protest. "Th' oven is too 'ot. The ware will be flown."

'Nay," retorted the dirty, perspiration-streaked fireman. "I wunna flown, dunt, crack, or make it crooked. The ware hasna been fired aright."

When the forty-eight hours allotted to the firing had elapsed, and the kiln had cooled for ten hours, the ware was ready to be drawn. Mr. Goodwin tore away the hot brick of the opening. The kiln was very warm, but it was possible to enter. He settled his padded cap more firmly on his head and went through the opening. Outside Thomas Croxall, Edward Tunnecliff, Benjamin Harker, and his two sons George and Benjamin, Jr., waited. No sound came from the depths of the round-bellied kiln. Tom Croxall became impatient and ran up the short flight of steps to the opening.

---

[1] For an account of the Bennett Pottery, see Bull. Amer. Ceram. Soc., 16 (1) 27–28, 30 (1937)

[2] The Harker Pottery Company celebrated its centennial anniversary in 1940. At this time, a history of the Pottery was published in Bull. Amer. Ceram. Soc., 20 (1) 25–27 (1941)

[3] Mr. Knowles later founded the Knowles, Taylor & Knowles Company and introduced machinery into ceramics in this country. For the story see Bull. Am. Ceram. Soc., 21 (8) 152–7 (1942)

"Comen out, John!" he called. "Whate're is th' matter?" he asked as he lowered his head and entered the kiln. "By Gonny!" His voice dropped to a shocked whisper. "Wun ye look at th' ware!"

The saggers and ware were fused into one solid, unmarketable lump and would have to be pried from the sides of the kiln with a crowbar.

It was a sad experience for John Goodwin — one that he never forgot. The severe financial loss, as represented by the worthless ware, did not, however, daunt the man. He used it as a steppingstone to greater achievements: In the winter of 1842–1843, he became dissatisfied with the arrangements at the Harker pottery and began manufacturing under his own name.

All the money he possessed was eighty dollars. With this small capital, he rented a vacant warehouse and remodeled it to suit the needs of a pottery doing all the work unassisted. It was a crude beginning, but it was the foundation for one of America's leading potteries of the nineteenth century.

The young potter labored long hours and lived frugally, and by the spring of 1843 had saved enough money to send for his wife and daughter. The young Englishwoman was not permitted to stay in America long, however, for she died the year following her arrival in the New World.

His wife's death, although a stunning blow to the potter, did not retard his ambition to become firmly established as a manufacturer. During the ensuing months, Mr. Goodwin astonished his fellow townsmen with his daring and initiative.

In 1845, he enlarged his production to include the making of Rockingham doorknobs, and he became the first potter in East Liverpool to make these necessary home accessories. These knobs were sold in the Pittsburgh market at four dollars a hundred, delivered.

Mr. Goodwin did not make his doorknobs by the same process used later by the Brunts[1]. Slip was mixed by the ancient "horse ring" method in a large vat sunk in the ground. Round and round the horse plodded in the vat until the clay and water were properly blunged. Then the slip was dipped from the huge tub into haircloth lawns through which it passed into containers known as "slip kilns." If the weather was sunny and the air hot, these kilns were left to dry naturally; otherwise fires were built beneath them. The clay was stirred constantly to keep it suspended until all the water had evaporated.

In the 1840s, the filter press and pug mill were unknown. John Goodwin took care of his clay as he had been taught in England. He wedged it by hand. The soft masses were pounded, cut, rolled, and pulled until every bubble had disappeared. It was then shaped into rolls. The clay was "thrown" into long "stalks," placed on boards, dried, turned, and "pinched" into the desired style.

Historians have accepted the belief that William Bloor was the first man to produce whiteware in East Liverpool.[1] From the records of John Goodwin, kept intact for many years by his son, James, and later by his grandson, the late Charles F. Goodwin, it has been definitely proved that John Goodwin made whiteware as early as 1846. According to Charles Goodwin, the entire story was set down in these record books by his grandfather at the time the whiteware was produced. He made several pieces of the ware, among them a custard cup which has been preserved until the present time.

The ware was made from samples of china clay mined near

---

[1] See "WILLIAM H. BLOOR," Bull. Amer. Ceram. Soc., 16 (1) 25–31 (1937)

Hollidaysburg, Pennsylvania, and from a specimen of clay from Missouri. The two clays had been sent to him for trial.

The potter mixed the widely separated clays, using no other ingredients. The combination produced a type of ware which took the uncertain glaze of that period perfectly. To the surprised workman, the ware closely resembled the Queen's ware of his native land. Mr. Goodwin was so impressed by the beauty of the pottery he had created that he recorded the process step by step.

The *East Liverpool Tribune* of October 24, 1891, printed the following story: "While digging the foundation for a new building at the pottery of S. & W. Baggott, workmen unearthed a relic of rare interest in pioneer pottery in the Ohio Valley. It was a small custard cup, made without handles, but with a foot and of handsome shape. It was a beautiful cream color, and the brilliancy of the glaze at once attracted the attention of the workmen. On the bottom of the cup, written in clay under the glaze in a bold hand, were the words 'J. Goodwin, 1846.' The cup was taken to the Goodwin brothers, who recognized their father's handwriting.

"Mr. James Goodwin consulted his father's memorandum books of 1846 and found the cup recorded. The clay used was a combination of clay sent to him from a mine near Hollidaysburg, Pennsylvania, and from Missouri.

"In those days, there were no such things as flint and feldspar. The remarkable thing is that the union of two clays and nothing else added to the body should produce such ware and take the glaze. The piece has stood the crucial test. For thirty-four years, since the fire of 1857 when the factory was badly damaged, this piece has lain buried in debris. The glaze has no sign of cracking or crazing.

"John Goodwin was then the first man to produce white- or cream-colored ware in East Liverpool. Other pieces of the same ware have been found, but the cup was the only whole piece. The Goodwin brothers have memoranda of these early tests, and Mr. Goodwin left his sons written testimony of his experiments."

The pioneer potter did not manufacture whiteware for sale. His production of it was brought about by the lucky fusion of two freak clays. He did, however, make whiteware almost at the beginning of the pottery industry in East Liverpool. Although this fact does not minimize the importance of William Bloor's contribution to American pottery making, it should establish some kind of record and obtain another bit of recognition for this famous potter of long ago.

Among the trials of the early potters was the problem of proper glazes. They could not be made according to formulas of the English potters for the simple reason that the necessary materials were not commonly used in America. The first ceramists in East Liverpool utilized the ingredients at hand, and the results were, to be conservative, quite remarkable.

John Goodwin was a master glazemaker. His reaction to the glaze used by his competitors was one of disgust mingled with impatience. The question baffled him, and no solution seemed possible because the proper materials were not available.

"I wunna turn out crockery with bad glaze," he declared emphatically to a friend one summer afternoon. "Any yet, I hardly know what to do about the matter."

"Come fishing with me," suggested his friend. "I always think better when I'm fishing."

John Goodwin laughed derisively. "I canna be making glaze out fishing." He took the man's arm and led him to the kiln-shed door. "See that pile of shard over yon? That is made from Pennsylvania and Missouri clays, and it turns out to be whiteware. Now, I've been thinking if I could grind up that shard and mix it wi' sand mebbe it 'as some 'idden properties. What think ye?"

"I wouldn't be able to help you," confessed his friend, wno was a prosperous farmer. "But there's sand along the river. Why not try it?"

A few weeks later, the two friends met in the village general store. "Well, John," the farmer inquired, "did the sand suit your purpose? I hear you've been doing a sizable amount of digging along the river shore. There's some people who think you're slightly batty."

"I will be soon, if I canna get a glaze to suit me," Mr. Goodwin replied wearily. "The sand was too dark and didna work. I must have white sand. And where can I be gettin' white sand about here?"

"Better come fishing," invited the farmer easily. "Out on Little Beaver Creek there's a good supply of white sand."

The suggestion was made so casually that Mr. Goodwin was about to refuse it impatiently when the import of the man's statement filtered through his harassed brain.

"Comen along," he shouted. "Let's go fishin'!"

The white sand along Little Beaver Creek proved to be the grade Mr. Goodwin needed. He mixed it carefully with ground white shard and produced a limited amount of exceptionally fine glaze, the pieces dipped in it were excellent and sold at prices heretofore unknown among the local potters. He could leave no written proportions of that early formula, however, for the hidden properties of the Pennsylvania and Missouri clays remained a secret he could not probe.

In 1846 the pottery industry of East Liverpool was very small. There were five potteries, and thirty men, beside the employers, worked in the shops. Union and wage agreements were unknown, yet the first strike in the local potteries occurred that year, and the cause was "lack of uniform wages."

One evening in the autumn of 1846, a workman from the John Goodwin pottery entered Josiah Thompson's general store. A group of men were gathered about the glowing fireplace. It was Saturday and payday in the shops. The weekly store orders, given in lieu of money, were filled and waiting in baskets to be taken home.

"It won't take long to fill your order," Thompson told the newcomer. "John Goodwin is the only boss who pays this way."

"Aye," replied the Englishman. "John 'as been in the ould countree and knows what it means to do without cash."

"We get paid in money, too," interrupted a tall potter, whose sallow complexion and quick cough was indicative of his occupation.

"That!" The first man spat contemptuously. "A shilling maybe, but no a fat sum alike we get. John pays us 'alf an' 'alf."

A hush fell over the group. The men shifted their feet uneasily and looked at each other questioningly.

"Alf an' 'alf what?" asked a man from the far edge of the group.

"Alf money, 'alf victuals," elucidated the Goodwin potter briefly. "Ye dinna get more than a few pence an' the rest in store orders. On pay nights, John gives us 'alf our wages in cash, th' other 'alf in store orders."

The seed of discontent was sown and began to bear fruit on Monday when the men returned to their benches. The rumbles of insurrection spread throughout the shops like wildfire. Wednesday afternoon, the three workmen on the payroll of the Ball and Morris pottery confronted Thomas Ball with the ultimatum that he pay them " 'alf an' 'alf" or they would refuse to work.

The scene was repeated in other potteries during the next few days.

The man at the bench was beginning to assert the freedom he had come so far to find. The manufacturers could not cope with the problem, and an indignant meeting was held in John Goodwin's pottery.

" 'Tis a lot o' foolishness," fumed James Salt. "Must ye be different from the rest o' us, John Goodwin?"

John Goodwin tilted his chair on its back legs and became interested in a small knife he held in his work-hardened hand.

"This time ten years ago," he responded slowly, "I was afraid to call my name my own. I worked sixteen hours a day and had no money for my 'ire, only orders on the tommy shops in the ould countree. Sumtimes I 'ad no store orders if the buttie at the James Edwards potbank saw fit to take out for breakage. I know what it means not to 'ave enough to eat or to wear. I'm treatin' my men alike I'd want them to treat me if I was aworkin' for them. You men," he raised his head and peered at them sternly, "are na so far from England's Potter's Quarters to be forgettin' what ye 'ad to put up with over there!"

The fearless words of the English potter brought an exchange of shame-faced glances between his visitors. Benjamin Harker cleared his throat loudly.

"Ye are right, John," he conceded hastily. "We almost forgot that we are no pot-masters in the ould countree, but we are in America now, free men. We've na right to put on our men what we left behind in England. I'll pay my men 'alf an' 'alf."

The strike ended almost before it began, and the men received their weekly wages the following Saturday night " 'alf an' 'alf!"

Labor troubles, poor materials, and lack of markets were only a few of the difficulties besetting the early potters. Among the legion of problems they had to overcome was the "wildcat" money flooding the country in the year preceding the Civil War.

The only stable pieces of money were the half-cent, cent, nickel, dime, quarter, half-dollar, and dollar. All paper currency was issued by banks in various large cities. A five-dollar note issued from a Wheeling bank would have a value of three dollars when redeemed in Pittsburgh. Thus the term "wildcat" money came into common usage.

As a result of the uncertain condition of paper currency, the readers of pottery history have a choice story to chuckle over — the story of John Goodwin and Joseph Cartwright. The latter operated a storeboat between East Liverpool and New Orleans.

Mr. Cartwright, in the spring of 1848, purchased ware from John Goodwin to stock his boat for his annual trip down the river. The only financial arrangement made between the two was the profit Mr. Cartwright was to make on the sale of the goods. A day or so after his departure from town, John Goodwin realized that he had not specified what kind of money the merchant was to use in paying him for the dishes. He knew that unless he did something immediately, he stood in a fair way of losing all his profits on the transaction. Accordingly, he boarded the next down-river boat and sighted the storeboat tied up at a wharf near Wheeling, West Virginia.

Joseph Cartwright was surprised to see his visitor. "Good evening to ye, John," he rose from his seat on the narrow deck and held out his hand in greeting. "What brings ye here?"

" 'Tis this," replied Mr. Goodwin without preliminaries. "We made no plans for payment of the crocks. Ye must not be payin' me in truck or bad money."

Mr. Cartwright was justifiably angry, and the conversation between the two men became spirited. Mr. Goodwin, however, left the store owner with the assurance that he would be paid in good money.

One evening late in the summer of the same year, Joseph Cartwright returned to East Liverpool on the steamboat Winchester. As the boat docked, he called to a small lad standing on the beach and instructed him to get John Goodwin. The latter was to bring a wheelbarrow with him.

A few minutes later, the potter, pushing a wheelbarrow, came hustling down the narrow path leading to the river's edge.

"Gud evening to ye, Joe," he greeted the other man breathlessly. "Just what do ye want with this barrow?"

"Your good money is here on deck. You best have help in gettin' it," replied Mr. Cartwright nonchalantly.

John Goodwin hurried aboard. It was as the merchant had said. He needed help. A gunny sack filled with clinking coins lay on the deck. The potter, with the aid of one of the deck hands, carried the bag down the gangplank and placed it in the wheelbarrow. He began his laborious trip to the pottery, followed by a number of laughing and curious townfolks.

When Mr. Goodwin arrived at his shop, the contents of the sack were dumped on the warehouse floor. It was good money as he had requested, but it was half-pennies and one-cent pieces. It took the greater part of three days to separate and count the financial return from the business deal he had contracted with Joseph Cartwright.

In the East Liverpool Historical Society collection is a handbill, printed in 1850, telling of the various pieces of merchandise produced by the Goodwin pottery. The ware was extremely diversified and speaks highly of the business acumen and ability of the man who had started his pottery eight years before with the meager capital of eighty dollars.

LIST OF MERCHANDISE PRODUCED BY THE JOHN GOODWIN POTTERY, 1850

Yellow Ware	Rockingham	
Chambers	Pressed pitchers	Pressed sugars
Pitchers	Flowerpots	Spittoons
Bowls	Turned ewers	Salad dishes
Milk pans	Pressed teapots	Butter tubs
Flowerpots	Bedpans	Turned washbowls
Twelve-in. dishes	Turned pitchers	Coffeepots
Twelve-in. nappies	Honey bowls	Pressed creamers
Pie plates	Pressed ewers	Sauce dishes

Some of the records of those early days tell that John Goodwin "made yellow ware and Rockingham so thick and heavy that a breakfast cup could be used in lieu of a carpenter's hammer."

In 1853, Mr. Goodwin sold his pottery to Samuel and William Baggott, eccentric Staffordshire potters, and for the next few years dropped out of the pottery business entirely. He sold real estate, entered politics, and tried his hand at various occupations. But not for long, for the art of making dishes was in his blood, and he could not remain away from his potter's wheel for any length of time.

An old history of Columbiana County, Ohio, relates the following concerning his activities during the next few years: "John Goodwin Sr., who had operated in real estate for several years after selling his original plant to the Baggotts in 1853, re-entered the pottery business in 1863 when he built a plant on the southeast corner of Broadway and Sixth Street in East Liverpool. The factory was composed of two kilns and was one of the first plants in East Liverpool to have been designed by an architect. In 1865, he abruptly withdrew from the concern and remained out of pottery making for nearly five years."

The centennial edition of the *East Liverpool Review*, printed in 1934, resumes the story of John Goodwin's ceramic efforts: "In 1870, John Goodwin went to Trenton, New Jersey, where he was interested in the Trenton Pottery Company for two years." Behind that bald statement of facts lies a story of a father's ambition for his sons and his hope that they would follow him as potters. He had three children by a second marriage, James, Henry, and George. As the boys neared manhood, he decided to launch them in the career of pottery manufacturing. The Trenton Pottery Company was comprised of James Taylor and Henry Speeler, former East Liverpool potters, and John Goodwin. The new firm was organized as Taylor, Goodwin & Co.

The American potters were suffering keenly from the unfair treatment they were receiving from foreign trade propagandists, and the factories were operating at partial capacity production. Buying of American pottery dropped away to almost nothing, and it seemed for a time as though American potteries would soon be only a memory. Then, an enterprising domestic manufacturer conceived the idea of marking his ware with a foreign trademark and offering it as English or French merchandise. The result was amazing, sales gained a new tempo, and the public was hoodwinked into believing the new patterns were of foreign creation. The trademark "T-G&Co." found on the bottom of John Goodwin's Trenton-made ware was interpreted as belonging to a then famous English ceramic company which had the same initials. When John Goodwin discovered the hoax and found that their spurt of prosperity was due to misrepresentation, he sold his share of the pottery to his partners and returned to East Liverpool in 1872.

The *Review* account picks up the story again: "In 1872, he returned to East Liverpool and purchased the Broadway pottery from James Foster and Timothy Rigby. He acquired additional land and engaged in the manufacturing of whiteware, which was then securing its start in East Liverpool. John Goodwin died in 1875, leaving the business to his sons, James, George, and Henry Goodwin, who formed the Goodwin Brothers pottery to manufacture white granite."

The factory John Goodwin purchased was equipped to make Rockingham and yellow ware. When the pioneer's death occurred in 1875, plans were afoot to make the expensive change to white ware production. The demise of their father placed the sons in a precarious position. They knew additional money was necessary before they could complete the projected plans, and the question of finance became serious.

"James, I am certain Father left more money than we have accounted for in the estate," George Goodwin told his brother wearily one afternoon as the two left their attorney's office. "I have literally turned our house inside out, and I can find no trace of it."

"We may have misunderstood Father about the bonds," his older brother replied thoughtfully. "Perhaps he used his surplus when we purchased that plant. We will have to do the best we can, but a few extra thousand dollars right now would mean the difference between our operation as white ware potters or our staying in the rut we are in now."

"I'm not going to give up," George answered doggedly. "I'm positive Father left bonds."

For several weeks, the brothers continued a diligent search for the missing bonds. Everyone knew of the aged potter's habit of hiding money in unexpected places. Carpets were lifted and presses and bureau drawers were inspected closely, but the bonds were not to be found. The two older Goodwin brothers were ready to give up the quest. They were convinced that the bonds were lost or their father had cashed them three years before.

One day, a few months after his father's death, Henry, the youngest son, called at his brother James' home for a romp with his four-year-old nephew, John. Before long, the two were playing boisterously on the floor.

"Watch out, lad," Henry cautioned John. "We almost knocked Grandpa's chair galley west."

He pushed the horsehair-upholstered rocker, which had been his father's favorite chair, out of the way. The child, seeing his opportunity, leaped on the back of his youthful uncle, and the two rolled against the chair, which crashed over on one side. They settled back, and Henry surveyed the chair with astonishment. The burlap webbing had been torn loose from the bottom, and a long packet of papers lay in plain view. Henry tore away the outside cover and there were the long-lost bonds — $5,000 worth. The brothers were able to make the needed improvements in their pottery and begin the production of white graniteware.

The era of machinery used in pottery making was in its infancy during the early years of the Goodwin Brothers pottery. The pulldown jigger and filter press were the first pieces of machinery used in making pottery, and they were operating in only a few of the plants. Wedging, slip kilns, blindfolded horses treading about slip vats, throwing, turning, and pressing were utilized in a large majority of the plants, particularly the trade of wedging. Every sliphouse had bricked-up plaster of Paris-covered wedging blocks, and the wedgers were men of great strength. Day after day, the wedger would lift heavy chunks of moist clay high above his head and bring them to his block with resounding thuds. His skillful fingers would knead and pummel the mass until all the air bubbles were removed. The introduction of a machine to replace this ancient trade came as a complete surprise to the potters and was brought about by James Goodwin.

The story of the first pug mill comes from the memory of the late Charles F. Goodwin, a son of the man who was responsible for its induction.

"In 1880," Mr. Goodwin related, "my father was vacationing in Wisconsin and visited a lumber factory where his attention was drawn to an ingenious machine known as a wood-pulp mill. As Father watched the uniform operation of the wood being fed into the hopper and emerging as pulp from the bottom of the mill, a fantastic idea flashed into his mind. Could clay be fed into a similar machine? Would the knives be sharp enough to find all of the air bubbles and would the pressure be sufficient to press the clay through the opening at the foot of the machine? He became so obsessed with the idea that before he left Wisconsin he purchased one of the machines and ordered it sent to our factory.

"A week or so after his return, the machine was delivered. It was an unwieldy contraption, and the wedgers in the sliphouse watched its installation with amused contempt. The mill was an upright type, standing six feet above the floor. A series of shafts, knives, and inter-meshing wheels was operated by steam from the engine room. The mill was set solidly on a stone foundation. The opening at the bottom of the large cask stood 18 inches from the floor. Everything was in readiness for the experiment.

"The workman hauled the leaves of clay to position by the large mill. The lever was thrown, and the wheels, shafts, and knives sprang into action. The pugger (as he was known later) folded the first leaf of clay and dropped it into the mill. The crowd was breathless. There was no sound in the sliphouse except the throbbing of the ex-wood pulp machine. Other leaves followed. Then from the hole at the bottom of the mill emerged a cylindrical stream of smooth clay. It moved into a trough and was sliced into long rolls for the jiggermen."

The pug mill became an accepted necessity to the potters, but it was protested for many years by the wedgers. For a long time, if a jiggerman wished to have his clay pugged instead of wedged, he had to pay the wedger for the accomodation. The pattern taken from the wood-pulp machine was used in the manufacturing of pug mills for many years. After a time, improvements were added, but the elementary principles remain the same today as they were in the machine James Goodwin brought from Wisconsin more than sixty years ago.

The *Review* centennial edition relates that "the Goodwin Brothers Pottery company was incorporated in 1893." The pottery was growing by leaps and bounds. Reduced tariff, walkouts, and strikes were accepted as part of a pottery manufacturer's life, and the pottery was well on the way to becoming one of the most progressive plants in the industry. They brought out a new shape in dinner ware, quite an innovation in the days when practically every pottery made Cableware year in and year out. The dinner set was named "Fawcett" after Thomas Fawcett, one of their ancestors and the founder of the town. Its introduction caused quite a furor among the potters. Every indication pointed to success for the Goodwin Brothers pottery when, in 1896, tragedy struck the firm.

On election day of that year, James Goodwin, who was the motivating power of the organization, was found dead from a heart attack. He had worked unceasingly to bring about the presidential election of his friend, William McKinley. His untimely death closed a successful career as a pottery manufacturer and ceramic authority.

The centennial edition tells simply and graphically of the closing days of the Goodwin pottery. "James Goodwin's place in the business was taken by his two sons, John S. Goodwin and Charles F. Goodwin, who continued in the firm established by their grandfather until the death of John 1909 and the retirement of his two uncles. The Company discontinued operation in 1911.

"Even though the Goodwin family was no longer identified with the industry as active manufacturers, Charles Goodwin remained as an important executive of the industry from 1912, when he was elected secretary-treasurer of the United States Potters Association, until his death in December, 1941."[6]

There is a number of descendants of John and Esther Goodwin living in East Liverpool and in scattered parts of America. Their occupations have taken them far afield from the art of making pottery. Most of them are successful in their chosen trades, and, although one or two members of the Goodwin family are employed in pottery making, none are manufacturers. The death, therefore, of Charles Fawcett Goodwin, which occurred while he was attending the annual convention of the United States Potters Association in Cleveland, Ohio, marked the end of the Goodwin family as pottery manufacturers and executives in ceramic endeavors, after a continuous span of ninety-nine years of service in that capacity.

For a biographical sketch of Mr. Goodwin, see Bull. Amer. Ceram. Soc., 21 (1) 5 (1942).

NOTES FOR CERAMISTS

JOHN GOODWIN — Story of Pioneer Potter

In the November, 1942, issue of *The Bulletin*, the feature historical story was of John Goodwin, written by Lucille T. Cox. On her feature stories Mrs. Cox is a painstaking research worker, and in this instance she relied on family records and legendary stories passed down through the generations of Goodwins. Those of the Goodwin descendants who read Mrs. Cox's story confirmed the story as being factual.

Legendary stories surely do get twisted far from the facts even in a short space of time, as each one knows from personal experience. No wonder that through a century history, stories of John Goodwin as passed on by the descendants became warped.

The only legendary Goodwin story that is not in line with the facts is that "During the opening years of the nineteenth century, England was faced with the problem of too many people. Her industrial towns were crowded centers of a teeming population living in filthy disease-ridden quarters. Compulsory emigration became the order of the day.

"The potters in Burslem were each given a number. At stated times, drawings were made, and the men possessing the called numbers were required to leave England in a fortnight or face life imprisonment. They could go to one of the English colonies or, by special permission, to America. John Goodwin's number was selected in January, 1842. He had no choice but to sell his belongings, poor and meager as they were, send his wife and young daughter to his wife's parents, and leave England."

The Goodwin story as presented by Mrs. Cox, based on family records, goes on to relate that in the spring of the following year (1843) John Goodwin had established a factory and had saved enough money to send for his wife and daughter. This he is said to have accomplished in a period of not more than eighteen months, and concerning this there is no doubt.

Mrs. Cox's attention was called by Dr. Andrew Dingwall to the probable inaccuracy of the statement that John Goodwin had been compelled to leave England. As the result of his communications with the British Information Services, the two following letters were received, and it is out of respect to the recorded excellent achievements and character of John Goodwin that they are now published:*

Letter No. 1

In reply to your inquiry about compulsory emigration from England in the 19th Century, we are unable to find any evidence that there was such emigration. The parliamentary Statistics of the period contain no provisions for enforced emigration.

The phenomenal growth of the population at the beginning of the 19th Century, together with the severe economic depression after the Napoleouic wars, were the chief causes which promoted emigration from Great Britian at that time. In 1817, a Select Committee on Poor Law had recommended "that all obstacles to seeking employment wherever it can be found, even out of the realm, should be removed, and every facility that is reasonable afforded to those who *may wish* to resort to some of our colonies." From then on the outflow to North America and the Colonies grew annually, and Parliament voted large sums of money for the assistance of those seeking to leave.

Emigration was at that time painted in such glowing terms, that far from being compulsory, it became the poor man's dream — to leave

---

* From "The Bulletin of the American Ceramic Society," Vol. 23, No. 11

behind him the acute economic distress at home and try his fortune in the New World. The chief difficulty was to provide sufficient funds for all those who wished to go.

Among other sources of assistance, various trade unions started emigration funds, and "The Potters Joint Stock and Emigration Co." at Burslem was the first to do so. It had for its object the purchase of 12,000 acres of land in the Western States which it proposed to sell in small lots to members at cost prices, repayments being made by installments spread over the years. People within the Staffordshire district paid a fee of sixpence weekly and became members emigrating in due course. Apparently John Goodwin was among them.

A system of numbers may very likely have been used to determine which members should be the first to leave, but any suggestion that departure was compulsory seems to be completely without foundation.

(signed) J.A.W. Bennett,
Information Division
British Information Services,
30 Rockefeller Plaza,
(1944)   New York, N.Y.

Letter No. 2

Whilst I was in England last month I discussed with several historians the story about John Goodwin which you drew to my attention some time ago, and we have since received a reply from the Home Office substantiating the view which everyone whom I consulted took, namely, that "In 1842, when John Goodwin is said to have drawn an unlucky number, the only system of compulsory emigration was that provided by the various Transportation Acts. These provided that for many specified offenses a person could be sentenced or ordered to be transported to some place out of the United Kingdom. It was essential, however, that in every case there should be a conviction of an offense by a competent court." But, of course, transportation to America had ceased with the American War of Independence in 1776, so the possibility of that sort of compulsory emigration does not arise in John Goodwin's case. One is justified, therefore, in making a complete denial of the suggestion that John Goodwin was forced to emigrate, and if necessary you may quote the Home Office as your authority.

(signed) J.A.W. Bennett

Hall China —
Red Cliff

1903 to present

My visit to the Hall China Company was one of the highlights of my visit to East Liverpool in 1973. This modern plant is a far cry from the early beginning as recorded in 1924 by the late Mr. Harold Barth in his *History of Columbiana County:*

In 1894 a company consisting of John W. Hall, Robert Hall and Monroe Patterson, purchased the defunct (Lincoln Pottery) plant and operated it as The East Liverpool Pottery Company. Ironstone and decorated ware were made. After nine years of successful operation the concern with seven others in the city combined as The East Liverpool Potteries Companies which held together for but two years. Out of the disintegration the Hall China Company was formed. It was composed of John W. Hall, Charles Hall and Robert Hall, Jr., the latter's father having died in 1903. After several years the company finally composed of Robert Hall, Jr., his brother-in-law, Frank I. Simmers, and Malcoln Thompson, stressed the manufacture of hard, vitrified fireproof china, which necessitated the purchase of the old Goodwin Bros., Pottery at Sixth and Broadway which is now plant number Two of the concern. Mr. Hall died November 20, 1920 and Messrs. Simmers and Thompson are now its motivating forces.

Now let us read the continuing history as recorded in the "Bulletin of the American Ceramic Society" for August 15, 1945, Vol. 24, No. 8, pages 280–281:

HISTORY OF THE HALL CHINA COMPANY
EAST LIVERPOOL, OHIO

On the afternoon of July 7, 1903, the former partners in the inoperative East Liverpool Potteries Company met in the home of Robert Hall to settle the affairs and distribute the physical assets of the Company. Mr. Hall accepted, as his share, ownership of the plant located on the southeast corner of East Fourth and Walnut Streets, which had previously been known as the West, Hardwick and George Pottery. Thirty-eight days later, on August 14, 1903, he founded The Hall China Company, East Liverpool, Ohio. Three oven kilns were fired, and thirty-three potters began to make bed pans and combinets, the first chinaware to bear the trade name, Hall China.

The Company, born among the depressing ashes of failure, arose, not phoenixlike, but feeble and struggling for the very breath of life. It suffered from lack of capital and scrambled in stiff competition with more than a score of other small potteries. What plans Mr. Hall had for its future, what success he might have made of his unpromising acquisition, were never to be known. For, before he had an opportunity to get well under way, he died, in 1904, the year following the founding of the Company.

Development of Single-Fire Process

Mr. Robert Taggart Hall, son of the founder, assumed the management. Very early in his new job he began to investigate the possibilities of developing a glaze that would stand the heat required for bisque firing, thus making possible single-fire ware that would be proof against crazing. He had little to guide him. Ancient history books reputed that a single-fire china had been made during the Ming dynasty (A. D. 1368-1644) in China, but the lore was lost, and beyond the encouraging fact that what had been done could be done again, Mr. Hall had no precedent to follow. His practical experience, and that of his superintendent, Robert Meakin, made it clear, however, that a leadless glaze was necessary to the successful development of the single-fire process, for lead could not stand the temperature necessary for bisque firing.

From 1905 to 1911, Mr. Hall experimented tirelessly to develop the single-fire process and struggled to produce, at a profit, sufficient white ware, such as combinets, bed pans, mugs, and jugs, to keep the Company in operation. Dinnerware, added to the line in 1908, was made in small quantities until 1914, at which time its manufacture was discontinued until much later in the Company's history.

The fact that the Hall kilns kept burning during the initial years was due largely to the efforts of Francis I. Simmers, who became associated with Robert Taggart Hall soon after the death of the founder. During those lean days, Mr. Simmers kept the orders coming in and laid the ground work for later development.

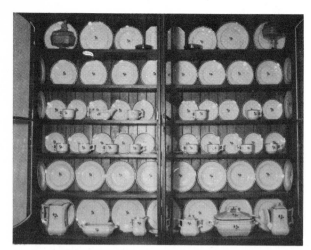

A beautiful reproduction line made for the Red Cliff Company of Chicago by Hall China Company and Walker China Co. This service-for-twelve collection was received by the owners as a wedding gift in 1960, just as Red Cliff was being discontinued in the stores.

RC-1   (67)

So meager was the Company's income during this early period that payday for the plant employees was often just another day of worry and struggle for the management. Looking backward, it now seems that 1910 was the year of darkness before the dawn. On Memorial Day of that year, vandals entered the sliphouse, slashed the engine belts to ribbons, tore the pug mill apart, and riddled the silk lawns of the slip sifters, leaving behind them damage to the extent of $3000, an almost catastrophic loss. The vandals, or the motives that impelled them, were never discovered.

This incident seemed to spur Robert Hall's determination to produce china ware by the single-fire process. Intensified research followed, and early in 1911, Mr. Hall and Jackson Moore, superintendent, who had succeeded Mr. Meakin in 1910, were to see the long search crowned with success.

First Successful Leadless Glaze

The first successful leadless glaze, in 1911, was mixed in a mortar with a pestle, and the quantity was just sufficient to dip half a mug. The mug was placed in the hottest part of the kiln, where the temperature was about 2200°F., and the result was "fair," which means that it was good enough to encourage further efforts. More of the glaze was prepared and a few bed pans were fired, and again the results were encouraging rather than successful. Next, it was decided to load an entire kiln with the glaze-dipped unfired bisque. The result pointed the way to complete success, for the pieces in the hottest part of the kiln were almost perfect, whereas those in the coolest part were unsatisfactory. It was obvious that a hotter fire was needed, so another load was fired at a maintained temperature of 2400°F., and when the kiln door opened, a new era was ushered in for The Hall China Company.

The ware that came from that kiln in 1911 was strong, hard, nonporous, and crazeproof. When Francis I. Simmers examined it, he turned to his partner and said, "Bob, if you continue to make ware like that, I'll sell so much of it you'll have to double the plant." Bob Hall did make the ware, and Ruby Simmers sold it in ever-increasing quantities.

In a few months, production had grown from two dozen to sixteen dozen pieces a day. And, although this is small in the light of today's output, it loomed large in comparison with the starvation years which had preceded it. If the Company was still a small youngster, it had now definitely survived and outgrown the vicissitudes of its enfeebled and precarious infancy.

The team of Robert Taggart Hall to make the ware and Francis I. Simmers to sell it worked in complete harmony. From 1911 to 1920, when Mr. Hall succumbed from a heart attack, the two men held the position of president alternately, a year at a time. Since the death of Mr. Hall, Mr. Simmers has served continuously as the Company's president.

1914 Brings Opportunities

The year 1914 brought opportunities of which the joint managers were quick to take advantage. Because of the war, European potteries, formerly the chief source of supply for stoneware items such as steam-table insets, coffee urn liners, and other vessels used in the preparation and serving of food, were unable to continue to make or ship their products to the United States.

All available production facilities at Hall were devoted to the manufacture of casseroles, teapots, coffeepots, coffee urn liners, and similar items for the institutional trade. The war thus gave impetus to the trend toward Hall China cooking ware that had started in 1911 with the introduction of the single-fire product.

The more widespread use of Hall China during this period demonstrated to hundreds of institutional men the difference between the European ware and Hall single-fire china. The imported ware was soft, porous, absorbent; the finish rough. Hall China was smooth, nonabsorbent, and glistening when new; it was still smooth, nonabsorbent, and glistening after extended use.

When the war ended, and cheaper importations entered the country, users of Hall China had learned that it was less expensive in terms of cost per year and immensely cheaper in the subtler items of food preservation and customer satisfaction. Hall China was in the market to stay.

Growth Continues

In 1919, Hall's production facilities were increased through the purchase of the plant of the Goodwin Pottery Company at East Sixth and

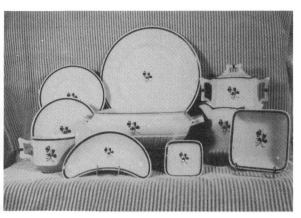

*This smaller service for six was received by the owners
as a wedding gift in 1980.* (36)

RC-2

Broadway, and an entirely new line was introduced — gold-decorated tea pots for the retail trade. Coincidentally with the introduction of Hall China gold-decorated tea pots, the Company engaged in a campaign, which has been sustained throughout the years, to educate the American housewife in the proper method of brewing tea and the proper pot in which to brew it. Hall soon became world's largest manufacturer of decorated tea pots, a position it has consistently maintained.

The Company's sales of institutional cooking ware and decorated tea pots continued to grow, and as they grew, new executive personnel was engaged. Malcolm W. Thompson, who joined the Company in 1920, is now treasurer and general manager. William J. Hocking started in 1921 and is today the Company's purchasing agent. Joseph D. Thompson, who became a member in 1925, is now secretary and sales manager. Robert H. Simmers joined in 1924 and has been vice-president since 1940. The Company's engineering and design staff was also enlarged and has been regularly augmented during the course of the years, and the policy of continuing research pursued by this staff, headed by L. H. Brown, has been largely responsible for the successful development of a wide variety of under-glaze colors, the series of design innovations that were issued by Hall before the present war, and the many advancements in manufacturing methods that have contributed to maintenance of high quality in finished ware.

In 1927, a third plant was opened and its facilities were used exclusively to produce a new line — soda-fountain jars. Another new line was introduced during the following year — decorated cooking china, distributed through retail-trade channels.

New Factory

Success brings its problems as well as its triumphs. Consequently, in 1929, the Hall management, realizing that the Company's growth was destined to exceed the capacity of its three potteries and that obsolescence of equipment made imperative the need for new and more efficient methods and facilities, decided to erect an entirely new factory and to abandon the three old plants upon its completion.

A tract of twenty-three acres in the East End became the site for the building which was first occupied in 1930. The new factory was 250 feet wide by 680 feet long, and there were approximately 170,000 square feet of floor space, all on one floor. The entire floor space was open, and the production layout enabled continuous, progressive movement of work. Firing equipment in the new factory consisted of three tunnel kilns — one open-fire multiburner, one muffle-fire, and one semimuffle-fire glost kiln. All were fired with natural gas. The open-fire unit was turned in when the building was first occupied. The glost kiln was turned in the following year, and the muffle-fire unit was placed in operation in 1933.

In 1933, The Hall China Company engaged in the manufacture of decorated cooking china, tea pots, and coffee-makers. The year 1936 brought further expansion in the line, when, for the first time since 1914, dinner ware took shape on the jiggerman's wheel, flowed through glazing, firing, decorating, and inspection processes to the shipping room, and thence to market.

The Company's activities in these fields have necessitated eight additions to the building and the installation of four other firing units. The additions, the first of which was made in 1934 and the last of which was completed in 1941, have provided a total of 385,000 square feet of floor space. The additional firing equipment consists of a circular electric kiln and a gas-fired multiburner turned in 1935, a circular gas-fired glost kiln turned in 1936, and a return-tray electric decorating kiln installed in 1937.

The war has brought new problems to The Hall China Company, as it has all other American manufacturers. Yet it seems that adversity has always been a stepping-stone to greater success at Hall, and those who keep their fingers on the pulse of the ceramic industry will continue to observe with keen interest how Hall solves its war and postwar problems.

(Printed 1945.)

Today modern potteries in America use every means at their command to provide pleasant working conditions. One of the greatest improvements is in the firing process. Originally the stovepipe kilns, fired by coal, were always belching out great black clouds of killing smoke; that, coupled with the dust from inside, produced "smog" — our new term for an old problem. Conversion to gas or electrically-fired tunnel kilns has eliminated this pall that hung over the Staffordshire and the American potteries. Today each machine which produces dust of any kind, or fumes of any sort, has a vacuum fan that pulls it away from the worker. Lung diseases in the potteries are now at normal levels with other industries.

Another method used to improve production is more pleasant surroundings so workmen are content to stay on one job. In the decorating department of Hall China Company I met four ladies who had been on the same job for forty years or more: Pauline Meigh, Dorothy Mountford, Zella Herbert, and Dorothy Kraft; and Mr. Eynon William ("Dutch") Friess, a gilder, who has been with Hall forty-eight years. The day I was there Mr. Everson Hall, the plant foreman, *asked* them to work an hour overtime; he did not *tell* them they had to work. The rapport I felt in that pottery is one of the outstanding memories of my visit. My guide was Mr. "Skip" Dawson, a color chemist, who missed his lunch that day. I had stopped to thank Mr. John T. Hall, the president, for his hospitality and cooperation. Mr. Hall had been most gracious in directing me to the proper sources for my research and in answering my inquiry about the Tea Leaf made by Hall China Company a few years ago. He even "scrounged" the neighborhood to find a sugar and creamer Hall had made for the Red Cliff Company. The few minutes I intended to stay in Mr. Hall's office stretched into several hours, but after a tour of the entire plant, with explanations by Mr. Dawson, I came away with the sure knowledge that Hall China Company has many employees who are living proof that our system of free enterprise really works!

During that visit some more interesting history came to light. One of the most important factors in the life of this company was the production of the Jewel Tea premium ware, which is so familiar to most of us. It was literally the life-blood of the company for several years and mute evidence of the fine quality of all Hall china is the durability of this modern day favorite.

Many people have confused this Jewel Tea design with Tea Leaf but the former, in shades of yellow, orange, and brown, is quite different from our favorite motif. Notice the comparison pictures. There is no copper lustre on the Jewel Tea design. This copper lustre was a provoking problem to Hall China Co. in their production of Tea Leaf for the Red Cliff Company in the 1950s and 1960s as shown in the following letter.

Dear Ms. Heaivilin:

I am sending to you, by UPS today, samples of a Sugar and Cream Set that Hall China made in the Tea Leaf pattern for

Red Cliff Company
1911 North Clybourn Avenue
Chicago, Illinois

This was made in the late 50's or early 60's and was an attempt to copy the English Ironstone Tea Leaf.

One of the main problems in this type of decoration was our inability to develop a bronze tea leaf which would withstand dishwashers. The English method of years ago was to decorate the item with a brown tea leaf underglaze, and then after the piece had been fired apply a luster and fire again.

This worked reasonably well for hand washing and in the case of the British product, as the luster wears off, the brown tea leaf remains. In our case, we were not able to apply the tea leaf underglaze and consequently tried to apply the tea leaf by decal only. This was not successful, and the item was discontinued.

As I mentioned before, we made these items exclusively for the Red Cliff

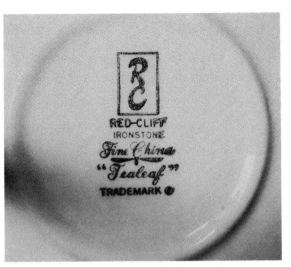

All Red Cliff china is well marked, even the cups. Any one of these marks may be found.
RC-3

Two more trademarks
RC-4

Company in Chicago and I am sure that if you write Mr. Fred Clifford, at that company, he will be happy to supply you with advertising literature.

Please let me know if there is anything further I can do to help.

Mr. Hall went on to relate how Mr. Fred Clifford of the Red Cliff Company had purchased original pieces of English Tea Leaf and sent them to Hall China Company to copy for reproductions of this fine old ware. It is very interesting to compare the Wedgwood fluted design with the Red Cliff shape; and the sharp square Clifford shape is so very much like the Meakin oblong tureen of the Jansen collection; and the Stancliff cake plate is very much like the Meakin cake plate. He also reminded me that gold or copper lustre is not microwave-oven safe and all Hall china ware is safe in these new type ovens.

The large photos and the sales brochure were furnished by Mr. Fred Clifford of Chicago, while the individually owned set was purchased as a wedding gift in the early 1960s from Ring's Department Store in Macomb, Illinois. Mr. Ring's advice to the purchaser was to buy all they would need or want as it was to be discontinued. Some of the service was still in the original boxes all marked "Oven-Proof." Our grandmothers evidently took for granted their Tea Leaf was "oven proof" as evidenced by the great amount of brown-stained ware we see today.

My first introduction to Red Cliff Tea Leaf was in Topeka, Kansas as Johana Anderton and I were on our way to photograph a huge Tea Leaf collection and "just couldn't pass up that garage sale." Johana spied the pieces first and whispered excitedly, "Buy it! Buy it! It's beautiful!" It was and I did and I've never been sorry because it really is very fine ware and fast becoming very scarce. That was the beginning of this entire chapter on Hall china — Red Cliff!

Mr. Clifford recalled that some of the flat ware (plates, etc.) were made for Red Cliff by the Walker China Company of Bedford Heights, Ohio but that all the hollow ware and the molded pieces were of Hall China origin.

From these photos it is plain to see there was never any intent to deceive — only to present a modernized version of our lovely old motif. Each piece of the ware is plainly marked — even the cups. We are all the losers because this beautiful ware is no longer on the market.

Today a potter is a respected individual in his own right; his work is accepted as a special art form, and his native skills can be enhanced and developed by advanced training and education in numerous colleges which have developed outstanding departments of ceramics. This is progress!

RC-5

Photos sent to the author by Mr. Fred Clifford, owner of the Red Cliff Company. Notice how faithfully the three major body styles of Anthony Shaw and Enoch Wedgwood (Tunstall) Ltd. have been preserved, yet each is distinctive in its own way.

RC-6

RC-7

RC-8

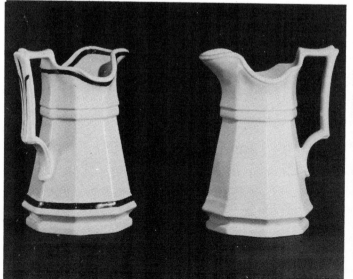

RC-9

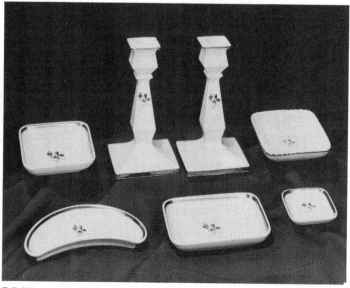

RC-10

C-11

RC-12

RC-13

RC-14

Harker Pottery Co.
1841-1972

This picture was a gift to me from Edith Harker Good-win, granddaughter of Benjamin Harker.

Benjamin Harker, who had established the second pottery in East Liverpool, certainly weathered hard times. His name will be remembered as one who helped James Bennett get started in the first pottery. The Harker Pottery was in continuous operation by members of the Harker family from 1841 until 1972 — a span of 130 years!

In answer to my 1973 inquiry about Harker China Company, I received a letter from Mrs. B. J. McLaughlin of the Harker China Company and Royal China Company, Sebring, Ohio, to the effect that Harker had ceased all manufacture as of March, 1972 and their stock was depleted. She felt sure they had made Tea Leaf, but had no records where she could check out the facts.

At that time Harker and Royal both were part of the Jeanette Glass Corporation.

If anyone has any Tea Leaf with a Harker trademark, let us hear from you.

Knowles, Taylor & Knowles Co.
1870-1934

Two cups and one saucer with familiar Star & Eagle. Warranted Ironstone China mark with KTK name or initials. (55)
KTK-1

*This gravy boat has the same trademark which is shown in **Playtime Dishes** by Lorraine Punchard, except for the KTK initials. A bone dish shown in the Odds and Ends chapter also has this emblem plus a star on either side of the ribbon banner, which was probably part of the KTK's dating system. The top gold band is wide and colorful but the first rim band is quite small. The design looks as if it were done free hand by a beginning decorator.*
KTK-2

Back stamp for above
KTK-3

As I began to tell the story of this early day pottery that made some of our Tea Leaf, I found that again Lucille T. Cox had superseded me with a wonderful account far superior to any I could piece together thirty years later. It is reprinted here with a word of gratitude to Virginia Voedisch, the librarian who sent to me this account as published in the "Bulletin of the American Ceramic Society" for August 15, 1942, Vol. 21, No. 8, pages 151–157. There are very few important details not mentioned in her account.

The account of the children's dishes in my collection is in the Children's Tea Sets chapter of this book.

Since I was sure there was Tea Leaf dinner ware made, I kept asking about it. Finally, six long years later Lois Lehner sent a photo of one cup and saucer — part of a set which belonged to a neighbor. An old man had given them to her long years ago so the story they could tell is lost. The free hand design is different than that on my little dishes, but there is no doubt it is American ware because the motif has no flower, only leaves. Also, it is in gold overglaze which is a common technique here.

It will be a great challenge to find other pieces of the dinner ware by this respected old company.

THE BULLETIN
OF
THE AMERICAN CERAMIC SOCIETY

Volume 21	August 15, 1942	Number 8

ISAAC WATTS KNOWLES, 1819-1902
By Lucille T. Cox

Isaac Watts Knowles, a potter of national renown, gave to the American ceramic industry a record of achievements, disappointments, triumphs, and discouragements unequalled in the annals of American pottery.

He came to East Liverpool, Ohio, as a skillful carpenter during the 1830s. Why his family chose the desolate river hamlet as their future home is not known, as there were no opportunities for a young cabinetmaker. Building was at a standstill, and money was so scarce that there were few silver coins to be found among the populace. Even the advent of James Bennett and his pottery in 1839 gave little impetus to prosperity. The majority of the people were skeptical of a man who dug clay from the surrounding hills and made jugs in a small clapboard shack on the river's edge. They did not believe that there was a future in this type of endeavor.

Young Knowles was keenly interested in the mysterious workings of the Bennett Pottery.[1] He spent hours watching the Englishman's skillful fingers throwing and shaping the clay and listening with rapt attention as the potter regaled him with stories of the "ould countree" and the potteries of Staffordshire. Raw clay being turned into objects of usefulness and beauty through the medium of fire and glaze was a constant source of marvel to him. During those visits to the town's first pottery, an interest and love of pottery making was born in Isaac Knowles. He was destined never to lose that interest as long as he lived.

In the meantime, however, he had a livelihood to earn that seemed almost impossible in a sleepy little village. One day he met James

---

[1] For an account of the Bennett Pottery and photographs of the Pottery and of James Bennett, see *Bull. Amer. Ceram. Soc.*, 16/1/27-28, 30 (1937) (story of William H. Bloor).

Bennett as the latter was attempting to cross the muddy main street of the village.

"Good morning, Mr. Bennett. If you bake those boots you have on you might sell them along with the rest of the mugs," he called jokingly.

The Englishman paused in the middle of the miry street and lifted one mud-encrusted boot to scrutinize it ruefully.

"Aye," he replied with a good-natured smile, "there's enough clay on that boot to make a sight o' jugs. But then I would have to be findin' a place to market them, an' that's sumthing I canna be doin'."

Knowles waited until the potter reached the boardwalk before he answered. His young face was serious.

"I'm thinking of building a flatboat and making a store out of it," he said slowly. "Then I'll go down the river and try to sell my goods among the farmers. I was calculating I might take a load of your dishes, providing you're willing."

As a result of this conversation, the carpenter-merchant a few weeks later loaded his boat with ware made in East Liverpool's pioneer pottery and started down the Ohio River, the first pottery salesman in the history of the town.

Many troubles and tribulations followed in the wake of the young merchant. It was the era of "wild-cat money," and, after spending the entire summer drifting down the Ohio and Mississippi rivers, he found himself in New Orleans early in the autumn with just enough good money to pay Mr. Bennett for his share of the enterprise. It was literally true that he did not have one cent to show for his work. His pockets were empty, and he was stranded in a strange town. In spite of the fact that he needed money for food and lodging, he refused to touch Mr. Bennett's silver coins which he carried in a moneybelt about his waist. One afternoon, he met a lifelong friend of his family who was master of the packet *New York*, who permitted him to work his passage back up the rivers to East Liverpool.

That was Isaac Knowles' first contact with the pottery industry. Through the next thirteen years, as he struggled to earn a living by making blungers and equipment for the potteries and by building an occasional house or creating new furniture, he never lost sight of the possibilities to be found in pottery making. Finally, in 1853, he made a decision which changed his entire life. He turned his dream of creating pottery into a reality.

The little town in which he lived was bankrupt. The years following the erection of the first pottery by James Bennett had been increasingly difficult. True, other potteries had been established during the ensuing years, but the great flood of 1852 had wrecked several of them almost beyond repair. Some potteries, including the old plant of James Bennett's, were wrecked completely. The town's first potter had moved his endeavors to Pittsburgh several years before the flood. It seems almost allegorical that Isaac Knowles should purchase the lumber of the wrecked Bennett Pottery to use in the erection of his factory.

The first shop of Isaac Knowles and his partner, Isaac Harvey, was as primitive as any in the previous decade. It was located north of the town, on top of a plateau near Tanyard Run. The one kiln was used alternately for bisque and glost firing. The two men worked long hours at the bench or in the kiln shed. They hired a few workers after a time, but whenever a kiln was to be loaded or drawn, Isaac Knowles was there to do it, sometimes unassisted.

Throughout the hard years of the Black Fifties and the Civil War, the little plant struggled for existence. Rockingham fruit jars, pie plates, bowls, and tea pots were produced. Every sale was important; all the material had to be accounted for, even the brick used in facing the kiln openings. Nothing was wasted, because every penny had to be used to the best advantage if the little pottery was to survive.

The struggle was heartbreaking and would have ruined a less intrepid man than Isaac Knowles. He now carried the burden alone, as he and his partner had dissolved their partnership. During the troublesome years following the Civil War, the potter was at times beset with fears that he might fail. Every avenue of assitance seemed closed to him. Drastic changes were taking place in the pottery business. The days of uncertain capital and primitive equipment were gone.

He was faced with the fact that his pottery must be changed to meet the demanding needs for whiteware, and he had no money for new equipment or additional buildings. The black cloud of discouragement settled over him, and he firmly believed that he had reached the end of his career as a potter.

One night, unable to sleep, the man left his home and went to his factory. He did not go inside, but stood in the bright moonlight and surveyed the dark buildings. The fire pots around the bisque kiln burned red. Their rays formed the only artificial light in the immediate neighborhood. Abruptly he sat down on a nearby log and buried his face in his hands. Failure seemed inevitable. How long he sat there he did not know, but a light touch on his shoulder aroused him. Looking up, he saw his friend, N. U. Walker, the owner of the most successful brickyards in the Ohio Valley.

"What are you doing out this hour of the night?" he said, trying to be nonchalant.

"Move over, Ike, I want to sit down beside you," replied his friend. The potter moved over.

"Ike," Mr. Walker began, without embarrassing preliminaries, "I couldn't sleep tonight. I had the feeling something was wrong with you, so I hitched up old Betsy and drove into town. I went to your house, but all was dark and I came on over here. I was just about to call myself an idiot and go home when I saw you sitting on this log. Ike, do you need money?"

"If we are to stay in the pottery business, we've got to change from Rockingham to whiteware," answered Mr. Knowles. "That will cost a heap of money. I do not have it," he finished succinctly.

Mr. Walker placed his arm about the potter's shoulders in a gesture of deep affection. "Ike," he said, "everything and anything I have in this world that can be converted into money is yours for the asking."

History does not tell if Mr. Knowles availed himself of his friend's generous offer, but his rise to fame in the industrial world during the next two decades more than justified Mr. Walker's faith in his abilities. It was the turning point in his career as a pottery manufacturer.

Making pottery during the early difficult years was not Isaac Knowles' only achievement. His obsession for good workmanship and his early training as a master carpenter opened new fields in ceramic manufacturing as yet unrealized by other potters. He knew the time would soon be at hand when the centuries-old method of making pottery by throwing and pressing would be inadequate to meet the demands. His inventive mind jumped ahead and met these possibilities. Consequently, he became the first man to introduce successfully machinery into ceramics.

In October, 1870, he turned inventor and succeeded in perfecting a shaft-driven jigger, the forerunner of all mechanized aids used in pottery making. Mr. Knowles outfitted his Old End clay shop with the jiggers, which proved their worth to such an extent that before long the other plants were clamoring for reproductions. The invention was fully covered by patent, and Mr. Knowles generously permitted his competitors to profit by his new machine. The original patent papers are in the possession of his son, Edwin M. Knowles, of East Liverpool, Ohio.

Bit by bit, the indomitable potter was paving the way for the manufacture of whiteware, a step he knew must surely come. In September, 1872, the new firm of Knowles, Taylor & Knowles Company drew its first kiln whiteware.[2] It was ironstone china and of a good grade. Isaac Knowles and his newly acquired partners, Colonel John N. Taylor and Homer S. Knowles, were content with nothing less than the best ware they could produce. The early efforts of this pottery reflect that characteristic to a high degree.

The little pottery had two kilns. The equipment, with the exception of the pulldown jiggers, was primitive, and the new ware taxed the production capacity to the limit. Strange problems were encountered which they did not know how to solve. Clays for ironstone china had to be brought into the village from outside sources. The blossom clays native to the Ohio Valley hills and used in Rockingham and yellow ware no longer sufficed. More machinery, quicker and more efficient methods of making ware, and a scientific knowledge of pottery making were needed. The potters could not quite understand why they could proceed just so far in their new endeavors and no farther. Lack of information barred the way. Science was their need, and where, in the 1870s, could a ceramic scientist be found?

The first man to recognize the need of a test tube in pottery making was Homer Knowles, the dynamic and brilliant young junior partner of the firm. He had grown up in the atmosphere of the "pot-bank," working with his father in the small yellow ware plant. When he became a man, it seemed natural for him to become associated with his father in the business. He chose to sell, and during those early years amazed his father by his sagacity and courage. The road of a traveling salesman was a rocky one, but the young representative accomplished results.

One evening, Isaac Knowles and his family were finishing their dinner when the father leaned back in his chair and eyed his oldest son quizzically.

"Homer, I saw a book on chemistry in your bedroom this morning. You aren't planning on becoming a chemist and pulling out of the pottery business?" he asked jocularly, with a hidden note of uneasiness in his voice.

The younger man's expression was slightly sheepish as he replied, "Not likely, father, but I believe there is a distinct need of chemistry in pottery making."

"Progressive, heh?" retorted his father. "Don't waste your time, lad, on such foolishness. How could books, written by people who never saw the inside of a pottery, tell you how to improve our established way of making dishes? The pottery industry will always be what it is today."

"Is that what you thought, sir," Homer asked curiously, "when you invented the pulldown jigger and started making whiteware?"

"Nonsense!" Isaac Knowles rose hastily to his feet. "Your travels haven't improved your manners!"

At the door of the dining room he stopped and glanced back at his family grouped about the table. Homer's grin was reflected on their faces.

---

[2] See Memories of Henry Goodwin; History of the Upper Ohio Valley, 1891; History of Columbiana County, 1905.

"Go ahead with your experiments," he growled, "and let me know if you need extra money."

During the next few years, Homer Knowles acquired a chemistry library. He studied on trains, in hotel rooms, at home, and in his office at the pottery. He made tentative experiments. Most of them he discarded; others he retained for the day when he could produce real American china.

In 1880, the Knowles, Taylor & Knowles Company needed a larger plant. The firm's five-kiln factory was taxed beyond its normal capacity. The backlog of orders was piling up. Production was stretched to a breaking point. Isaac Knowles and his partners knew the time had come when something had to be done, but once again they were faced with the lack of funds; furthermore, there did not seem to be any way to obtain them.

The junior partner was brimming with plans for expansion. Some of his plans were overly ambitious; others were practical and completely workable. The older men, however, opposed every plan Homer Knowles had to offer, for they would not borrow money, as they did not know when they could repay it.

"All I want to do is to try to get the money," the younger man pleaded. "I give you my word of honor, if I fail to get a loan on the plan I have in mind, I will take your advice and forget a new addition."

After days of discussion and argument, the older men consented and the young partner left town. He did not tell his wife or family where he was going. For several days he was absent; then late one afternoon he walked into his father's office and with a gesture of unconscious drama handed his father a folded paper.

Isaac Knowles opened the document; his partner leaned forward to read over his shoulder. It was a copy of an agreement drawn up between the *Pittsburgh Dispatch*, a wealthy newspaper, and the firm of Knowles, Taylor & Knowles Company, in which the former agreed to loan the pottery the necessary amount of money to built an eight-kiln pottery. The principal of the note was to be paid from the earnings of the new factory.

The New End was erected immediately, thus raising the capacity of the pottery to thirteen kilns. In 1886, the pottery was producing twice as much ware as any other two potteries in the country. It employed five hundred men and women in its shops, used fifteen tons of clay daily, and turned out a crate of ware every ten minutes. Its sale of ware aggregated a half million dollars a year.

The meteoric rise of the Knowles, Taylor & Knowles Company left the other pottery manufacturers gasping. The organization had only begun, however, to show what it was capable of doing. It was now firmly established as a manufacturer of white graniteware. It had the largest pottery in America, and its output in those days, more than fifty years ago, was considered to be enormous.

Despite their continued successes, Isaac Knowles and his partners were not satisfied. The potters of this country were facing an unfair battle, the battle for the recognition of American ware. The homemakers of the nation knew no other ware except that made in foreign markets and would accept no other. The feeling that merchandise must bear a foreign stamp to be worthwhile had been handed down from the era of Colonial days, and the feeling of condescension toward domestic products was rampant. The pottery of this country was classed as a poor joke, and the situation became so serious that some of the manufacturers were driven to stamping their ware with a foreign trademark in order to sell it.

The two earliest pottery companies to fight this condition were the Homer Laughlin China Company and the Knowles, Taylor & Knowles Company. Long before any of the other manufacturers decided to assert their independence, these firms were planning ways of reprisal; e.g., Knowles, Taylor & Knowles planned to manufacture bone china.

Homer Knowles, the dynamic junior partner, had been making cautious explorations in the field of china, and he was determined to produce a ware so beautiful that it would end for all time the insults of the foreign trade promoters. His plans hit a snag when he broached the idea to his superintendents. They did not know how to make bone china. After an extensive search, which delayed his plans for months, he secured the services of Joshua Poole, a young Englishman, who was an authority on Belleek or bone china.

Mr. Poole, though young in years, was well versed in the art of making fine china. His boyhood had been spent in his father's pottery at Stoke-on-Trent, England. The *East Liverpool (Ohio) Tribune* on December 14, 1889, gives the following account of the potter: "Joshua Poole came to America in 1887 and came to East Liverpool on the advice of the owners of the English clay mines who gave him a splendid recommendation to the Knowles, Taylor & Knowles Company. He has been manager of the Belleek Pottery in the west part of Ireland, famous for its fine ware."

The young man was thoroughly capable of directing the new work of making American china at the Knowles, Taylor & Knowles Company. At that time, there was probably no one else in this country better equipped to do the work. Before the actual process could be put into operation, however, a new factory for the express purpose of producing hotel and bone china had to be built.

In 1888, the firm completed the erection of the noted China Works. Old records describing this building called it a "mammoth building," and, according to the standards of those days, it was awe-inspiring in size, as it contained six large double kilns. The firm was now satisfied. They had a man who knew how to make bone china and the factory in which to produce it. In the meantime, they would produce hotel china and keep their plans pertaining to bone china undisclosed.

It was five o'clock in the afternoon of November 18, 1889, eighteen months after the completion of the new factory. The citizens of East Liverpool were alarmed by the ringing of the fire bell in the city hall tower. Quickly the volunteer fire department assembled, and in a few minutes the hook-and-ladder wagon dashed through the streets headed toward the north end of town.

The China Works was afire! For two hours the firemen fought the blaze, but it was useless. The magnificent modern pottery burned like a tinder box. The burning of the China Works meant a serious loss to the firm. It had been operating at peak capacity, and the backlog of orders was larger than any in the history of the organization. Now, in a few minutes, all that remained of the once splendid plant were the kiln stacks and windowless walls charred by fire or ruined by smoke and water.

On the north wall of the East Liverpool Historical Society rooms is a mute testimony to the complete destruction of what was then considered the finest pottery building in America. It is a single pane of glass bearing these words:

"Of the 9400 lights of glass in the China Works, this is the only one found whole after the fire of November 18, 1889."

The economic tragedy of the fire was lightened somewhat by the attitude of the workmen. The following letter was sent to the firm at the completion of the second China Works:

"We, the employees of the China Works, desire to express the sympathy which was felt by every one of us on the occasion of the destruction of the factory by fire on November 18, 1889, and our admiration (which was shared by the whole city) of the courage, energy, and promptitude displayed by the firm in rebuilding and re-establishing the works on a large and more complete scale; and last, but not least, our gratitude for the kindness shown by you in providing us with employment elsewhere during the winter.

"Now that the new establishment is completed and will soon be in operation, we feel that we have just reason to congratulate our employers and ourselves on so much having been accomplished in such a short time. Our earnest hope and confidence is that the success of the new China Works may be commensurate with your deserts."

In the spring of 1890, the plant was completed, and everything was in readiness for operation and for the making of bone china. Joshua Poole was given carté blanché and consequently devoted his entire time to the production of the new china. In a few months, the Englishman, working under great secrecy, produced one of the most exquisite china bodies in the history of modern pottery making.

It seemed strange that anything so lovely as this new china could rise above the malodorous manufacturing connected with it. The bones used in the manufacture of the new china were hauled from the slaughter houses along Tanyard Run. Great wagonloads of bone were brought to the factory and dumped into large vats, where they were boiled until every particle of meat dropped away. The bones were then dried, placed in kilns, and burned to a powdery ash. A ventilation system was installed to carry the fumes throughout the shop and to prevent any of the overpowering stench to escape into the neighborhood. Consequently, the rate of illness was very high among the workmen during those trying days.

Joshua Poole produced his ware. It was startling in its loveliness, its grace of line, and its perfect glaze and body. The workmanship left nothing to be desired. One of the most unusual pieces was a tall, graceful vase, its wide-lipped edges rolling back like the petals of an unfolding flower.

According to tradition, Homer Knowles examined the vase minutely, his face alight with triumph.

"This piece," he said slowly, "looks like a lotus flower."

From this comparison came the name of the rare ware. In spite of its supreme beauty, however, the firm realized that something more was needed to raise the ware from the beautiful to the realm of the artistic. Fragility was not enough. The decorations used on it must be unusual and in keeping with its delicate loveliness.

An eyewitness account of the decorating of lotus ware and the artist who did it was given to the writer as follows by Will T. Blake of Columbus, Ohio, who, when a boy, was the assistant of Henry Schmidt, the German artist who gave the new china its final beauty:

The name of the young German potter was Henry Schmidt. He came to this country early in the 1890s and, except for a brief period of employment in New York City and Trenton, N. J., he obtained his first steady job with the Knowles, Taylor & Knowles Company. A workbench was provided for his use at the China Works. The clay shop employees at that plant spoke of him as a "fancy worker," but the firm members referred to him as an "artist."

His specialty was the ornamentation of vases and bowls that were made for him in the casting shop. These ornamentations usually consisted of flowers and openwork which he made very quickly with the aid of his rubber bag and copper tube that was inserted in the end of the bag. A similar instrument is quite frequently used by bakers to ornament cakes.

This receptacle was first filled with a small portion of pliable jellylike clay which could be squeezed through the copper tube upon the slightest pressure of the hand when forming floral or openwork designs.

Mr. Schmidt originated his own floral decorations and openwork designs. When he was ready to put his clay flowers on a lotus bowl, he would first center the bowl on a whirler and trace out his particular pattern on the bowl with an undulating movement, much like one would trace an imaginary lead-pencil line around the bowl. The stems, leaves, and flowers of his patterns were produced with remarkable rapidity and skill. He used a small piece of plaster of Paris, a little thicker than a lead pencil and shaped like a petal, to give a more realistic impression to his flowers. This always was done after the clay petals had reached the proper hardness. The stems of these floral designs, and sometimes the leaves that were attached to them, were indented with a sharp tool to give a roughened and more natural effect to them.

His openwork patterns were first worked out on a small plaster of Paris mold. He would do a quick penciling of his design on the mold and then etch it out slowly with a sharp tool so that, when he went to work on it with his cornucopia bag, these minute indentations served to support the moist clay while the design was drying. When the drying process was complete, the openwork would be removed from the mold by a slight jolt of the plaster form from the hand.

He would next take the openwork design into his hand and apply a little fresh slip to its outer edges. Then he would attach the design to the vase or bowl on which he was working. This required much care. If too much pressure were applied, the pattern would be crushed and rendered useless.

Lotus ware was never produced in large quantities. It was created for one purpose, to be a challenge to foreign trade supporters. It was the irrefutable answer to the question, "Can any good thing come out of American potteries?" The cost of manufacture, however, was prohibitive. Mr. Blake continues his account:

"The Company experienced heavy losses in firing lotus ware, chiefly because it had to be fired in the same kilns used for firing the thick, heavy hotel and restaurant chinaware. The kiln men who handled lotus ware were not always able to handle it with the requisite delicacy necessary to prevent breakage, and serious breakage frequently occurred."

Lotus ware was considered to be a luxury line by the firm, and it was common knowledge among them that it cost ten dollars to make one piece of ware which had a market value of one dollar. Virtually every piece in existence today is considered to be of museum value.

When the World's Fair in 1893 opened at Chicago, lotus ware was displayed and captured blue ribbon after blue ribbon. It was adjudged the loveliest bone china on display at the fair. The French Commissioner for the museum at Seares purchased one of the vases, and a second piece was secured for permanent exhibition at the Swiss Government Art Gallery. The dreamy, fascinating appeal of lotus ware with its delicate flower work and fragile tracery won the admiration and praise of all the critics.

Genuine lotus ware, the co-product of Joshua Poole and Henry Schmidt, was produced by the Knowles, Taylor & Knowles Company for less than a decade. By 1900, the ware was no longer produced. Only recently have the art collectors realized that some of the world's finest bone china was made in East Liverpool more than forty years ago.

Creating the exquisite body and designs for lotus ware was not the only accomplishment of Joshua Poole, for he produced unusual colored-bodied ware which was shaped into vases of exquisite lines and decorations. The decorations were applied by Henry Schmidt, who used his flower work on these pieces of ornamental ware as well as on the lotus ware. The colored-bodied ware was produced in light and dark blue and in green. The rich shades were not obtained by glazes, but by colored bodies, a secret Mr. Poole had obtained from his father during the years he spent under the older man's supervision in England. There are today few of these vases extant.

Joshua Poole remained with the Knowles, Taylor & Knowles Company as superintendent of its china production until about 1907, when he accepted a similar position with the Homer Laughlin China Company. He was also vice-president of the Edwin M. Knowles China Company until his death in March, 1928.

During the years Isaac Knowles, a man in his seventies, and his associates were producing lotus ware, the other lines of the pottery were swinging along in full production. The firm, under the name of "K. T. & K. Co.," had a capital stock of one million dollars, and Homer Knowles' dream of having the largest pottery in the world became a reality.

Isaac Knowles died in 1902, and the decades following his death found the pottery classed as the leader of pottery making. It continued as such until thirteen years ago when the disastrous merger of many important potteries under the name of the American Chinaware Corporation brought about the failure and eventual closing of the pottery.

In 1931, the merger declared bankruptcy, and the Knowles, Taylor & Knowles Company became a memory. The plants were razed, and the sites of the Old End, New End, Buckeye, and China Works gradually were rebuilt to accommodate garages, markets, recreation fields, and gasoline stations.

The pottery founded by Isaac Knowles in 1853 carved a place for itself in the annals of pottery history on two counts, at least, if for no other reasons — it introduced machinery into ceramics and it created lotus ware.

According to personal correspondence with Mr. W. L. Smith, president of Taylor, Smith & Taylor Company of East Liverpool, that company purchased the name of the Knowles, Taylor & Knowles Company when they went into bankruptcy in 1934. The Taylors that were originally in their company were the same that were in the old K. T. & K. Co. However, there are none now, nor have there been for nearly fifty years.

Taylor, Smith & Taylor Company did not make Tea Leaf, but they made a line called Oak Leaf on their Conversation Shape in the early 1950s. It was popular at the time but manufacturing difficulties caused them to eliminate the entire shape line. They now are a part of Anchor Hocking of Lancaster, Ohio.

Homer Laughlin China Co.
1873 to present

Homer Laughlin of East Liverpool was the first United States potter to aggressively advertise American-made dinner ware. His initial insignia, his badge of honor, was the eagle rampant, lion supine, as described in their privately printed *Makers of American Pottery*. It was first used in 1874, continuing to 1904. The original drawing is on display in the East Liverpool Ceramic Museum.

Sentiment had continued pro-British in spite of, and long after, the American Revolutionary War. This attitude, plus the European propaganda that American products were inferior, caused many housewives to refuse to buy American-made goods. As a result there were many sly attempts to deceive the buying public. The most common ruse was the use of trademarks which were often slightly altered, and/or blurred versions of the Royal Arms mark which was used by English potters. Initials of a company were substituted frequently, especially if the

Pie plate, 9¾" × 1¼" deep with one center and six rim Tea Leaves. Glaze on back is perfect but front has been sprayed so it is rough and grainy looking. The motifs are stenciled on, just as if a stencil for the whole plate was prepared and all done at once in a dull, light colored, gold paint, some of which has worn off. We wonder what other pieces came with it . . . a server? plates? **HLC-1**

Insignia on above
HLC-2

American firm name or initials were alike, or similar to, those of the original British potteries.

Mr. Laughlin's exhibits at the Centennial Exposition in Philadelphia in 1876 were quite outstanding, and won for him many honors, but without his firm stand on proud identification of American-made ware, our prestige in the ceramic world market place would have been missing for a much longer time.

Today this all sounds trivial to us, but at that time (1870–75), the proper mark could easily have made the difference in profit and loss to many small, poorly financed "pot-banks," or possibly complete failure.

Even though patronage had been a standard practice in England, it was almost non-existent in the United States; however, there were a few instances when potters were given government grants. An outstanding case is that of our friend, Homer Laughlin. James McCord, in his *History of Columbiania County* relates that Homer, son of a pioneer storekeeper, Matthew Laughlin, at nearby Calcutta, returned from the Civil War and came to East Liverpool about 1867, with twenty-five dollars in his pocket. With it he bought some locally made yellow ware which he readily sold. He was soon joined by his brother, Shakespeare, in an unsuccessful venture in the manufacture of stoneware, then later he did a short stint as an importer of English goods in New York City. In 1873, the City of East Liverpool gave these two brothers the only public bonus ever given a pottery venture in the history of that community — five thousand dollars for the erection of a pottery for the exclusive manufacture of "white ware." In later years Homer Laughlin often declared he "would willingly have contributed many times the amount of the bonus to remove the record of that public contribution to his original enterprise." Seemingly patronage was simply not a part of his philosophy. His pride of personal achievement as well as practical experience, and expertise in ceramic chemistry, made him an outstanding asset to the entire pottery industry. Much of the later progress in production methods, improvements in quality of ware produced, and reconciliation in labor-mangement relations were due to his business acumen and his fertile mind. These are the facets of his story which I deem more important than the number of kilns or buildings or their dating methods.

Mr. McCord went on to relate how, early in his career as a potter, Mr. Laughlin had one miserable failure. Right after receiving the grant from the city in 1873, part of the ware from two kilns which he drew was a total loss; it consisted largely of tea cups and all the handles dropped off as they came from the kilns! "Hundreds of the old "village croakers", thinking of that five thousand dollars, marched up the railroad track to the new pottery and gazed sadly at the heap of worthless cups dumped over the river bank into the water, shook their heads gravely, and slowly walked home predicting early disaster for the new firm." I wonder if any of the cups are still in the river!

Homer Laughlin stood above these damaged cups and turned blunder into beauty. He went abroad and studied foreign methods and wares, then adapted the best of their government financed techniques, and concluded that the new white ware production demanded chemical expertise. He brought chemists from England and France, and soon his plant was humming with the production of beautifully decorated china and art wares.

Less than three years from the time of the cup disaster, his company was awarded a medal for their ware at the Philadelphia Centennial of 1876. And three years later at a similar exposition in Cincinnati, the firm was given their highest honor, a gold medal for the supreme quality of their exhibits. By then his leadership in the American ceramic

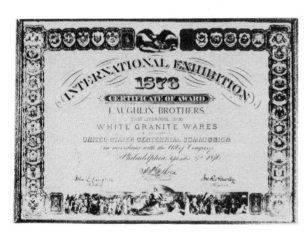

industry was firmly established. These awards at various exhibitions are verified in a recently discovered company catalog from 1901, according to Mr. E. S. Carson. He included these two copies for our pleasure.

Today, Homer Laughlin China Company is the largest pottery in the world. Mr. A. V. Bleininger, followed by Mr. H. W. Thiemecke, both long-time employees, have "led the pack" as ceramic engineers for the entire industry for most of this twentieth century. Now a ceramic engineer is one of the most important employees; no pot-works can do without at least one!

From the lowly beginning in East Liverpool, the company expanded numerous times, and gradually by 1929, was moved just across the Ohio river to Newall, West Virginia. As a result a host of improvements of great benefit to the entire area were made; the Newall-East Liverpool bridge, a new power plant, a new water system, and a plant for making barrels were among them. This was long before the day of cardboard packaging which came into general use after 1915. New type automatic jiggers and continuous tunnel kilns were only two of the plant improvements.

In a phone conversation of January, 1980, Mr. Ed Carson, long time employee, remarked that the plant covered 76 to 87 acres. (They have the same roof but had not measured it lately.) He also commented that Homer Laughlin China Company was the (old) Henry Ford of the dish world in the United States just as Alfred Meakin had that distinction in England.

Homer Laughlin was reported to be a well educated but shy, retiring gentleman; this only enhanced his success. In 1889 he hired Mr. W. E. Wells who, with his sons and grandsons following, have given more than a century of meritorious service to the company; some are still with the firm.

Laughlin slowly began to relinquish operation of the plant; it was incorporated as the Homer Laughlin China Company in 1896, he retired in 1898, and in 1899 he sold his interest to the Marcus Aaron group of Pittsburgh, Pennsylvania and Mr. Wells.

Mr. Laughlin moved to California and was a very successful real estate developer in the Los Angeles area. Aarons have carried on the ideals of the founder: quality merchandise at reasonable prices made by employees who work in pleasant surroundings and are paid reasonable wages.

Collectors well might wish this company *had* decorated some of their old ware with the Tea Leaf design. While in the area, I went to the plant to see if they might have, but was told to my disappointment they had not made my favorite pattern. Mr. Arthur Wells, the plant foreman, was my guide through their "morgue"! He was in his eighties, a delightful historian with an accurate memory of past production. He had been an employee of the company for well over sixty years, beginning as a teen-age boy. Their "morgue" was a large room where examples were stashed for future cataloging and display, but was not open to the public. Mr. Wells seemed to have total recall of events in the history of the company and showed me the lines they did make in the 1880s–1890s. Alas! No Tea Leaf. That appeared later.

In conversation with Mr. Carson I inquired about a 10″ pie plate with their Kitchen Kraft Ovenserve back stamp which had been sent to me from Kutztown, Pennsylvania a short time before. It had a small Tea Leaf in the center with six more placed around the edge. The glaze was perfect on the back but the front had been reglazed with some lint/dirt embedded so part of the plate looked moldy. Upon close inspection it was easy to see the tiny leaves in pale gold had been stenciled over that glaze, and part of them were showing signs of wear. No — I did *not* put it in the oven — I am afraid the piece is strictly for show.

Later there was an article in a collectors' publication stating the pattern was called *Fleur-de-lis*. There was a picture of a squatty jug (about a quart size) typical of HLC ware of the 1930s.

Mr. Carson explained: They had sold first quality as well as seconds in both decorated and undecorated wares. Sometimes those outside decorators placed their designs so small blemishes on the body were concealed (apparently not the case on this plate). This was an old English trick — used by Mason's Patent Ironstone decorators among others. He indicated it would be hard, if not impossible, to say what company or person might have added their own designs. But *it was not done in the Homer Laughlin China Company factory.*

It will be most interesting to hear from someone who knows the "who," "where," "when," and "why" of this 1930s reproduction.

J. & E. Mayer
1881 to present

Probably the best known of all the American producers of our Tea Leaf was J. & E. Mayer Company of Beaver Falls, Pennsylvania. E. A. Barber* in 1893 was the first to record, ". . . the Mayer Pottery Company — manufactures stone china, lustre band and spray and decorated goods." W. P. Jervis, in 1902 in his *Encyclopedia of Ceramics* related: ". . . but after considerable experiment and adaptation of English methods to American materials, a very superior grade of underglaze lustre band and sprig ware is produced which gave the company considerable prestige." As late as 1948 John Ramsey, writing in his *American Potters and Potteries*, commented, ". . . they copied the English shapes and some of the relief decorations — but their sole decorative inspiration is the gold lustre bands and sparse leaves — one to a piece — used by the Mayer Pottery Company of Beaver Falls, Pennsylvania after 1881."

These three are the only references I found to the pattern having been made by a certain potter, and it is interesting to note they all referred to the Mayer Company.

Ernest and Joseph, founders, were the sons of Joseph and Frances Withers Mayer, a family of pottery pioneers at Dale Hall Works in Burslem, but known throughout all England. They migrated to the United States after Ernest had served his apprenticeship at G. W. Turner and Sons, Tunstall potters, and later worked for a time at the Bell Works and the Phoenix Pottery, Hanley, which belonged to the Clemenston brothers. He was born in Burslem in 1857, and first attracted attention to his pottery after publication of a paper on his new method of mixing clay bodies; and shortly afterward he invented an improved type of jigger. He arrived in New York in 1878, spent some time in the import business with his two brothers, then served for a short time as superintendent of a Baltimore, Maryland pottery.

After he and Joseph bought the Beaver Falls plant he served forty years as manager of the manufacturing end of that business; but he took time to serve as vice-president, and later as president, of the American Ceramic Society where his influence was felt nationwide. He passed away in 1920.

By the time Joseph was twenty years old he had come from Burslem to the United States, and was president of the Arsenal Pottery of the

Group of Mayer items: the square bowl, (left center) is more shallow than the English made; the platters have the clipped corners like Enoch Wedgwood (Tunstall) Ltd. but without the vertical ribbing; the tea pot is on the familiar Cable body style (the finial is a replacement); the milk jug comes in a variety of sizes (see page 199); prize of the group is the creamer and sugar in the center. I have used all these pieces on my table. All Mayer ware is underglaze decal decorated with dark copper lustre overglaze.

JEM-1

---

* Barber, *Pottery and Porcelain.*

Cup and saucer should be shown in cup section but look for this oak leaf variant in a full dinner line; it is very attractive with super lustre. (72)
JEM-2

10¾" plate with molded handle decoration; possibly part of a tea set. Owner's husband is from Derbyshire, England. (70)
JEM-3

9½" square plate with molded-in handles added. May be service tray for a tureen or the usual tea set plate.
JEM-4 (82)

Mayer Pottery Manufacturing Company (in Trenton, New Jersey) according to Barber. He was still listed as the proprietor in 1902. He also was born in Burslem, educated in Sanback, England and in Belgium; later he was in the import business with his brother, Arthur, in New York, and left there with the third brother, Ernest, for the new frontier which turned out to be Beaver Falls, Pennsylvania. He died in 1930 from injuries sustained in a fall at his home in New Brighton, Pennsylvania, leaving fifty years of successful pottery history at Mayer China Company. Surviving him were his wife, the former Helen Townsend, and his two sons, Arthur and Walter.

Modern legend recounts that Joseph and Ernest were on a train en route to East Liverpool, Ohio, and expected to arrive there late at night. The two towns are less than thirty five miles apart. Naturally when the train stopped at Beaver Falls, they assumed they had reached their destination; but when morning came and they fully realized their mistake, they took a look around that strange, beautiful place and had some second thoughts about leaving.

Among the enticements was an operating pottery which was for sale by the Economy Society (sometimes called Harmonists), a German religious group who wanted to move elsewhere. That pottery was completely powered by water from the Beaver River Falls. These were three falls which the Indians had hated so very much because of treacherous portage problems; the river drops about seventy feet in seven miles. The waters furnished at first mechanical, and later electrical power to operate the pottery, and the generating station was still used as a stand-by power supply in 1973. This pottery is one of the very few in the world and the only one in the United States with this distinction. This certainly must have been a far cry from the coal-fired kilns of Staffordshire with their ever-present smoke pall.

In a minimum of time after buying the holding of the Harmonists, Joseph and Ernest were once again, in 1881, in the pottery business, this time as J. & E. Mayer.

Their family history is one of the most interesting and best documented of all the English potters; a full account would be tedious but a review of their family accomplishments will help us better understand the excellence which was the Mayer tradition for several centuries. Since this is not an exercise in genealogical research, and proper family ties were not always recorded by historians, I call attention only to the outstanding achievements and recognize how some in each generation raised the standards of quality and advanced pottery technique throughout the industry. By this we can learn what kind of people and potters they were. Not all the Mayers mentioned are *immediate* ancestors of our American subjects.

The name Mayer had several spelling variations, due possibly to human error or lack of knowledge. Among them were Mare, Mares, Meir, Mear, and Miers. The name was known in the Norman Conquest times, and many of their facts and artifacts have been preserved in various British Museums, one of which is the Mayer Museum at Liverpool.

One china works, in Chelsea, near London, was founded in 1747 by some firemen and other workers from Staffordshire (one of them was a Meir), but it soon failed and the workmen returned to Burslem. This was probably a normal process of moving which accounts for so many Mayers in various areas. There is hardly a town in the Potteries which has not recorded at least one Mayer on their rolls.

Posset-pots are very interesting bits of history in clay, common in England and Wales three hundred years ago. Posset is a delicious drink

This was introduced to me as a water bucket but on comparison with an 1894–95 catalog it proved to be the waste jar to a bedroom set. It is a beauty! (18)
JEM-5

Common trademark; may or may not have letters or numbers at top and bottom of diamond as part of their dating system. **JEM-6**

mixture of hot ale, milk, sugar, spices, and sippets (small dices of bread or oat cakes). This was almost a universal Christmas Eve drink and the posset-pot was often an heirloom brought out for such special occasions. Tradition called for the wedding ring of the hostess and a silver coin to be dropped into the brew. As the pot was passed around the table the one who fished out the ring with his spoon was slated to have a happy marriage, and the one who retrieved the coin was supposed to have good luck the coming year. This may have been the story behind John Mier's posset-pots — one of which bears his name and is dated 1686.

Another speciality of the very best potters of that day was a selection of huge bowls or pots on the order of the posset-pots. One of these vessels was filled with food and set in the center of the table so each person could dip his own spoon into the mess and help himself from that one pot. (I wonder if this was the beginning of our fondue pots?) Bowls large enough for this purpose required special skill in throwing as well as firing; evidently the Mayers were masters of that art as they made them also.

Dr. Plot, in *Natural History of Staffordshire*, 1686, listed a Hugh Mare in his role of Burslem potters in 1686, and Professor Church† wrote of Richard Mare as a Hanley potter in 1697. This was authenticated by the Mayer China Company in their own brief twentieth century publication *China From the Dawn of History* when they mentioned a two-handled cup found in a cottage in Cheltenham (which is seventy five miles south of Stoke and eighty miles west by north of London) bearing on the bottom: *Richard Mare 1697*. It would seem various family members were active in Staffordshire before those in Derbyshire, but be that as it may we read of many more outstanding Mayer artisans from The Potteries such as: Elijah of High Carr who, with one Mr. Moss, was reputed to have made greater quantities of goods than any other potters.

His son, Elijah, of Hanley, an enameller of great talent, is mentioned in most of the older histories. He was considered, by many, as an equal of Josiah Wedgwood for his similar works of black basalts, Caneware, and Queensware. He was, at one time, a china merchant for Chatterly's in Holland.

In turn, his son Joseph, Esquire, who lived in a *modest* mansion above the church in Hanley, was famous as a historian, a collector, and an unusual potter. According to Elizabeth Collard, writing in her *Nineteenth Century Pottery and Porcelain in Canada*, Joseph was instrumental in preserving one of the largest and most complete collections of documents concerning the Josiah Wedgwood Pottery, both of which are still in existence in Staffordshire. About five years after the death of Josiah Wedgwood II in 1843, Joesph Mayer rescued, and helped preserve, old ledgers and huge bundles of pertinent old papers which had been sold for scrap shortly after the Wedgwood death. They were being used to wrap groceries and butter in a Birmingham shop.

As an innovative potter Joseph made transparent stoneware, a true parian, forty years before it was rediscovered, and a sample of it is in the Victoria and Albert Museum. This was in addition to his usual wares.

He was considered the best linguist of the European languages in all the Potteries. Several of these Mayer family members had inter-married with the Ridgway family who were very active in the Methodist movement; evidence of Joseph's high principles was his well known spirit of great generosity to those less fortunate than himself, as recorded by his friend Simeon Shaw in his *History of the Staffordshire Potteries*, 1828.

Joseph quit potting at the prime of life (1830); rented out parts of the

---

† Sir Arthur Church, *English Earthenware* (London, 1895).

two family pot-works; stored vast amounts of his very best black basalts, Cane, chocolate brown, and Queenswares, some of which was elaborately perforated and decorated. He locked the doors on this jumble of beauty and there it remained until his death in 1860. His sons dispersed the collection at auction, much of which was purchased by foreign collectors, consequently it was soon scattered all over the world. What an antique auction that must have been!

Three other Mayers, who had great impact on the economy of the Cobridge potters in 1770, were J. and R. Mare and William Meir, who were part of a group of thirty who signed an agreement to sell their pottery at stated pre-set prices. This was done to stablize the market and improve the profits. These men were well known makers of salt glaze ware, which was so popular at that time.

From 1829 to 1838 Mayer and Mawdesley, Tunstall potters, were busy making black basalts and china toys. Goeffrey Godden‡ explains these earthen figurines were originally called *toys* and their makers were known as *toy manufacturers*. They were usually products of extremely small pot-banks, owned by one man who hired only a dozen or so people, who all worked in a sort of regulated informality where each worker felt important. Many of these toys were figures of famous people, lovers, animals, small decorated boxes, and the like. They were on the order of fairings but larger, higher quality, and better decorated.

Thomas Mayer, master potter of the Cliff Bank Works, Stoke, from 1826 (an uncle of Joseph and Ernest) made one of the most unusual specimens of solid earthenware ever crafted. It is a table thirty-two inches in diameter, on a beautiful pedestal, and profusely decorated by painting with subjects from natural history. To the best of my knowledge it is preserved in the Mayer Museum in Liverpool. I was told by a ceramist friend, Lucille Wren, that this type of pottery making is most difficult under modern, ideal conditions; and that even a six inch flat tile is a real challenge, therefore we can appreciate this table as a master creation of one hundred fifty years ago, made under much less than ideal conditions.

Thomas was also an outstanding producer of the American views in old Blue Staffordshire ware and much of his trade was with the American market. The Cliff Bank works in Stoke, which he left when he joined his two brothers at Dale Hall in Burslem, had formerly belonged to David Bird, known as the flint potter. Bird, by accident, introduced the use of flint in pottery making, quite an innovation in the 1820s! While on a trip his horse required treatment for a sore eye; he was intrigued when he saw the hostler burn common flint stone to a fine white powder and blow it into the animal's eye. But *he* was astounded with the whiteness of the calcined flint and decided to try mixing it in clay. He not only produced a whiter, more beautiful body, but Bird soon determined the exact proportions necessary to prevent dishes from cracking in the oven. Nothing was recorded on the success of the treatment of the horse, but it is inevitable to me that Thomas Mayer inherited and improved on this potting technique and carried it on to greater success at Cliff Bank.

It was also quite an accident that in 1752, young children playing around the print shop of John Sadler and Guy Green, in Liverpool, stuck discarded transfer papers onto pottery shards from near-by potteries and found the designs firmly imprinted. Mr. Sadler was quick to perfect and patent the process, but it was the Mayers who developed three to five color transfers, to be completely printed at one time, thus reducing time and labor costs and ultimately the price of pottery.

Another mark frequently seen on Mayer ware. It may or may not have numbers on either side of the royal arms mark.
JEM-7

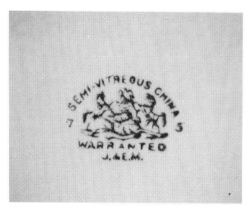

A twentieth century mark; note the semi-vitreous china substitution at top.
JEM-8

‡ Godden, *British Pottery and Porcelain.*

As artists the Mayers were original in use of shape and design of their wares; painstaking in the execution of delicately modelled raised flowers used to decorate vases and such; yet practical in their planning for "fit" in the nesting of dinner plates and similar dishes. These little items add so much to our pleasure.

As I researched various histories of the family it was mind-boggling to realize the wide range of talents and interest represented: an enameller, a collector, a linguist, a philanthropist, a foreign chinaware agent, a rival of Wedgwood, historians, wealthy businessmen, well educated gentlemen, importers, exporters, high volume producers, labor movement leaders, inventors, and makers of such difficult wares as the huge pots, large tables, parian and Queensware, Staffordshire scenic ware; in fact all types of high class earthenware known in their time, yet practical enough to enrich us all.

Joseph, the father of the American chinamen, did not live to see the successful developments of his sons, for he died as a young man from overwork. He had learned the pottery trade well, and saw to it that his two sons were thoroughly indoctrinated in the art and technique of pottery manufacturing. Even more important, they had been taught by example from ever so many other preceding illustrous family potters.

It is no wonder that Joseph and Ernest knew their "pots" when they arrived at Beaver Falls.

The Mayer Pottery was opened just six years after Alfred Meakin began potting at the Victoria Works in Tunstall, therefore, the two companies were contemporaries and possibly rivals. Many other companies were also involved in making the avalanche of Tea Leaf to satisfy demands of the American housewives; there were also many other potting Mayers – even to the present day, who contributed to pottery progress in varying degrees. The years following their purchase of the Beaver Falls factory must certainly have been hectic. They enlarged and modernized the plant as well as launched an extensive advertising program. One of their 1892-93 ads read: "Lustre Band and Sprig — already over ten years on the market. Will not wear off — Indestructable as the Rock of Ages.§" But by the end of the century they turned attention to other dinnerware as the Tea Leaf design was past its prime.

The late Thelma Shull in her *Victorian Antiques* quoted Walter S. Mayer, vice-president of the company as saying that ware was decorated as follows:

"Lustre must of necessity be put over the glaze. The method used to produce this kind of ware was to print the pattern underglaze, then put the lustre overglaze exactly over the under-glaze print."

This indicates they used a decalcomania process for decorating. The Mayer Company was the first in the United States to make our favorite pattern, and the only one I have found so far who put their design underglaze.

We know the term "ironstone" was applied to ware, from Mason's patent in 1813, until as late as 1890. From then until 1899 it was called "white granite' by the trade; and after the turn of the century the term was generally "semi-porcelain." The early J. & E. Mayer ware was called "stone china," but a little later the term "ironstone" was part of their back stamp; later yet the term "semi-vitreous" was incorporated in the trademark. To vitrify means to change the structure by heat in such a way as to make a semi-fluid mass which is transluscent and nonporous. Mayer maintained an average standard of two one-hundredths of one percent absorption. Their perfect union of body and glaze eliminated crazing which is caused by the two components expanding

§ Kamm, *Old China.*

and contracting at different rates of time or degrees of temperature. Their underglaze decorations were superior because they used proper knowledge of the chemistry of colors in a modern tunnel kiln. They also chose the proper glaze to best bring out the beauty of colors obtainable only in an even fire, and they chose proper colors that withstood continuously higher temperatures. Only a few are suitable. Without these, other manufacturers had to resort to placing colors on the surface which were bound to wear off long before the china has given proper service.

"The work of final selection-inspection-is a very skilled job and it requires constant alertness and sound judgment as to what pieces are satisfactory and what should be rejected and broken. The manufacturer who makes a piece of china to sell at the lowest possible price has to skimp many places in the long and complicated process and it is here at the end of its journey and in this department that defects manifest themselves. The sorters of such a manufacturer cannot examine wares for defects in the same spirit as one who gets an equitable price to enable him not to have to cut corners in the process. A number of our sorters are the oldest employees of the company, having a lifetime of experience.

In fact, in many parts of the plants there are father and son working side by side who represent the third generation working for the same company. We hear it often lamented that our modern industrialization with its mass production has dealt a death blow to the old spirit of craftsmanship. This may be true of some other industries. In the making of pottery there seems to have been a happy union of science and mechanical invention to enable the expert craftsman to do the things he could not have accomplished without their aid, and to see the results of his art and skill carried, through the economics of mass production into every home.

The heritage of a hundred years is quality in business record and product. That is the watch word in every department today and has never been sacrificed to increased production or added profit.*

The old pottery was completely destroyed by fire in 1896, but a larger, more modern plant was immediately built, and the two hundred previous employees were soon at work again. The company now occupies a thoroughly modern plant that covers well over two city squares. It is bright, cheerful, and clean, providing pleasant working surroundings for the employees, which is, in return, reflected in the standard of work so pronounced in their china.

Before my visit to Mayer's in 1973, correspondence with them brought this information from Lois McKean: "In checking our archives, we are sorry there is very little information. Tea Leaf was made on a semi-vitreous body and Mayer discontinued production of semi-vitreous ware in 1912. Mayer China now manufacturers vitrified china exclusively for fine hotels, restaurants, air lines etc. . . . and it is considered the cadillac in this field.

"There are no Mayer catalogs illustrating Tea Leaf . . . Mayers were well known potters in England before coming to the United States. They sold the company several years ago, and there are no Mayers associated with our company at this time.

". . . our back stamps are only to 1914." Since then the back stamp has changed quite a number of times:

J & E Mayer established in Beaver Falls, Pa., in 1881 by brothers Joseph & Ernest Mayer 1881-1888

The Mayer Pottery Company 1888-1923
Mayer China Company   1923-1968

Mayer was sold to Shenango Ceramics, New Castle Pa., in September 1964, but continued using the name Mayer China.

---

* Mayer China Co., *China From the Dawn of History*, p. 14.

Interpace (International Pipe & Ceramics Corp., Parsippany, New Jersey), purchased Mayer and Shenango January 25, 1968, but later sold it (June 15, 1979) to Richard P. Rifenburgh. The name Mayer China has been retained continuously since 1923.

Also in 1980 (June 13) Mayer China Company bought the Walker China Company of Bedford Heights, Ohio and it is now known as Mayer Plant No. 2.

The late Arthur E. and late Walter S. Mayer were sons of the late Joseph Mayer.

Robert T. and Richard D. Mayer are sons of the late Walter S. Mayer.†

Is this the end of this brilliant family of potters who have given the world so much quality and pleasure? I think not.

This jug (pitcher) is similar to one given to one of the early day Meares (Mayers) by King Charles II after the battle of Worcester in September, 1651. Eliza Meteyard, in her *Life of Josiah Wedgwood*, reported it was still (1878) called King Charles' Cup. It was 7¾" high and the diameter at the top was 3", probably of "Flemish or German make, and a very appropriate gift to one of a name so closely identified with the history of Staffordshire pottery." In Miss Meteyard's time it was in the possession of John Mare of Etruria.

Since modellers were always on the lookout for new ideas, it would appear reasonable for J. and E. Mayer Company men to copy a specimen of such historical importance.

Most of us would agree the new shape, body, and glaze are superior and it certainly is easier to pour from. The one I have is 7" high and 3" in diameter at the top. It was made in several sizes, and the other one I saw like this one was part of a wash set — 13" high and about 5½" in diameter.

This unique shape jug came in graduated sizes to hold from 1½ pints to a gallon or more. Notice the similarity in this and the print from page 178 of Meteyard's book on Josiah Wedgwood.
JEM-9

(Fig. 47.) KING CHARLES II. CUP.

One of the faithful Mayer employees invented a unique sand vibration machine to evenly distribute fine sand into and all around the bisque ware in the saggers before it was fired. Since vitreous and semi-vitreous wares require extremely high temperatures — 2440° for 55-60 minutes — it becomes soft and tends to twist and fall out of shape unless it is evenly supported. This one invention obviously saved a great deal of material, labor, and money.

*The Bulletin of the American Ceramic Society*** reported a problem and the solution concerning use of this process. Semi-vitreous bisque (which requires very high firing temperatures) was defected with numerous black specks and/or brown stains after having been imbedded in sand and fired in a continuous tunnel kiln, but when fired in an old type updraft kiln no spots or specks were present. Extensive research provided a simple answer: Lack of oxygen caused iron particles in the sand to melt at lower temperatures and cause the staining. The solution: increase the air-flow through the kilns by either cutting holes in the saggers, or adjusting the dampers to provide sufficient air at all times; and to preheat the ware to oxidize the organic matter completely before reaching the maximum temperature. "It is now regular practice to fire ware bedded in sand in tunnel kilns in saggers with holes." Another example of science and industry working hand in hand for mutual benefit.

† Information from correspondence with Lois McKean, Mayer China Co.

** *Bulletin of the American Ceramic Society:* Vol. 13 No. 11 Nov. 1930 pgs. 871-873

Sebring Pottery Company
1887-1934

This unusual piece came to me from the home of the Kentucky Derby. Seemingly, Tea Leaf by Sebring is as rare as a Derby winner. The shell shape lip on this jug is spectacular, but, even though I have no other information about it, it does tell us that this fine old company made Tea Leaf. Look for it. (4)
SB-1

Backstamp on above
SB-2

Sebring is the name of a man, a family, a pottery, a tradition, an empire.

To separate one from the other is impossible. For our purpose we will adhere to the story of only the pottery where our Tea Leaf pattern was made in the early 1900s — The Sebring Pottery Company of Sebring, Ohio.

Back in 1887 the five Sebring brothers (along with two partners whom they soon bought out), purchased the two story brick pot-works at Second and Market Street in East Liverpool. It had been known as the old Agner & Fouts & Company place ever since it was built in 1863. Just previous to the Sebring purchase of this four kiln plant, it was known as Agner & Gaston, but owned by a Mrs. Campbell. After bankruptcy and idleness for five years the $12,500 purchase price was just the beginning of expenses — three kilns had to be rebuilt, new machinery installed, and a general renovation effected; all were necessary in preparation for the production of white granite instead of the old yellow ware and Rockingham.

Frank was the president and head of the sales department and the youngest son, William, was the secretary-treasurer. George and Oliver worked at Knowles, Taylor, & Knowles plant where George was a foreman. The other brothers, Ellsworth and Joseph, were interested but not actively engaged, according to historians.

That first venture was literally a "one-horse" operation. They truly did have a single horse on a treadmill to furnish their horsepower! But don't laugh.

In eighteen years time they had three plants with fourteen kilns. George was manager of the East Palestine Pottery in East Palestine, Ohio, which the boys had leased on a percentage basis. Success came quickly; before long that town raised money for the Sebrings to build a brand new plant in the east end of town — The Ohio China Company. This was their second new works; in 1889 they had built the six kiln French China Co. plant in the east end of East Liverpool, commonly known as the Klondike. They sold it in 1901 to the Smith-Phillips Pottery people.

According to McCord, by 1905, Sebrings had under their control twenty-five kilns, 1200 employees, and a capitalization of $1,500,000.00. Not bad for eighteen years' work!

Money from the previous projects was used to buy land to establish the city of Sebring, on the county line near Alliance just a few miles northeast of East Liverpool. That Sebring saga would fill a book much larger than this one; we shall concentrate on the Sebring Pottery Company, which was just a part of the whole Sebring complex.

The boys, plus the two girls, were soon residents of the new town and active in business after shaking the dust (or mud) from East Liverpool off their feet. Frank concentrated on this new pottery which was completed about 1900, to make white ware and tea sets along with other decorated wares.

Another brother, Ellsworth (Evis), was head of Sebring China Company. Mixups on the mail caused so much trouble the post office finally held the mail until one man from each firm came in to sort the mail by clues from inside the envelopes (if possible!).

Sebring men had the uncanny ability to adapt or devise new merchandising plans or schemes, whereby their wares — sold on various premium plans — brought more profit than hum-drum routine sales methods could ever return. Their emphasis was on marketing, so quality was secondary but not inferior.

It is difficult now to relate how many pottery operations there were in this Sebring empire, but part of them went down the drain with the failure of the American Chinaware Corporation in 1933. Sebring Pottery was *not* one of them because Frank liked to run his own show and refused to join that merger which had begun about 1927.

The Sebring family had realized another dream about 1908 when they established the city of Sebring, Florida and put it on the map. It was their winter home; several passed away there but all were brought back to rest in Sebring, Ohio. They were all active in various churches, as well as fraternal and charitable organizations, and the American Ceramic Society for over thirty years. Frank was active in or near Sebring, but so far as we know, none of the others made Tea Leaf.

After his death in 1936 the old pottery plant "went to pot." It was outmoded and run down. Rather than being renewed and renovated it was partially dismantled and the rest was sold. Around 1944 the remainder was rented by the Stanford Pottery where art pottery was produced. The plant was not rebuilt after a 1960 fire.

Perhaps if Frank had trained as a potter (like his brothers had) instead of a grocer, as he and Evis did in East Liverpool before buying the first pottery, there would be a modern Sebring Pottery Company today.

I wonder what KOKUS in the trademark means?

C. C. Thompson Pottery Co.
1868-1938

There have been Thompsons in the East Liverpool hills and valleys for 142 years and for twenty years before that they were at nearby Calcutta. There has been hardly a function or board of directors that has not carried at least one Thompson name and many are still active today. Most of them are direct descendents of William Thompson, who in 1818, with his sons, migrated (via Fawcettstown briefly) to Calcutta from Beaver County in western Pennsylvania and operated a tavern and a general store. In 1848 they moved to East Liverpool. William bought the store and house of George Smith; his son, Josiah, bought the home of Anthony Kearns in what is now Thompson Place.

Around 1837 when talk of a railroad spurred interest in the town — a big "sugar tree" grove was cut into firewood to clear riverfront land. Lots were sold in this area bounded by presently named streets of Union to College, and Water (Front) Street north to Robinson (Fourth) Street. This is an area about three to four long city blocks square, with alleys between each street. The waterfront area was wider than the Fourth Street end. A depression panic slowed progress a little bit but several Pittsburgh families came, including Anthony Kearns who built a sawmill and improved the land to the east of College Street and developed Thompson Place. George Smith had built three brick houses there and when Josiah bought the Kearns house, Smith and Thompson became partners in a store. They gave credit to James Bennett while he was building the town's first pottery.

One of the most important projects the family was ever involved in was the city water supply. Shortly after his arrival in 1850, Josiah Thompson built a reservoir, on the east side of Walnut Street, which was 40 x 100 feet and 6 feet deep, and was fed by a spring. Many early families got water there, or at two other Thompson springs; one at the pottery and one up the hill at a stone house. These were just three of many springs that dotted the town site. In 1879 a new water works was built near his home with a large reservoir 350 feet above the river on Thompson Hill. With other later additions, output was multiplied four or five times. Josiah Thompson and Isaac Knowles were two of the first four trustees of that project.

Footed oval vegetable dish with lid, 7" × 10". Mint. The Tea Leaf is more horizontal than most, but one of few American companies that has the flower along with the leaves. (60)
CCT-1

Trademark for above
CCT-2

The western part of that old "sugar tree" grove is now part of the older business district of the city. In 1845 the Sandy Beaver Canal was opened; 1856 was the year the Cleveland & Pittsburgh Railroad began service; oil and gas were discovered in 1860; and in general use in the potteries by 1866. Thompsons saw it all! Thus, they concluded the climate was right for yet another pottery.

In 1868 Josiah and his son Cassius C., with their partner, Col. J. T. Herbert, built the C. C. Thompson Pottery on the riverfront just east of Sugar Alley (the southwest corner of Thompson Place). In a couple of years Josiah bought the Herbert interest, took in B. C. Simms and John C. Thompson as partners, and their style was C. C. Thompson & Company. They boasted five kilns and were one of the largest producers of Rockingham and yellow ware, and continued longer than most with that line. It occurred to me they may have owned extensive clay beds and continued using this native clay to meet the demand for the cheaper ware after white ware came in vogue. I have no authority for this but they were extensive landowners. One of the prerequisites for use of improved machinery was change from the "old bodies" made with local clays to more refined ones for white granite, Queensware, or ironstone.

The company had the same management from the beginning; in 1884 the plant was enlarged and they finally began producing cream-colored ware. After the death of Josiah, the boys incorporated in 1889, and the next year they added a decorating department which was a very important factor in their future success. They also added another trademark (the one on the lone sample which I show). This dates their Tea Leaf production after 1890. Since the plant was right on the riverbank high flood waters required suspension of operations. That was not too bad with the old type kilns but when the circular decorating kilns were installed they had to be put on the second floor.

What of the man C. C. Thompson? He was one of the few men of his day with any advanced education; this perhaps accounts for some of the company's success. Born in Beaver County, he came with his father to East Liverpool in 1848. When he finished school at Mt. Union College he joined in the business. During C. C.'s time the pottery business was like a yo-yo, up and down, with the protective tariff laws helping make rich men out of poor potters in only ten years time. Some of the largest profits earned were in 1880s when plants ran at full capacity and there was a 55 to 60% ad valorem on imported wares. In 1887 Senator John Sherman of Ohio remarked that this American industry could not afford to do without the protective import taxes which had removed English goods from competition, brought English laborers in, and that skilled men were making finer and better goods than the English, and selling them cheaper. President McKinley also was a staunch supporter of the potting people. But, by 1892 the bubble broke and the industry was at the mercy of tariff reduction forces until 1896.

In 1905 Cassius Thompson died after twenty-five years in business; he was succeeded by his son George C. and the last name change took place — to C. C. Thompson Pottery Company. With his accension control passed to the New Breed. He was very active, possessed great enthusiasm, and carried on plant operation as long as his health permitted. George C. was president when another era of development began and firms grew up in months — not years. The keen competition could be met only by using modern methods, new machinery, and men who changed with the times as succeeding Thompsons did, until 1918 when they finally added semi-porcelain. In 1905 they had one kiln but added one more later. A stroke was the ultimate cause of George's death.

Another son, Stewart, took the helm for a while but by 1938 the plant was finally dismantled and the building adapted for other purposes. Steward was elected secretary-treasurer of the United States Potters Association but passed away in December of that year, 1963.

In 1947 the Croxall Chemical and Supply Company which was owned by Russel Smith was a tenant of the modern fireproof building, formerly occupied by C. C. T. Company. Croxall handled an English line of color supplies for ceramics, iron, enamel, glass, jewelry, and enamel colors. (This is according to the *American Ceramic Society Bulletin*, September, 1947.)

During a phone conversation in late January, 1980, with Mrs. J. D. Thompson (Josiah Donald [Don], a grandson of Josiah), she related that Don was sales manager for many years. Around 1930 he went to the Homer Laughlin China Company in the same capacity until his retirement thirty-five years later. He passed away at eighty-five in 1975. According to his wife Marian, she was an "outsider." She was a native of Delaware who had been in college at Smith College in North Hampton, Massachusetts, and was the house guest of one of the Smith girls from the old Taylor, Smith & Taylor Company, when she met J. D. Thompson. She had been in East Liverpool only fifty-seven years! J. D. was a 1912 Yale graduate and spent his life and expertise improving East Liverpool pottery.

She also recalled their favorite uncle was Will Thompson, the song writer-composer-musician. (My children learned piano from instruction books written by him.) In 1900 he gave 100 acres for a park up on hills overlooking the city. He stipulated there was never to be any intoxicants or intoxicated persons allowed there; no horse racing with betting; no gambling of any kind; and no games or sports allowed on Sunday. She remarked that most of the churches hold their picnics in the park. Many of the family members built homes around the park perimeter early in this century and several still reside there.

She also added that the late Malcom Thompson, a brother-in-law, had been a lifetime employee at Hall China Company.

She further advised me that the home of Dale Thompson, a nephew who was also in the C. C. T. pottery, was given to the East Liverpool Historical Society for their permanent headquarters, at the death of his widow, Dorothy, in late 1979.

Another subject we spoke of was the old Thompson Hotel at Third and Broadway. It had been built in the late 1800s. The floor tile contained the names of seventeen of the potteries at that time. It was *the place* to stay. It is too bad it was torn down to make way for a new highway in 1974.

Vodrey Pottery Company
1848-1928

Jabez Vodrey was widely known as an "outstanding Staffordshire potter" during his entire American potting career, which began in 1827 when he, with a Mr. Frost (also a Staffordshire potter), established a pottery at New Liberties, Pennsylvania (now part of Pittsburgh). Known as Vodrey and Frost, they were reputed to have brought other Staffordshire men to help make white ware but were unsuccessful because of unsuitable clay. However they did make yellow ware and a coarse salt glaze stoneware for a couple of years, then, in 1829, moved on.

Vodrey *may* have come from the Tunstall area of Staffordshire because Little* records a pot-works of Baggaley and Vodrey in 1810 at

---

* Little, *Staffordshire Blue*.

Unusual small pitcher, 3½" across and 4" high with a lip on each side. Looks as if it had been made for something else, like a brush vase for a toilet set, and the handle added to make a creamer. The decoration in bright gold is partly worn off. The piece is quite heavy, and very white.
VP-1

The only mark is a banner with the word Ursilla on it. The banner is identical to Vodrey's "Winona" banner. This may be an erroneous attribution. If not Vodrey, who? (82)
VP-2

Golden Hill but it was not listed in an 1819 census. However, one David Vawdry was. Spelling variations were so common that this is not too important. No other historian's account I read had any record of Vodreys. Be that as it may . . . Jabez Vodrey evidently had a good reputation: A group of investors, including one Jacob Lewis (also from Staffordshire) invited Vodrey and Frost to move their company to Louisville and operate the first pottery in Kentucky. They did so in 1830 and met with moderate success in making cream colored ware. Perhaps part of this success was due to forty men they brought from Staffordshire to work. No specification was made as whether this was the same group of men which was at New Liberties, or if it was a new crew of immigrants.

After two or three years Frost retired and the partnership was then Vodrey and Lewis, until 1839 when Lewis moved just across the river to Troy, Indiana, to help James Clews in the ill-fated Indiana Pottery. It is a very mediocre grade white ware.

Clews finally inveigled Jabez Vodrey to also come help at this trouble spot. Probably because of English friendship ties, he disposed of the Louisville works and put all his energy into making acceptable wares in Troy until 1846. He was unsuccessful only because the clays were unsuitable. Unknown to him, this fact was verified by chemists and geologists later on.

Upon leaving Troy he went, as James Bennett had done just a short time before, to East Liverpool to try again in another pottery. The 1840s were the decade when several Englishmen began there: Benjamin Harker, John Goodwin, William Bloor, and William Brunt, to name a few.

The first partnership was Woodward and Vodrey, beginning in 1848 as the Herculaneum Works, with good success in making the usual Rockingham and yellow ware. After a fire in March of the next year they rebuilt to come back later in the summer, bigger and better than ever. The inclusion of new investor/partners, John and James Blakely and Richard Booth, caused the name change to Woodward, Blakely, and Company. Jabez was the "and Company" — the expert, experienced potter, and under his hand they kept growing until soon they were one of, if not the largest in town who made only the best Rockingham and yellow ware. In 1856 they were awarded a gold medal, the highest honor given by the American Institute, for beauty and finish of Bennington ware. Another line added was terra-cotta but this was their undoing: They took a contract for work on St. Paul's Cathedral in Pittsburgh, using the terra-cotta. They lost at least $10,000 on it and this, in conjunction with depressed economic conditions, caused them to fold. Assignment was made in 1857. Blakely and Woodward left town.

Vodrey exhibited "stay power" and was able to salvage the east end of the building on the east side of College at Fourth streets. He got one of the three kilns (see the Brunt story) and with the aid of his sons, William H., John, and James N., he began again as Vodrey & Brothers *Palissy Works*. They kept in step with the times by making white ware in 1875, and adding semi-porcelain in 1879.

Jabez Vodrey retired after the 1857 reorganization was completed but lived until 1861. In 1880 the title was changed to Vodrey and Brothers, and in 1897 they incorporated as Vodrey Pottery Company, continuing to use that until they closed in 1928.

One piece I have seen *may not be* by Vodrey but I am of the firm opinion the name on it is the pattern name or body style. The banner is identical to their *Winona* mark.

In later years a son, William H. Vodrey, was a participant in a love story that had a happy ending, thanks to his perseverance:

Mr. William Brunt had purchased the first white ware pottery in East Liverpool from the founder, William Bloor, and when Mr. Brunt went to war he left his foreman, young John Thompson, in charge of the pottery. Upon his return two years later (1864) he found Thompson had left town to avoid the draft and the pot-works idle and grown up with weeds. However, Thompson soon returned and, along with several other men, bought interest in the company. Early in the life of this new firm, John Thompson died, leaving his estate in the hands of Colonel William H. Vodrey, for payment to an old-time sweetheart in England. Colonel Vodrey, a son of Jabez Vodrey, held the money for many years but finally traced the whereabouts, in England, of the legatee who was by then an old woman. His mission was completed when he delivered the money to her.

The Vodrey family was involved in pottery production until about 1928 and is still active in community life in East Liverpool.

The late William H. Vodrey Jr. passed away in September, 1979. I now have no direct contact with family members to verify information. Perhaps someone else will come to my aid.

Walker China Co.

1923-1980

Plate, 9¾"; cup, 3" high; and saucer, 5½" wide, all in heavy hotel ware. Underglaze decoration, beautifully executed; no hint of crazing; cup has a comfortable handle. **WAC-1**

Trademark on above **WAC-2**

To the best of my knowledge this is the only company presently (1980) producing Tea Leaf with the exception of Cumbow China Decorating Company, who decorates *only* — they do *not* manufacture. Consequently, Walker is left in a very unique situation. Their production of Tea Leaf, according to an early letter, is limited to filling custom orders for institutional use.

Lois Lehner related in her recent book on *Ohio Pottery and Glass* that Walker China Company began as Bedford China Company and was reorganized as Bailey-Walker China Company in 1923. They produced hotel ware with the label of "The Bailey-Walker Vitrified China." At some point Albert Walker purchased the interest of Harry Bailey and began the manufacture of a line of fine dinner ware along with the hotel ware. The style of that company was Walker China Company and it still operates under that name.

In personal correspondence Mrs. Lehner stated that Walker was a division of the Alco Standard Corp., which made vitreous china and table ware under that label until November 15, 1976. At that time the company was purchased from Alco by the Jeanette Corporation.

I have seen and photographed the cup and saucer in the accompanying photos in order to show their trademark. These are not what could be termed "reproductions." There appears to be no intent to deceive. This line is simply a 1970s production of this century-old favorite.

The cup and saucer are excellent quality, hotel-type heavy goods which can "take the heat of the kitchen" as Harry Truman used to say. The decoration is under the clear white glaze and even with the weight, the cup is comfortable to hold, and coffee retains heat for a reasonable length of the time. I would assume the full line is similar.

In an earlier phone conversation with Mr. Fred Clifford of the Red Cliff Company he related that the production of flat ware (plates, etc.) in the Red Cliff line was done by the Walker China Company, while the Hall China Company made the hollow ware for Red Cliff. This line was made during the 1950s and discontinued in 1960 — see Hall China chapter.

Perhaps in time, more information on this twentieth century Walker China Company will become available.

Sure enough, just during proof-reading word came to me from Lois McKean of Mayer China Company of Beaver Falls, Pennsylvania that the Walker China Company had been purchased by that firm on June 13, 1980 and is now known as Mayer Plant No. 2.

So ends the Walker China Company as such, but a better day is here in pottery history with the Mayer people. See the Mayer chapter.

Wheeling Pottery Company
1979-1908

Those of us who are fortunate enough to own a piece of Tea Leaf made by the Wheeling Pottery Company of Wheeling, West Virginia are proud possessors of another scarce item, and one of the better quality wares produced in the United States. Perhaps this is due to the very early influence of Mr. Edwin Meakin Pearson, general manager of the original Wheeling Pottery and several succeeding companies under the same organization. Other men in this group included George K. Wheat, president; William A. Isett, secretary; Charles Craddock, decorating department manager; J. Nelson Vance and Charles Franzheim, two important financial backers.

The first organization took place upon the arrival in Wheeling by Mr. Pearson in November, 1879, after his departure from East Liverpool, less than sixty miles up the Ohio river. In 1887 this same group organized and operated the La Belle Company, and in 1889 the two companies were consolidated. The original Wheeling Pottery made white ware, both plain and decorated, while the La Belle works made a different ware they called "Adamantine" china, along with various other lines of utilitarian and decorated goods. After Mr. Pearson left in 1893 or 1894, Mr. Franzheim became president and general manager and under his guidance the capacity was increased until those two works had a combined total of fifteen kilns and thirteen decorating kilns — one of the largest potteries in the United States. Mr. Franzheim boldly advertised their ware as "Made in America." This was at the crucial time when our goods were considered inferior and well could have contributed to the later failure of the company.

There were numerous other mergers, consolidations, and reorganizations during the next twelve or thirteen years, but in December, 1902 the Wheeling Potteries Company was incorporated, absorbing the Wheeling, La Belle, and Riverside potteries as well as a plant at Tiltonville and Avon Faience; each was then operated as a department of the Wheeling firm, according to Mr. Paul Evans, writing in *Spinning Wheel* magazine, January-February, 1974. He went on to record: "The Wheeling empire was seriously affected by the 1907 panic, and the following year it abandoned the general ware plants (La Belle and Wheeling departments) which produced semi-porcelain table, toilet, china, and commerical decorative wares. Operation of the Riverside and Tiltonville plants was anticipated for the production of sanitary goods.

"Attempts at reorganization were not successful and the firm went into receivership in late 1908."

Mr. Edwin A. Barber in his *Pottery and Porcelain of the United States* (pg. 309–311) places Mr. Edward Meakin Pearson in proper perspective for us to enjoy learning more about this member of the famous Meakin family, the best known of all the Tea Leaf producers.

He was born in Burslem, England in 1848. His middle name came from his mother's family, and his father owned the Abbey Pottery at

Cobridge which had been built in 1703. Mr. Pearson was thoroughly trained there and admitted as a partner in 1869 at the age of twenty-one. Just before he was taken into the family business he made two trips to the United States and liked what he saw.

In 1873 he terminated his English partnership and came to East Liverpool, Ohio, to assess the possibilities of producing white ware there, and stayed on for some time. I am sure he found many potters there whom he had known a short time before, back home in his native Staffordshire district.

At that time Knowles, Taylor, and Knowles China Company was the principal pottery engaged in experimentation prior to their production of white ware, the newcomer to the American market. They, in cooperation with private citizens of the town, were most generous in their contribution of land and $10,000 to establish a plant exclusively for this purpose, which Mr. Pearson helped plan, build, equip, and later managed for a while. This plant was opened in 1874 in conjunction with Mr. Homer Laughlin and his brother, Shakespeare. Mr. Homer Laughlin continued to operate this plant while Mr. Pearson planned and built eight more facilities which produced this ever-in-demand white ware. He was connected with five of them in some capacity until he moved to Wheeling in 1879 and became involved with the Wheeling Pottery.

Mr. Pearson's greatest services to the entire pottery industry were felt through his effective tariff legislative recommendations to both houses of Congress, and as an active member and office holder in the powerful United States Potter's Association. He is buried in East Liverpool.

Two other well known English potters, who at one time were connected with the Vance/Avon Faience works of the Wheeling Potteries, were William Percival Jervis and Fredrick Hurten Rhead. Although they may have had little or no direct contact with the white wares division, I believe they were carefully chosen by the company officials who had earlier established extremely high standards of excellence for each key employee. It was most interesting to learn that Mr. Jervis, in addition to writing such fine books as the *Encyclopedia of Ceramics*, *A Dictionary of Pottery Terms*, *A Pottery Primer* and others which I have used for reference work in this book, was also a working potter. Besides the Craven Art Pottery of East Liverpool, which he established in 1905, he had extensive facilities at his home at Oyster Bay on Long Island where Mr. Rhead was associated with him sometime after they left Wheeling. Rhead's pottery path led him to California via Zanesville, Ohio, and University City, Missouri. Finally, he returned to eastern Ohio and was art director for Homer Laughlin China Company from 1927 until his death in 1942. His writings also, along with his work, have influenced art potters and is still felt, even indirectly, today.

According to Minnie Watson Kamm in her *Old China* book, the popular table nicety of 1895-1908 was to have a set of bone dishes which were curved to fit close to the edge of the plate. The one shown in her book was made by La Belle. I have photographed numerous ones of these by various companies, some by potteries which had closed long before 1895; even if this was the height of their popularity, they were in use almost a quarter century before. By the way, they make very nice salad dishes to conserve space on our crowded tables of today.

Notice the motif on the nappy: It does *not* have a flower on the leaf design. This seems to be common to the American wares; compare the East End Pottery and Wick designs. Apparently Mayer China Company of Beaver Falls, Pennsylvania, was one of the few who followed the

4½" square nappy with bright gold motif and fine edge-trim. Some crazing but very white.
WH-1

Trademark on nappy, used
1886–1896.
WH-2

English style. There is some suggestion that this may have been one mode of silent rebellion against the rose as the flower of England — remember — "There will always be an England?" These potters were an independent lot and Alice Morse Earle in *China Collecting in America* acclaims them very well. "Working the earth makes men easy-minded. A community of potters is always orderly, law-abiding, thrifty, and industrious."

There were some fifteen trademarks used by this company but the only one I have seen on Tea Leaf is their version of an Americanized Royal Arms mark as shown here, used 1886-1896.

Wick China Company
1889-1918-19(?)

Berry set on Aurora body shape; the large bowl is about 10" in diameter and very shallow; the smaller bowl, about 6" in diameter. More suitable for strawberry shortcake than juicy fruit sauce. Very attractive swirls inside each piece. *(60)*
WC-1

So very little information about this company has come to me, but since I have seen and photographed a number of items bearing their trademark, I feel they may well have done a thriving business in Tea Leaf, for a little while at least.

Part of the site of Wickboro (Kittanning) in western Pennsylvania was on land previously owned by a Capt. John Armstrong. In 1872, George H. Fox and Valentine Neubert platted a town to be known as "Germantown," but in four years just twenty-one houses had been built with only a saw mill, a brick works, and a lime kiln to support the economy.

Adjoining this village, John Donaldson had been in the nursery business since before 1843 when he had built three hot-houses. By 1878 he had over 300,000 trees of all kinds growing; was shipping about 20,000 of them each year to all parts of the country; in addition he was operating a large truck garden with only about twenty men. Evidently, outsiders felt this was not "good use of the land" or not furnishing employment for enough men and "progress" demanded something different.

However it was, John Wick Jr. bought about 300 acres, uprooted the orchard, and leveled the ground. He proceeded with dispatch to lay out the town of Wickboro right in the middle of the old orchard site. Along with the platting of the town he donated ground for a school, contributed to the building fund, and gave land for two other large industries — a plate glass manufacturing company and a brick and fire clay company; *and* he built a pottery — all to bolster the economy and put Wickboro on the map.

In 1889 The Wick Chinaware Company was organized and operated by the Pennsylvania China Company. They kept several hundred employees busy making tableware, plain and decorated wares, and ornamental vases. They used at least seven clays: two from England, one from Florida, and four native types.

Towards the end of 1913 the pottery closed without warning — a terrible blow to the workmen, most of whom owned their homes and/or other property. Many sacrificed this property when they had to leave the area to find work. W. S. George of East Palestine, Ohio, eventually purchased the works and continued operation.

W. S. George had been in and out of various pot works in eastern Ohio and western Pennsylvania for a good many years; consequently, he was well qualified to handle the floundering Wick China Company. He had grown up in difficult times, with little formal schooling. At one time he was a semi-pro boxer which may also have enhanced his standing among the work-hardened pottery men. His success as a pottery salesman stemmed from his warm, outgoing personality mixed with these other attributes, and it paid off: He was the owner of four

Enlarged Tea Leaf design   *(60)*
WC-2

Flat soup, 9″, and a little bit deeper than most. Lustre slightly darker and better preserved.
WC-3

Butter dish with lid (and one hole drainer) with rope-like handles as well as finial, and one of six butter pats; tea pot (no lid), 6″ high. All very white and heavy. One of six matching butter chips unmarked. All with gold overglaze.
WC-4

Sugar with lid; 9″ high. Very attractive rope-like finial.
WC-5

scattered pot-works instead of a laborer in only one. His plan was to leave a pot-bank to each of his four sons.

His health failed and while he was ill, certain underhanded competitors planned to "freeze" out the entire family if he died. He fooled them all and recovered to throw the rascals all out. His plan did not work quite as he expected because only one son, Campbell George, was interested and capable of carrying on at his demise.

At the time W. S. bought the Wick Company in 1913-1914, he owned the Continental China Company in East Palestine, Ohio where nearly half the town people worked for him. He changed the Wick to the George China Company, which was in operation until after World War I. When the doors closed for the last time the buildings were abandoned and finally torn down. Today a cement block manufactory stands on the site.

On December 29, 1919 Wickboro merged with the town of Kittanning and the name was changed to Kittanning.

W. S. George continued in business at some of his other locations until at least 1955.

"Aurora" is the body style we are most familiar with since it is part of Wick's most common trademark. A collector in Vancouver, British Columbia was the first to report owning Tea Leaf with that insignia; then in 1979 I photographed the bowls with the unusual swirls inside. These are similar to present day ironstone, made by Johnson Bros. in England. Also, the finials on two pieces of Wick I have had for several years remind me of a twisted rope finial shown on articles made by Johnsons as pictured in a 1902 Montgomery Ward catalog. My soap dish, along with a covered sugar are a slightly greyed white, quite heavy, but pleasant to hold. The KNOBLE trademark on other pieces had me baffled until I purchased a large jug on which the decoration was typically Wick and T W C CO which stand for The Wick China Company.

We can expect to see more Tea Leaf by Wick, so keep looking.

Large jug, about 1¾ qt. capacity. Heavy and somewhat hard to hold; top is quite brown. Note Knoble as part of trademark (probably shape). (90)
WC-6

Children's Tea Sets

China Toy Tea Sets.

25155

25155 Set consists of cups, saucers, tea pot, sugar bowl and cream; small size; packed in paper box. Price......... $0.10
25156 Same description as above but larger. Price. $0.25
25157 Set consists of decorated plates, cups, saucers, tea pot, creamer, sugar bowl; good sized dishes. Price.................................. $0.50
25158 Same description but larger. Price....... .75
25159 Same, but larger size and assortment. Price................................ 1.00
25163 White Stone China Tea set of 24 pieces, as follows: 6 plates, 6 cups, 6 saucers, 1 sugar bowl and cover, 1 tea pot and cover, 1 creamer, 1 slop bowl. This set is large enough for a miss from 8 to 14 years of age. (Not safe to send by mail.) Weighs 8½ lbs. Per set.................. $1.25
The pieces in this set are larger than usually sold in toy sets; the cups stand 2 inches high, and the plates measure 4¼ inches across.

25164—Fancy Decorated Tea Set, same size and assortment as above; elegant patterns. Packed in wooden box, weight 8½ lbs. Price. $1.75

Montgomery Ward 1894–95, winter catalog

Toy China Tea Sets.

No. 29R377 Toy China Tea Set, consists of cups, saucers, teapot, sugar bowl and cream-er, about 16 pieces, small 25-cent value pack-ed in paper box. Per set 15c

Shipping weight, 10 ounces.

No. 29R379 Toy China Tea Set, consisting of dec-orated plates, cups, saucers, tea pot, creamer, sugar bowl, about 23 pieces. Price, per set................ 25c
Shipping weight, 20 ounces.

No. 29R381 Toy China Tea Set, consisting of about 17 pieces, decorated plates, cups, saucers, tea pot, creamer and sugar bowl. Larger size, and very interesting for a child. Splendid 75-cent value. Price, per set........ .... 50c
Shipping weight, 48 ounces.

No. 29R383 Toy China Tea Set, consisting of about 25 pieces, finely decorated plates, cups, sau-cers, tea pot, creamer and sugar bowl. Large size and extra value. Price, per set.............. .... 75c
Shipping weight, 56 ounces.

No. 29R385 Toy China Tea Set, consisting of about 25 pieces, decorated cups, saucers, plates, tea pot, creamer and sugar bowl. Our larger size set. and suitable for misses up to 14 or 15 years of age. **Unmailable on account of weight.**
Price, per set.. $1.00
Shipping weight, 7 pounds.

No. 29R387 Toy China Tea Set. This, our finest set, consists of 23 pieces finely decorated cups, sau-cers, plates, teapot, creamer, sugar bowl, etc., larger cups and saucers, and suitable for young misses for an afternoon tea. Equal to any $2.00 value. Price, per set.. $1.40
Shipping weight, 9 pounds.

Sears in 1902

Oh, to have been a child in 1894-95! Montgomery Ward and Company advertised children's tea sets for 10 cents up to $1.75. The cheapest set, packed in a paper box, was a service for six. The most expensive one was for a "Miss, 8-14 years of age." It was a twenty-four piece set for six: six plates, cups, saucers, a sugar/lid, a tea pot/lid, a creamer, and a slop bowl. It was stone china in an elegant pattern, fancily decorated, packed in a wooden box, and weighed 8½ pounds.

The waste bowl mentioned above was to hold the dregs of tea from cups, before refilling with fresh brew. It was considered poor taste to pour fresh tea on old leaves or dregs.

Sears, Roebuck and Company the same year carried a slightly different assortment. Their beginning price was fifteen cents for a sixteen piece set for four (in a paper box), total weight ten ounces. The prices increased to $1.40 for twenty-three pieces. They left out the waste bowl. This set was suitable for a "Young Miss for afternoon tea."

The late Thelma Shull, writing in *Hobbies*, October, 1948 recalled that in 1889 a Chicago store advertised "Moss Rose": 100 piece dinner set for $13.50; and children's china tea sets "decorated with delicate leaf sprays on each piece" sold for eighty-five cents. This children's set included six plates, cups, saucers, two platters, a creamer, covered sugar bowl, and a tea pot.

Since Tea Leaf and Moss Rose were popular at the same time and often placed on the same body styles, we are safe to assume the prices quoted above were also valid for Tea Leaf children's dishes. It would also appear that most of the children's dishes we see today were made for older children . . . "Young Misses" . . . so to speak.

A suggestion I have heard repeatedly is that many items we consider to be children's dishes were actually salesmen's samples. For many years, after the days of the peddler who traveled by horseback, or in old noisy wagons on which he hung all sorts of pots and pans that clanked and clanged as he drove, the sales territories were covered by these "drummers," who traveled by train and then by livery "hacks" to the outlying areas. My own father at one time drove one of these livery hacks on a regular route, carrying mail, passengers, freight, and news. He recalled how often these drummers (traveling salesmen to us now) made life much more interesting with their news and stories of other people, places, and events. The obvious answer to their need to show true quality of their wares was a good supply of samples. I can just see a little girl's eyes light up in anticipation, as she watched the local general storekeeper look over all those samples, and bargain with the drummer on how many barrels of Tea Leaf or Blue Willow dishes he would buy for his Christmas trade. His order also would include the necessary bedroom sets, adult dishes, and lamps; all the time he was hoping to get some glass-ware premiums thrown in for good measure. I have yet to hear definitely that any of these samples ever reached a little hostess, but how else do we account for so many unusual items in larger size "children's" dishes?

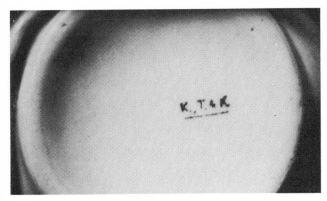

Trademark on child's tea set by KTK.

CTS-1

Part of a child's tea set by KTK; overglaze gold decoration.

Doll's set; 4 cups and saucers; gift from Johana Anderton. Unmarked. (2)
CTS-2

Kathy Mast dishes by Edward Walley (53)
CTS-3

The partial set of child's dishes I have, bearing the only mark I had found for the old Knowles, Taylor, and Knowles Company, came to me in two parts. The first, a tea pot, sugar bowl with lid, one cup, and a chipped saucer, were from my young friend, Rob Lee, who enjoys the "old brown" Tea Leaf so much. Such a small beginning of a child's set of dishes was of slight interest to an effervescent, high school junior-year young man, so we traded tit for tat. Several years later a dealer friend, Roger Harper, asked what I would give for four Tea Leaf child's plates. We agreed on a price and everyone reading this page can share my utter delight when those three plates and a perfect saucer matched exactly the pieces I had with the old K. T. & K. mark! Since there is a distinct difference in this American version, these are rare indeed! The dishes are rather thin, but quite heavy and very white. The glaze is slightly gray, quite thick, and very lightly crazed on some of the plates and a saucer, as if many tea parties had been served by the little girl-owner of long ago. The design is gold overglaze and some has worn off with numerous washings after these mini-social events.

Compared to a Japanese made set (not Tea Leaf) given to me that first Christmas, from my "new Mama," Emma Mason Doring, in 1923, this K. T. & K. set must have been part of a larger, much more expensive set made for the older girls, as it is just twice the size of my first play dishes.

I felt sure regular dinner ware was also made in the Tea Leaf pattern by this company; sure enough . . . six years later an Ohio friend sent a photo of a cup and saucer. (See the K. T. & K. chapter.)

One of the early delights in my Tea Leaf hunting was a gift from Johana Anderton: a set of four tiny porcelain cups and saucers, with the larger design on the saucer somewhat resembling an oak leaf, but the unmistakable Tea Leaf was on the cups which were only 1-5/8" across and 1-3/8" high, while the deep saucers were 3" across. The gilt overglaze decoration came off easily as I learned while mending one tiny cup which was accidently broken. This may well have been part of one of those Lilliputian sets which sold for twenty-five cents or fifty cents. I have seen smaller size cups in cheap imported ware but none so well executed as these. Logic would indicate this set was meant for a small child four to six years old. We probably will never know what other pieces, if any, were in the original set, because it is unmarked.

As I researched collections for items I had not seen, I found Kathy Mast owned the oldest child's set, a variant made by Edward Walley of Cobridge. It was a beautiful blue-white, heavy ironstone, free from all crazing, in the popular Niagara shape, as verified by the back stamp. There is a service for four with only the lids for the tea pot and sugar bowl missing. The lustre was mint and any little girl of 1880 or 1980

Three childrens' tea plates: #1–4", Meakin; #2–4", American, maker unknown. Notice no flower on motif. #3–4¼", Meakin. All are crazed. (35)
CTS-4

Tea party for six, with close up of larger pieces. (39)
CTS-5

Trademark on above **CTS-6**

could be a proud hostess at her tea party to show off these dishes. Walley was in business from 1845-1856, so this may be one of the oldest child's sets we are likely to see. The design is almost identical to one used by Elsmore and Forster.

The only children's dishes by Alfred Meakin which have come to my attention have been plates, from 3½" in diameter to a larger 5¼", with ever so much variance in condition, from mint to crazed, brown stained, little or no lustre and some with hairline cracks and/or chips which bespoke of long, happy, childhood play days.

The families of the Mellor, Taylor Company of Burslem must have had little girls, as the majority of Tea Leaf children's dishes I have heard of or photographed were made by them. I like to imagine they made for other children what had given their own little ones so many days and years of pleasure.

The prize of all the children's sets I have seen belonged to a dealer-collector in northern Illinois. Upon arrival at his home we found the table laid with a complete set of Mellor, Taylor ware in service for six, plus child size pewter flat ware, and napkin rings, complete with miniature napkins. This surely must have been the pride and joy of a very loving and careful young hostess. Each piece was mint, as if it had been kept for "Sunday best." Since visiting there and photographing these beauties, along with many other rare items in the dealer's possession, I have been told the dishes are now in the care of a southern Missouri belle, for the purchase price of $1,000.00!

Another famous English potter, Anthony Shaw, made some Tea Leaf for children and Laura Ady shared photos of her collection bearing this trademark. It is a service for four in which the plates are larger (4-7/8" across) and the cups are smaller (2" high and 2" wide) with the design in the bottom of the cup as was the custom of the Shaw decorators. It seems to me it took more time and labor to put the flowers inside at the bottom of the cup than to casually apply them to the side or front as other decorators did. Perhaps there was a special effort on the part of the Shaw people to keep alive the legend of "reading" the tea leaves left in the cups and hoping for tidings of good luck to come. Shaw's Tea Leaf is usually very white with a blue tint, the lustre of good quality and more than adequate, while the body shapes are pleasant and comfortable to hold. This set is no exception.

Tea party for four by Anthony Shaw, 16 pieces. Tea pot, 5" high; plates, 4⅞" in diameter. Tea Leaf in bottom of cup. Trademark—A. SHAW WARRANTED.
CTS-7

Part of Clemenston's Coffeeberry tea set for the little girls. Creamer, 4" tall, teapot base, 4¼" without lid; cups, 2" high and 2½" in diameter (42)
CTS-8

Ewer for child's bedroom set or possibly for a mush and milk set. 5" high, in the Cable body style. (60)
CTS-9

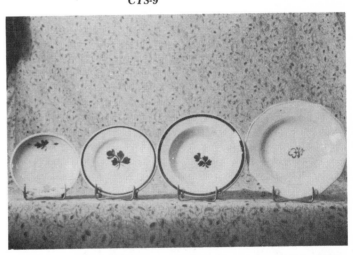

Another child's handleless cup; unmarked; 2¼" high (78)
CTS-10

Left to right: doll saucer, 2½"; cup plate, 4"; conserve, 4½"; child's tea set plate, 5½".
CTS-11

Child's handleless cup; Lily-of-the-Valley by Shaw. 2⅛" high × 2¼" wide. Tea Leaf inside bottom. (1)
CTS-12

Some time ago I ordered by mail what I thought were two large flat soup plates by Anthony Shaw. I first saw them pictured in the "Western Collector" magazine and later in *Antiques Past and Present* by Katherine M. McClinton. When they arrived I was delightfully pleased to find I had not two large flat soup plates with Lily-of-the-Valley embossed on them, but two little 4" plates less than an inch deep that may have been salesman's samples or possibly cup plates; but I think they are conserve plates. See page 22.

Another order brought two pieces, one with a clover leaf design, which I feel is a child's plate, quite yellow and crazed under the glaze with well executed overglaze design. This is too large for a cup plate, 4½".

I have been told of two sets in the Coffeeberry variant; this is one of them. Perhaps there are others and someone will share a picture for us all the enjoy.

Surely there are other children's tea sets in regular Tea Leaf or one of the variants, which we can show at a later time, should knowledge of them become available.

Odds and Ends

Seven cups. Top: Edge Malkin. Center: (left to right) Clemenston, 12 panelled; unknown; Shaw. Bottom: (left to right) Wick; Furnival; Meakin. (86)(45)
OE-1

Row 1: unkown. Row 2: Meakin, Meakin, Shaw, Davenport, Wilkinson. Row 3: unknown. Row 4: Adams, Powell & Bishop, Clemenston, Mellor-Taylor.
OE-2

Gift to author (37)
OE-3

Included in this chapter are cups and cup plates; mugs and egg cups; butter chips and bone dishes; conserve/honey plates and salesmen's samples; mustard pots, syrup pitchers, and toothpick holders; salt and pepper shakers and candlesticks; foot tubs; spittoons and cuspidors; and reproductions.

1. Cups

Gourds, sea or coconut shells, or even ostrich egg shells were likely the first cups our ancestors used. No one seems to have thought of putting handles on drinking vessels until the early 1770s when the English tried to improve on the tea bowls (cups) which they had copied from the Chinese by making them larger. When the additional size made the cups too hot to hold when full of steaming brew, Englishmen simply added handles. To keep everyone happy, they continued making cups without handles, as well as the handled ones, for almost a century.

The myth that England did not know how to apply handles and make them stick to the cups must have been started by a jealous European potter. Pictures of very early British ware show handles applied to all sorts of items. The handles of tea cups are applied the very same way as the handles of the largest jug: The handles were molded from a bit of the same clay used in the body of the cup, then the two pieces were stauked (stuck) together with slip and fired. The intense heat of the kiln melted it all into one solid piece — the cup, the glue (or slip), and the handle. Today cups and handles are often moulded in one piece so handles are not easily broken.

From 1815–1850 single cups with two saucers were usual parts of larger dinnerware services and most households had two sets of dishes — one of earthenware for everyday use, and one reserved for company, made from some type of porcelain. But by 1900 a set of dishes in a service for twelve included two sizes of cups — the larger one for coffee and the smaller one for tea.

Coffee cups were usually taller (3–3½"), while teacups were more shallow; both were about 3" in diameter, but since there was no set rule they were likely interchanged.

In the accompanying picture there are eighteen cups, all varying slightly. Maybe one is ¼" taller or wider than another. Variances in decoration and shapes of handles are noticable differences; body styles and glazes also help identify manufacturers. Only the reproductions are marked so the makers are not all definitely known.

Who cares what size or weight a cup is when longing for that first cup of good, hot coffee, tea, or chocolate in the morning? One of my prize possessions is the big Tea Leaf coffee cup in the common St. Denis shape, given to me by my sister-in-law, Dorothy Samuelson Heavilin. It had been the favorite cup of her Swedish grandfather for as long as she could remember as she grew up near his homestead farm in central Iowa. In 1897 Tea Leaf cups and saucers like Mr. Samuelson's were listed at $2.10 for a dozen sets. In the same catalog, shaving mugs varied from five cents to fifteen cents each, while mustache cups ranged from eighteen cents to thirty-eight cents each.

Four cups. Second from left embossed on outside and has Meakin trademark; other three seen frequently unmarked. (73)
OE-4

Oak Leaf cup and saucer by Mayer (72)
OE-5

Three cups, all sold with Meakin saucers. (84)
OE-6

Three cups: (left to right) East End Pottery; handleless tea; Mellor-Taylor. (84)
OE-7

Four Chelsea shape cups by Meakin (71)
OE-8

Davenport handleless cup (33)
OE-9

Edge, Malkin & Co. mustache cup and saucer in rich yellow color — Rare! (35)
OE-10

Three of Shaw's Lily-of-the-Valley handleless cups and saucers, one regular, two child's sets, with/without handles. (60)
OE-11

Shaw's service for four, Cable style; design in cup. (58)
OE-12

Another Shaw, 12 panelled. Extra large saucer is 6¼". (69)
OE-13

Shaw's Lily-of-the-Valley chocolate cups. RARE! 3½" high. (82)
OE-14

Two of four demi-tasse cups; 2½" high and saucers 5⅛" wide by Meakin. Spoon for comparative size. (1)
OE-15

Farmer's cups, so called because of their size, were used for several purposes: to serve a double portion of brew, since the cup held at least a pint; or as a porringer to serve mush and milk or bread and milk — common suppers of our grandparents' time (before we began to eat our main meal at night and call it dinner!). Coffee was precious until about 1870, so this helps to limit the time of popularity of oversize cups to the Tea Leaf era. The first "farmer's cup" I saw in Tea Leaf was in a restaurant in Illinois, where Tea Leaf is on display. When I returned to photograph it someone had stolen it!

It was common practice a century ago to make use of "Regency Sets," tea sets in which each piece was different. There were many delicate, ornate, unusual styles included, and today we can use our purchases or gifts of Tea Leaf cups and saucers to make our own "Regency Sets." These make great conversation items and we are getting good use of whatever cups we can find on the market today.

A style we may see revived is the *mustache cup.* No explanation is necessary to extol the advantages of this protective device. Any gentleman in need of one should certainly welcome a beautiful Tea Leaf mustache cup as a special gift. The price for a left-handed style will naturally be higher than that for an ordinary right-handed type — but well worth the money — if you can find one! I have been told of them but have not seen them.

While some cups had no handles and others had covers, there were some which had saucers that fit so snugly there was no chance for the cup to slip or tip. I can imagine that a sailing ship captain invented this style; or if not him, then surely a future airline pilot, in a previous life, thought of this idea. This type was called a trembleu'se from the Greek word tremein which means "to tremble." It will be no surprise to me to see one that was taken from the galley of a sunken sailing ship off the American coast as this type would suit their need precisely.

Something not seen in common use today but available a century ago was a custard cup with a lid. These were very popular for serving custards, baked or boiled, and the lid obviously was to keep the food warm. Along the same line were caudle cups, used to serve food to sick people. Caudle was a mixture of warm milk, wine or ale, sugar, and spices, with small bits of bread. One of the cups or mugs shown here *may* have been made for this purpose. See page 215.

2. Cup Plates

The Chinese tea cups of the 1600s were quite small, as their idea of a proper cup of tea was 3½ sips; consequently, later when the price of tea went down in England, the size of the cups went up and the size of the saucers was equalized. Eventually it became proper etiquette to sip the beverage directly from the saucer after it had cooled. This, of course, called for something to set the cup in to protect milady's fine homespun cloth and handmade table. Cup plates were the answer. Cup plates came into fashion here in the United States around 1800 and were in use for most of the century; and "merrie ole" Englishmen did not miss the

Handleless cup and saucer by J.F. Wileman (90)
OE-16

Wileman cup and another variant—possibly Elsmore & Son. (90)
OE-17

Four panelled cinquefoil design variant on cup. (64)
OE-18

*3½" diameter tiny cup plates; anything larger than 4" is **not** a cup plate; these are by Meakin.* **OE-19** (71)

No, not Shaving Mugs, but Hot Soda Water Mugs

Take a good look at these pretty mugs. For years people have been thinking of them as shaving mugs. They're the same size, they're decorated and of course not a few collectors have converted them to mugs for serving today's refreshments.

The firm of Crandall & Godley has set us straight in the matter. These are not shaving mugs, but mugs for a beverage which few, if any, of today's collectors have ever heard .... hot soda water. Yet this was a rage in the 1880's. Most soda fountains had heaters in which charged water was made as hot as water for tea. Only this hot water was ready for flavoring with coffee syrup, or ginger, chocolate or lemon. They tell us that thousands of fountains had hot soda water taps, offered these four flavors, and served it in these mugs. Such documentation should require no further words. We are most grateful to Crandall & Godley for this information that we hereby pass on to collectors and dealers for their edification and, shall we say .... amusement?

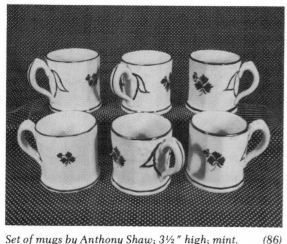

Set of mugs by Anthony Shaw; 3½" high; mint. (86)
OE-20

chance to please the American housewives and fill their coffers at the same time. Many of the cup plates seen today are of ironstone in old Staffordshire-blue patterns but Tea Leaf decorations are rather scarce and expensive. As stated earlier, there were two saucers for each cup: The large one was about 6" wide and rather deep — big enough to hold the liquid from the cup so it could cool. Meanwhile, the cup was placed in the smaller "cup-plate" which was 3" to 4" across and fit closely around the cup. My friend, Vere Kneeland, writing in the *Antique Journal*, November, 1973, described a cup plate as one on which the "rim stood away from the table." Another author warned that if a "cup plate" was more than 4" in diameter, it was *not* a cup plate! China ones matched the sets of dishes but did not always come in a pre-packaged set, but were sold extra. Mamie Hackley, in a personal letter, said they could be round or square. Glass ones were strictly American and "users choice." The production of cup plates ceased by 1880–1885. It was reported seventy years ago that one collection of that day had over 550 cup plates in it.* No wonder they are so scarce today, and so expensive!

The custom of cooling the beverage was called "saucering"; it was perfectly acceptable, even in the best homes, well into the twentieth century, to drink the brew from the saucer. I can remember my own grandfather, Charles Doring, a native of Switzerland, and, yes, even my own father, regularly enjoying their coffee in this old manner. This seems to be another part of Americana which is gone forever. Today, more than often not, we dispense with the saucers too.

3.   Mugs

Mugs were another product of the potter's hand. Shaving mugs were "big business" from 1840 until about 1925, and it is reasonable that many of the ironstone potters making mugs decorated scores of them with Tea Leaf. Perhaps the mug we thought was a shaving mug was really a "hot soda mug." *Spinning Wheel* magazine, August, 1953, carried this small item to pique our interest.

Do we have a shaving mug or a hot soda mug? Cider mugs have been mentioned in some antique publications, but since there have been no pictures for comparison, I doubt a mug was made expressly for this purpose. It is likely the same mug was used for cider as for hot soda. The set of six matching ones are a fine example, and today they could easily be used as coffee mugs.

A small round mug for a child probably came with a little bowl and perhaps a pint size pitcher and/or a small plate. These (not Tea Leaf) were sold by Sears in 1897 for fifteen cents and were still shown in the 1927 catalog for fifty-eight cents. Some had two pieces, others had four pieces in the set.

4.   Egg Cups

These two words should always be capitalized if that will indicate price. Seemingly, they have simply disappeared; or perhaps they are all in 500-piece collections I have not heard about. From inquiries I get, no one has any, and everyone wants a set.

From Anna Long in Pekin, Illinois, who cooked for royalty in Germany and Switzerland in her younger years, comes this information on the proper use of egg cups: The small part of the egg cup is the base, so the egg is placed in the larger (top) half of the egg cup, with the egg shell left intact. A small portion of the top of the egg shell is cracked and removed carefully and the egg is eaten directly from the remaining large section of shell. Never take the egg from the shell and then place it in the egg cup! A second egg was served in a second egg cup, if another one was desired.

---

* *Good Housekeeping Magazine*, July, 1909.

Two egg cups, 2½" × 4" high; left, very brown and crazed, while right is white and pretty. Both unmarked.
OE-21 (85)

Boston egg cup or footed sherbet? **Buffalo Pottery Book** *calls it a Boston egg cup and my friend Mary Jane from Colorado suggests it could be perfect for a poached egg. 4" diameter × 2¼" high.* **OE-22** (82)

A wall hanging of several butter chips (13)
OE-23

Scalloped 2½" square by Wedgwood (78)
OE-24

Upon looking at the *Buffalo Pottery* book (pp. 38–39) I was quite surprised to see listed a "Boston egg cup," and it looked just like a picture I had received from Mark Ward, labeled a "footed sherbet." Numerous inquiries of dealers, collectors, librarians, and finally a call to Mr. Seymour Altman, co-author of the Buffalo Pottery book, shed no light on why this was called a "Boston Egg Cup"! Perhaps some proper "old-line" Bostonian will brief us all on these amenities. Neither could Mr. Altman explain why a "double egg cup" was necessary when it would still hold only one egg in the shell. We both jokingly questioned if they were meant to be used with larger duck or goose eggs! From all indications, this little footed dish was meant to hold one or possibly two cooked eggs, removed from the shells. Or they may have been meant to be used for serving a poached egg or even a baked egg. I can see no reason why it could not be used for serveral purposes — if you can find a set. It would be a pleasant sight on a sick-bed tray with fresh fruit or jello in it, or even a big scoop of ice cream. Let us get all possible from our "good old Tea Leaf"!

In 1979 my attention was called to some single egg cups offered for sale in the midwest, which were obvious reproductions: They were unmarked and very poorly executed. The dealer who offered them for sale expressed doubt about their age and authenticity. Consequently, he removed them from the market. *If* you are not sure of the merchandise, then be doubly sure of your dealer. These reproduced egg cups may well have come from a china painter, working in her home in a north-central state. So far her name eludes me. **Please** be cautious about buying newly painted ware for prices of genuine antiques.

5. Butter Chips

Butter chips (or butter pats) are some of the best-loved replicas of Victorian china, but there seem to still be a great many in circulation yet. They were concurrent with the popularity of our Tea Leaf pattern; consequently, every barrel of dishes shipped from England which contained a service for twelve, held a dozen little butter pats as part of the set. They were probably used on special occasions. Thus, they were not subjected to breakage as were pitchers or plates. More than twenty years ago, someone reported there were over 65,000 butter chip collectors, and most of the interest stemmed from childhood memories as related earlier in this book by Sally Wright.

In my own collection of butter chips, there are various sizes and styles — round, square, fluted corners, octagonal — all match the Tea Leaf dinnerware of some potter, either English or American. It was so easy to carry an afternoon's "find" in my purse or pocket.

One of the prettiest arrangements I have seen is a wall hanging of a group of these miniatures in the home of a prominent Illinois physician.

Why not a "Regency Set" of butter chips for our own pleasure? Any number can be used to make an enchanting arrangement for a china cabinet or a wall display.

As reported in other chapters, possession of these miniature dishes was a dream-come-true for many little girls. To our sorrow, it seems the day of those Tea Leaf "play-dishes" for those little darlings in the family is over.

The butter chip era faded with the passing fancy for our beautiful Tea Leaf and by 1910 both were just memories.

6. Bone Dishes

Many of us have bone dishes which we treasure; proof that they are desirable is that they too have been reproduced recently. They were quite useful on the Victorian tables where there was plenty of room, but on our small tables they serve a better purpose as salad dishes. Some are

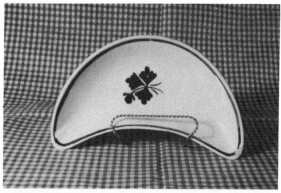

Bone dish by Meakin, 3″ × 6″; very light-weight. (87)
OE-25

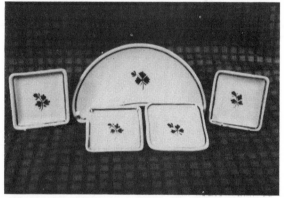

One of ten bone dishes by Mellor-Taylor; and four butter chips, 2⅝″ square; very shallow. **OE-26** (41)

Biggest little prize of all! Mustard jar, lid, and ladle, 3″ tall × 3¼″ wide; ladle 4″ long. Made by Shaw. Sale price was $100.00 in 1973. **OE-27** (21)

Bone dish and egg cups by Powell & Bishop **OE-28** (3)

plain, others are scalloped, but all are curved to fit the edge of the dinner plate. They were not part of the 102-piece set, but were an added nicety. Today the "Regency Set" idea has been applied to bone dishes, and a set of miscellaneous Tea Leaf bone dishes by English or American potters is perfectly acceptable for use with other dishes. The lovely Red Cliff line made by Hall China in the 1960s show bone dishes and may be easier to find. They are well marked; there is *no* intent to deceive, as with those that Jabe Tarter reported in 1971 in *Collectors' Weekly*.

Old bone dishes are usually in good to mint condition, because they were not in constant use.

7. Honey/Conserve Plates

The items that puzzle me most are the honey or conserve plates. Minnie Watson Kamm, in her *Old China* book, describes the conserve plate as too large for a cup plate, with a well to hold the conserve (sugar-preserved fruit). Another authority noted that the honey plate was to hold an individual serving of honey and butter or small servings of butter mixed with lemon, spices, or herbs. Yet another little plate mentioned by Carl Dreppard* is a toddy plate, in which the toddy glass was placed (used for the same purpose as the cup-plate). I suspect any tiny plate could serve for any of these three purposes; all can be found with the Tea Leaf motif.

8. Salesmen's Samples

If you still have small plates less than 5″ across you cannot identify, and are sure they are not part of a child's set, consider the possibility they may be salesmen's samples. As stated before, it was a common practice from the late 1800s to carry samples, as catalogs were too expensive to send by mail and regular sized wares were far too expensive and bulky for "drummers" to carry along, so sample dishes were the answer to show actual wares which were available from the china houses. I do not have photos of items which I am absolutely sure were made for this purpose.

9. Mustard Pots

The mustard pot pictured was in a fine antique shop in Galena, Illinois, and carried a price tag of $100.00! It was one of two I have seen or heard about, but if there were two, there must be more and I would like to hear of them also. This one is quite heavy, 3½″ wide and the same in height, with a lid and indentation for a spoon. The other was bulbous shape with about the same dimensions.

10. Syrup Pitchers

Another item — one I have not seen or photographed — in this catch-all chapter is a syrup pitcher. It surely must be a show piece on some lovely table. From meager information, it seems to be 5″ to 6″ tall with a domed metal top which closes with a spring-hinge. Would not this be an elegant addition to a Sunday brunch table set for serving waffles and tiny sausages, with fresh strawberries and steaming hot coffee?

11. Toothpick Holders

No one seems to have remembered to make a toothpick holder, one of the most collectible miniatures of today and an old-time favorite item. Two have been reported, but the consensus of opinion is that they were both handleless cups to a child's tea set, made by Anthony Shaw. One was for sale in California; the other sold for over $100.00 at a Kansas auction a few years back. If there are toothpick holders made we would all like to be enlightened.

* Carl Dreppard, *A Dictionary of American Antiques*, 1952.

Wm. Adams Co. reproduction from 1960–1972. Very attractive. (89)
AD-1

Trademark on shakers
AD-2

Flat; top removes for cleaning. Cuspidor is just a nicer name for a spittoon. (82)
OE-29

Cuspidor, 12" tall, 8" in diameter; by Anthony Shaw. No handles. Spittoon was the term in general use 100–150 years ago. (54)
OE-30

12. Salt and Pepper Shakers

There is one new Tea Leaf item which makes us wonder why "no one thought of that before" — salt and pepper shakers. The set shown was made by the William Adams Company, who made one of our beautiful English reproductions from 1960–1972, when their Tea Leaf line was discontinued. (See the full Adams story elsewhere in this book.) This pair of shakers belong to an avid Illinois collector who has been on the Tea Leaf trail for a long, long time. Sets of shakers were pictured in Sears' 1897 catalog in glass and metal, but none in pottery, much less in Tea Leaf. Why did we not see Tea Leaf salt dips or master salts?

13. Candlesticks

The Red Cliff Company offered these candlesticks from 1950–1960, but I have not seen them in a private collection. At least we have something here in the United States that is uniquely our own and not copied from Staffordshire. These were made by Hall China for Red Cliff Company. (See that chapter in this book.) This is the *only* mention of candlesticks I have ever seen!

14. Foot Tub

One other piece I have heard about is a foot tub decorated with Tea Leaf that sold at a Parke Benet auction some years ago. In an old magazine of the 1950s there was an ad for a "big, oval, ironstone foot-tub — $20.00." What next?

15. Spittoon/Cuspidor

Last, but not least on this list, are spittoons or cuspidors. These photos were the only ones I have seen. The snapshot was sent to me several years ago but I am unable to find the owner, so I have no way to identify the trademark of the potter. There surely must be many more of these around. They would make fine flower holders for plants, and certainly memorable conversation pieces. The other photo came from Texas and the owner identified it as a cuspidor. Some cuspidors are taller than others but "cuspidor" is just a "nicer" name than spittoon. These are *not* reproductions. There is a fine collection on display at Landis Valley, Pennsylvania.

Mug, 3½″ tall × 3¼″ in diameter; *unusually wide band and extra large design on only one side. Unusual handle and shape unlike any seen before in marked ware make this cup look like a reproduction. Unmarked but pretty.* **REP-1** (82)

Handleless cup, 2⅞″ high × 3″ wide. *Extra heavy (11 ounces). Looks like plain old hotel ware recently decorated in a dark mahogany reddish copper lustre, then fired again. It was reported that such items were on sale in Iowa in late 1979.* **REP-2** (43)

7″ plate with double band, poorly executed; lustre too bright, and gaudy. It is too thick, smeared, and uneven. There is underglaze crazing. Unmarked. **REP-3**

Porcelain cup and saucer marked "Germany." Both pieces sprinkled with Tea Leaves. Very pretty. (6)
REP-4

16. Reproductions

I am anxious to hear of other things made and decorated in our favorite style.

a. Please indicate if the item is old or is a reproduction and circumstances surrounding the acquisition.

b. Also, please include black and white photo of the *item and trademark*, if possible.

c. Indicate any unusual qualities of weight, glaze, color, decoration, etc. This is especially important if it is a suspected reproduction and is unmarked. A prime example of this last item is this 6½″ plate. It is unmarked, a creamy white color, instead of the usual white. The double band around the edge is most unusual, and the motif is so poorly painted it is not even a good reproduction. But I *had* to have it to perhaps learn one day where it came from.

I have heard of egg cups being decorated on old plain blanks in central Illinois, but I have not seen the quality work and very little information leaks out.

Several reports of Tea Leaf coming in from Japan and Germany have floated for years; finally I received a photo of a very pretty little German-made porcelain cup and saucer in a rich ivory shade with tiny gold Tea Leaf designs scattered all over both pieces. How I wish someone was proud enough of their hand work to sign their name! Keep looking, maybe one of you will locate the remainder of this set, or one from Japan, which you cannot resist.

Several references have been made to Tea Leaf having been made in New Jersey; I am anxious to hear from those who have items like this.

Early in 1981, I attended an Antique show and bought two pieces which later I was able to identify as having been made by Fell and Thropp in Trenton, New Jersey, 1889–1894. But that is a story for another book. Keep looking!

Correspondence can be sent to me through the Wallace-Homestead Book Company or mailed direct to me at Box 9285, Kansas City, MO 64168.

Unmarked

Oyster bowl, 5½″ in diameter; *deep rim foot; some discoloration. Part of a hotel set. All oyster bowls are similar, round, rim foot; wider than deep, and heavy. Can be from 5½″ in diameter to almost 7″. Some have motif on outside, others inside, on the bottom. There may or may not be a lustre ring around the base. More of these come unmarked than most other pieces, but all companies made them if they made a hotel ware line, which most of them did.* **UM-1**

Unmarked

Relish tray, not a service tray as it is rounded in bottom.
UM-2

Gravy boat
UM-3

Sauce ladle, 3" × 6¼" (19)
UM-4

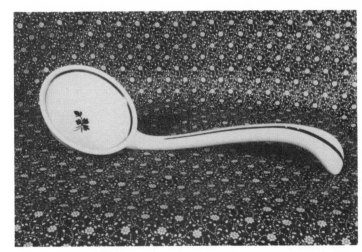

Soup ladle, 4" × 12" (40)
UM-5

Egg cup, 4½" high × 2¾" wide. American-made, or reproduction? (82)
UM-6

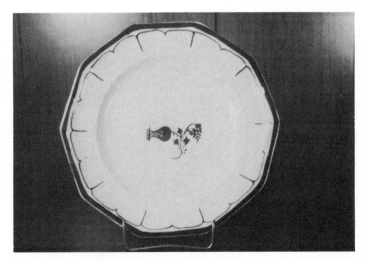

10 sided plate, 9½"; with Thistle and Berry. (90)
UM-7

Museums, Historical Houses

These are some museums and historical houses displaying Tea Leaf dishes:

Amana Colonies, Iowa; Don Shoup, Secretary
"Star of India"; San Diego, California
Campbell House Foundation, St. Louis; Theron R. Ware, Director
Mundelein Historical Society, Libertyville, Illinois
Madison County Historical Society, Inc.; Mrs. Thomas Harris, Superintendent
Minnesota Historical Society; Janis Obst, Curator
Heritage House, Monticello, Illinois; Glenna Musgrove, Curator

About the Author

The author, a native Missourian, brings to life, in this her first book, a bit of history from deep in the Ozark Hills which are so dear to her. Like the rising sun, this love of Tea Leaf dishes has spread to all parts of our country and through her eyes we can truly look into a bygone era and find a measure of contentment through *this* Grandma's Tea Leaf Ironstone.

Annise Heaivilin is the mother of five: two daughters; and three sons, who have served, or are now serving in some branch of the military service. She has eleven grandchildren and one great-grandson.

As Annise Doring, she graduated from Chanute High School, Chanute, Kansas, and after her marriage to James A. Heaivilin, they lived for a time in Wichita, Kansas, Houston, Texas, and Phoenix, Arizona. They settled permanently in Kansas City, Missouri, in 1941 and have been busy in a wide variety of private business enterprises including her present motel operation. Mr. Heaivilin is totally disabled due to a stroke in late 1973, but this has afforded Annise even more time to read, write and research as she has been forced to stay at home.

Annise says she will never live long enough to get done all the things she wants to do: take some interesting college courses; go to Staffordshire, England; catch up on correspondence; visit the other twenty-four states she has missed; finish a Tea Leaf quilt; meet in person each one who contributed to this book; learn to type; get all of her scrapbooks in order; write a bunch of magazine articles; finish a five-year Bible study course; and, last but not least, write another book.

Bibliography

Altman, Violet and Seymour: *The Book of Buffalo Pottery*. New York: Bonanza Books, 1969.

Barber, Edwin Atlee: *Pottery and Porcelain of the United States*, 2nd Edition. New York: G.R. Putnam and Sons — Knickerbocker Press, New York: 1902.

------- *Anglo — American Pottery*

------- *Marks of American Potters:* Philadelphia: Patterson — White, 1904.

------- *The Ceramic Collectors Glossary:* New York: DaCapo Press, 1967.

Barth, Harold B: *History of Columbiania County*, 1924.

Beers, J.H.: *Armstrong County Pennsylvania:* Her People Past and Present, Vol. I. 1914.

Bedford, John: *Old English Luster Ware*. New York: Walker and Company, 1966.

Bemrose, Geoffrey: *Nineteenth Century English Pottery and Porcelain*. London: Faber and Faber, 1952.

Blacker, J.F.: *Nineteenth Century Ceramic Art*. Boston: Little, Brown and Company, 1911.

Bohn, Henry G.: *A Guide to the Knowledge of Pottery, Porcelain and other Objects of Virtue*. London: H.G. Bohn, York Street Convent Garden, 1857.

Burton William: *A History and Description of English Earthenware and Stoneware*. London: Cassell and Company Limited, 1904.

Burton, W. and Hobson, R.L.: *Handbook of Marks on Pottery and Porcelain*. London: McMilliam and Co. Ltd., 1909.

Chaffers, William: *Marks and Monograms on European and Oriental Pottery and Porcelain*. London: 14th Edition, William Reeves, Bookseller, 1954.

Church, Sir Arthur: *English Earthenware*. London: 1895.

Clark, Garth: *A Century of Ceramics in the United States 1878–1978*. E.P. Dutton IV, 1979.

Clement, Arthur W.: *Our Pioneer Potters*. York, PA: Privately Printed, Maple Press, 1947.

Collard, Elizabeth: *Nineteenth Century Pottery and Porcelain in Canada*. Montreal: McGill University Press, 1967.

Comstock, Helen (Editor): *Concise Encyclopedia of American Antiques*. New York: Hawthorn Books Inc., 1968.

Cooper, Ronald G: *English Slipware Dishes.* 1650–1850. New York Transatlantic Arts, 1968.

Dreppard, Carl W.: *A Dictionary of American Antiques,* 1952.
First Reader for Antique Collectors
Primer of American Antiques, 1944.
Charles T. Bankdford and Co. Boston, MA.
Victorian, The Cinderella of Antiques. New York: Award Books 1970.

Earle, Alice Morse: *China Collecting in America.* New York: Empir State Book Company, 1924.

Eberlein, Harold Donaldson and Ramsdell, Roger Wearne: *The Practi cal Book of Chinaware.* Philadelphia and New York: J.P. Lippin cott, 1948.

Emmett, Boris and Jeuck, John E.: *Catalogues and Counters, A History of Sears, Roebuck and Co.* Chicago: University of Chicago Press 1950.

Fisher, Stanley W.: *British Pottery and Porcelain.* New York: Bell pub lishing Co., 1962.

Freeman, Larry: *Ironstone China, China Classcs IV.* New York: Cen tury House, Watkins Glen, 1954.

Godden, Geoffrey A.: *Antique Glass and China.* New York: Castle Books, 1966.
British Pottery and Porcelain Marks, 1780–1850. A.S. Barnes and Company, Inc., 1963.
Encyclopedia of British Pottery and Porcelain Marks. New York Bonanza Books, 1964.
An Illustrated Encyclopedia of British Pottery and Porcelain. New York: Bonanza Books, 1965.

Greaser, Arlene and Paul: *Homespun Ceramics.* Des Moines, IA Wallace-Homestead Book Co., 1973.

Grigson, Geoffrey: *Wild Flowers in Great Britain.* London: Collins 14th James Place.

Hagger, Reginald and Mankowitz, Wolf: *Concise Encyclopedia of English Pottery and Porcelain.* New York: Hawthorn Books, 1957.

Hartman, Hazel: *Porcelain and Pottery Marks.* New York, 1943.

Hayden, Arthur: *Chats on Old Earthenware.* New York: Frederick A. Stokes and Co., 1909.

Hillier, Bevis: *Master Potters of the Industrial Revolution, The Turners of Lane End.* London: Cory, Adams and Mackey Ltd., 1965.
Pottery and Porcelain in 1700–1914. New York: Meridith Press 1968.

Home Guide to Trees, Shrubs and Wild Flowers. Harrisburg, PA: The Stack Pole Company, 1970.

Honey, W.B.: *Old English Porcelain.* London: G. Bell and Sons Ltd., 1928.

Hughes, G. Bernard: *English and Scottish Earthenware 1660–1860.* London: Abbey Fine Arts
Victorian Pottery and Porcelain. New York: The McMillan Com pany, 1959.

Hughes, Therle: *Cottage Antiques.* New York and Washington: Fredrick A. Praeger, 1967.

Jackson, Mary L.: *If Dishes Could Talk*. Des Moines, IA: Wallace-Homestead Book Company, 1971.

Jervis, William P.: *A Pottery Primer*. New York: The O'Gorman Publishing Co., 1911.

Encyclopedia of Ceramics — 2 Volumes. New York: 1902.

Rough Notes on Pottery. Watkins Glen, New York: Edited by Serry Wood as European China, China Classics III Century House, 1896. Reprinted 1953.

A *Dictionary of Pottery Terms*. First published in the Pottery, Brass, and Glass Salesman. Feb. 1917 thru Dec. 1918. Later issued in bound form by J.F. O'Gorman and W.P. Jervis, New York.

Jewitt, Lewellyn: *Ceramic Art of Great Britain*. 1883, Revised new edition, Ward Lock Reprints, 1970.

Kamm, Minnie Watson: *Old China*. Grosse Point, MI: Kamm Publications, 1970 Reprint.

Ketchem, William C. Jr.: *Early Potters and Pottery of New York State. The Pottery and Porcelain Collectors Handbook*. New York: Funk and Wagnalls, 1971.

Kovel, Ralph M. and Terry H.: *Dictionary of Marks Pottery and Porcelain*. New York: Crown Publishers, Inc., 1974.

Lehner, Lois: *Ohio Pottery and Glass Marks and Manufacturers*. Wallace-Homestead Book Co., 1978.

Lehner, Lois: *Complete Book of American Dinnerware*. Wallace-Homestead Book Co., 1980.

Lewer, H. William: *The China Collector*. Dodd, Mead and Company, 1913.

Little, W.L.: *Staffordshire Blue*. New York: Crown Publishers, Inc., 1969.

Lockett, T.A.: *Davenport Pottery and Porcelain. 1794–1887*. Rutland, Vermont: Carles E. Tuttle Inc., 1972.

Madden, Betty I.: *Arts, Crafts and Architecture in Early Illinois*. University of Illinois Press, 1974.

Maddock, Thos. Maddock's Sons Company: *Pottery*. Privately printed by this company, 1910.

Martain, W. Klebe: *The Concise British Flora in Color*. New York: Holt, Rinehart, and Winston, 1965.

McCord, Wm. B.: *History of Columbiania County*. Chicago: Biographical Publishing Co., 1905.

McKee, Floyd W.: *A Century of American Dinnerware*. Private Printing, 1966.

Meteyard, Eliza: *The Life of Josiah Wedgwood*. Vol I. London: Hurst and Blackett, Publishers, 1865.

Moore, N. Hudson: *Collectors' Manual*. From Delineator Magazine, 1905. Reprint 1935.

The Old China Book. New York: Tudor Publishing Company, Reprint, 1936.

Mountford, Arnold B: *The Illustrated Guide to Staffordshire Salt-Glazed Stoneware*. New York: Praeger Publishers, 1971.

Peterson, R.T. and McKenny, M.: *A Field Guide to Wild Flowers of North Eastern and North Central North America*. Boston: Houghton, Mifflin Company, 1968.

Rackman, Bernard: *Early Staffordshire Pottery*. New York: Pillman Publishing Company.

Ramsey, John: *American Potters and Pottery*. New York: Tudor Publishing Company, 1947.

Ramsey, L.G.G.: *Complete Encyclopedia of Antiques*. New York: Hawthorn Books Inc., 1967.

The Connoissuer New Guide to Antique English Pottery, Porcelain and Glass. New York: E.P. Dutton and Company Inc., 1961.

Revi, A.C.: *The Spinning Wheel's Complete Book of Antiques*. New York: Grosset and Dunlap, Publishers, 1972.

Shaw, Simeon: *History of the Staffordshire Potteries*. New York: Praeger Publishers, Inc., Original 1829. Reprint 1972.

Shull, Thelma: *Victorian Antiques*. Rutland, VT: Charles E. Tuttle Company, 1963.

Spargo, John: *Early American Pottery and China*. New York: Garden City Publishing Company, Inc., 1926.

Stoke-On-Trent, The City Of: *Official Handbook*. Issued by Authority of the Stoke-on-Trent Corporation. London: Ed J. Burrow and Co., Ltd., 1973.

Symonds, George W.D.: *The Shrub Identification Book*. New York: M. Barrow's and Company, 1963.

Thorn, B. Jordan: *Handbook of Old Pottery and Porcelain Marks*. New York: Tudor Publishing Company, 1947.

Watkins, Laura Woodside: *New England Potters*.

Wedgwood, Josiah, M.P., C.C.: *Staffordshire Pottery and its History*. New York: McBride, Nast and Company, 1913.

Wedgwood, Josiah, M.P., C.C. and Ormsbee, Thomas: *Staffordshire Pottery*. Robert M. McBride and Co., 1947.

Wenham, Edward: *Antiques A to Z*. New York: Thomas Y. Crowell Company, 1954.

Wood, Serry: *English Staffordshire, China Classics VI*. Watkins Glen, New York: Century House, 1959.

Young, Jennie: *The Ceramic Art. A Compendium of History and Manufacture of Pottery and Porcelain*. New York: Harper and Brothers, Publishers, Franklin Square, 1878.

Index

(E) English (A) American
Boldface type indicates main discussion of topic.